FASHIONING DIASPORA

FASHIONING DIASPORA

BEAUTY, FEMININITY, AND SOUTH ASIAN AMERICAN CULTURE

VANITA REDDY

TEMPLE UNIVERSITY PRESS

Philadelphia • Rome • Tokyo

TEMPLE UNIVERSITY PRESS
Philadelphia, Pennsylvania 19122
www.temple.edu/tempress

Published 2016

LIBRARY OF CONGRESS CATALOGING-IN-PUBLICATION DATA

Names: Reddy, Vanita, 1977– author.
Title: Fashioning diaspora : beauty, femininity, and South Asian American culture /
    Vanita Reddy.
Description: Philadelphia : Temple University Press, [2015] | Series: Asian American
    history and culture
Identifiers: LCCN 2015039136 | ISBN 9781439911549 (cloth : alk. paper) | ISBN
    9781439911556 (paper : alk. paper) | ISBN 9781439911563 (e-book)
Subjects: LCSH: East Indian Americans—Ethnic identity. | Women, East Indian. |
    Feminine beauty (Aesthetics)—Social aspects—United States. | Femininity—Social
    aspects. | Fashion—Social aspects. | Transnationalism. | East Indian diaspora.
Classification: LCC E184.E2 R43 2015 | DDC 305.891/4073—dc23 LC record available at
    http://lccn.loc.gov/2015039136

Printed in the United States of America

9 8 7 6 5 4 3 2 1

A book in the American Literatures Initiative (ALI), a collaborative
publishing project of NYU Press, Fordham University Press, Rutgers
University Press, Temple University Press, and the University of Virginia
Press. The Initiative is supported by The Andrew W. Mellon Foundation.
For more information, please visit www.americanliteratures.org.

To my parents, with love and gratitude

Contents

ACKNOWLEDGMENTS

The writing of this book has taught me much about the virtues of patience and perseverance. More importantly, though, it has humbled me with lessons about the intimacies and communities that intellectual labor—which is never merely intellectual—makes possible. I am deeply indebted to the various forms of support that I have received from a great many people over the years, beginning with my dissertation cochairs at UC Davis, who not only served as aspirational scholarly models but promised they would continue their mentorship of me beyond the confines of graduate school and did. Bishnu Ghosh's steadfast belief in this project from its inception as a dissertation chapter has sustained me in more ways than she will ever know. Her brilliance and professional stamina are formidable, and I hope that these pages reflect even some of what she hoped this project would look like. Gayatri Gopinath's continued support of me within and beyond academia has been invaluable, and I am so grateful for my friendship with her, which has continued to grow in unexpected ways over the years. Beth Freeman gave me a much-needed kick in the pants during the writing of my dissertation, and I will be forever grateful to her for that initial rearward force. During the writing of this book, emerging Asian and Asian American feminist scholarship on fashion and beauty provided me with the intellectual fortitude to keep writing. This body of work has greatly refined my thinking on beauty, fashion, gender, race, globalization, materiality, and affect, as is evident in the pages that follow. I am excited to be part of this growing cadre of feminist scholars.

My current and former colleagues at Texas A&M University have provided me with the kind of community that I could never have imagined upon my arrival—Neha Vora, Zulema Valdez, Aisha Durham, Angie Cruz, Qwo-Li Driskill, and Jenelle Troxell sustained me intellectually and emotionally during my first several years here. Their empathy, humor, and camaraderie were incomparable, and I miss them all so dearly. My daily online check-ins with Neha and Zulema have helped keep me on track during the most arduous parts of the writing process, and I feel lucky to have been invited into their community of accountability. Cara Wallis, Lisa Ramos, and my colleagues in the Department of English—Nandini Bhattacharya, Margaret Ezell, Bob Griffin, Emily Johansen, Mary Ann O'Farrell, and David McWhirter—have supported and encouraged me during the various challenges of a tenure-track job. In particular, Nandini, Mary Ann, and Mikko have been steadfast mentors and lent their listening skills and acumen, and I owe them a very special thanks for their mentorship and support of me and my work. My wonderful colleagues in Women's and Gender Studies—especially Jyostna Vaid, Dan Humphrey, and Joan Wolf—have also provided welcomed support. TAMU's Melbern G. Glasscock Center for the Humanities' Publication Support Grant helped to cover the costs for image permissions. Several small grants from the Department of English and the Glasscock Center allowed me to present various portions of the book at conferences. A large grant from TAMU's Division of Research's Program to Enhance Scholarly and Creative Activities provided much-needed research support from 2011 to 2012.

Over the past ten years, I have benefited in large and small ways from the advice, collegiality, and support of a number of other amazing colleagues: Jigna Desai, Patty Duncan, Inderpal Grewal, Rick Lee, Nhi Lieu, Bakirathi Mani, Anita Mannur, Mimi Nguyen, erin ninh, Leah Lakshmi Piepzna-Samarasinha, Joe Ponce, Jasbir Puar, Junaid Rana, Kasturi Ray, Cathy Schlund-Vials, Priya Shah, Sima Shakhsari, Nitasha Sharma, and Caroline Yang. Several workshops and institutes provided venues in which I presented various portions of this project. Elizabeth Dillon's working group at the Futures of American Studies Dartmouth Summer Institute in summer 2006 pushed my ideas in new directions. I am grateful to Badia Ahad for her expertise and support during her proposal-writing "boot camp." The East of California Junior Faculty Workshop in Asian American Studies at Penn State University in summer 2011 introduced me to a wonderful community of Asian American scholars, including Sue Kim, Judy Wu, Eric Hung, and Tina Chen. I am privileged to have had the audience of remarkable feminist and queer South Asian women artists at a summer 2013 South Asian Women's Creative Collective Process/Practice/Portfolio workshop. A one-year fellowship in the Department of Gender Studies at Indiana University, Bloomington, in 2013–14, came at just the right time in my career. Marlon Bailey, Claudia Breger, Jordache Ellapen, Jed Kuhn, Maria San Filippo, and LaMonda Horton Stallings were a wonderful community of support and helped me to brave the Bloomington "polar vortex"—I look back with great fondness on my time there.

Janet Francendese is the kind of editor with whom every writer should be lucky enough to work. She expressed unwavering support of this project at every stage until her last day at the press. Though she could not see this project through to its completion, I am indebted to her responsiveness, flexibility, and firm hand, when needed. Aaron Javsicas skillfully stepped in during the final stages of the submission process and helped me to navigate the entanglements of book production. I am also grateful to Sara Cohen for her swift responses to my many questions about images. The two anonymous readers at Temple University Press provided incredibly thoughtful and engaged feedback, and this book has benefited greatly from their input. I owe a special thanks to Laura Morris, Alma Villanueva and Sarah Alarcón for their meticulous research assistance and to Catalina Bartlett for our occasional Saturday work sessions. I am especially indebted to the writers, artists, and filmmakers whose work I discuss in these pages. In particular, Pallavi Dixit, Swati Khurana, Prema Murthy, Shailja Patel, and Harjant Gill forced me to grapple in new ways with the intellectual and political stakes of my arguments about diasporic beauty and fashion.

There are a handful of people whose unrelenting faith in me motivated me to keep writing in my darkest and most despairing moments and whose consistent engagement with my ideas have been absolutely vital to the realization of this book. I am lucky to have met Tamara Bhalla during the Junior Faculty Workshop in Asian American Studies at Penn State University. I am so grateful for her various forms of feedback and to have taken a significant part of this journey with her. Anantha Sudhakar was always willing to read and comment at a moment's notice, and she read every word of this manuscript in its final stages. Her friendship has been a constant source of inspiration, joy, and kindness in my life. Our meeting at "nerd camp" in summer 2006 was nothing short of serendipitous. I remain in awe of her generosity and of the grace and dignity with which she meets the most difficult life challenges. Victor Mendoza has been an exacting reader and ardent ally, and this book simply would not exist without him. His unassuming brilliance shaped the earliest version of this project, and he convinced me that beauty and fashion lay at the heart of this book's ideas. His enthusiasm for my work lifted me out of my most paralyzing moments of self-doubt, and his commitment to our friendship in the face of social constraint has buoyed me. I am so glad I chose that conference seat.

My parents constantly amaze me with their generosity to others and with their demonstrated commitment to live their lives with integrity, dignity, and intention. My mother, Suchita, is a model of industry and skill that I can only hope to match. Her ability to practice medicine, sew, knit, and garden with equal deftness is truly admirable. My father, Jithender, has provided me with a soft, stoic love and sound financial support and advice, both of which have kept me afloat. Though my choices in life have presented them with many challenges, they have continued to support and love me through it all, and I love them fiercely for it. My sister-in-law Salima is the sister I always wanted. Her genuine concern for my well-being and happiness is an unexpected gift, and our online chats are the best part of my mornings. My brother, Rajneesh, has been one of my most exacting critics, and at the same time an incredibly sympathetic ear during uncertain times. My cousin Sonya Reddy's willingness to help me with the most thankless of tasks in incredibly stressful times is humbling; I admire the quiet and thoughtful ways in which she shows her love. Marsha Saben, Jamie Saben, Gurvinder K. Saben, Lewis Higgins, Ravi Reddy, Cornelia Reddy, and other members of my San Diego family sustained me with good meals, laughter, and some of my most meaningful conversations. My summers writing and recreating in San Diego have been wonderfully restorative; I cherish every moment that I get to spend there. My thirty-year friendship with Sonia Kakkar, even with its ebbs and flows, has been incredibly dear to me, and I admire her tenacity in maintaining our friendship. Other members of my extended family in the United States, India, and elsewhere have supported all of my goals and aspirations, and I owe them my deepest gratitude.

Finally, Jacey Goddard's love, companionship, loyalty, and cheerleading have kept me going over the past eight years. Her strength and humor have carried me through the most difficult moments of my career and beyond, whether from afar or by my side. Her desire to keep learning and the way she lives her life with purpose and courage continue to inspire me. Her unwavering advocacy on behalf of animals is simply stunning; I have learned so much from her about human-animal intimacies. For all this and more, she has my deepest love and gratitude. Two nonhuman beings have seen me through some of the densest thickets of life: Shea was not only my canine running partner, cuddle buddy, and bedtime co-snacker but also a confidant, and losing her has marked me indelibly. I owe a great deal of my sanity to my dog Gypsy. Her goofiness, sweetness, and protection of me and our frequent games of hide-and-go-seek have made me feel loved every day and in every circumstance. I can only hope that she feels my love in return, with all of its human limitations.

A version of chapter 1 appeared in *Contemporary Literature* 54.2 (2013): 337–68. Portions of chapter 2 appeared in *meridians: feminism, race, transnationalism* 11.2 (2011): 29–59.

Introduction: Beauty Matters

On September 14, 2013, Nina Davuluri, a twenty-four-year-old Miss New York beauty-pageant queen, became the first Indian American to win the title of Miss America. Within minutes of Davuluri's history-making win, Twitter was abuzz with racist tweets, some calling Davuluri a "terrorist" and a "member of Al Qaeda." Others misidentified Davuluri, a Hindu whose family hails from South India, as both "Muslim" and "Arab," religious and geographic identities that, in the wake of a post-9/11 cultural backlash against Muslim, Arab, and South Asian populations and rampant Islamophobia, were intended to disqualify Davuluri from the title of Miss America—as one racist tweeter put it, "This is Miss America not Miss Muslim." Yet, just as quickly, countertweets came pouring in to defend Davuluri, whose political platform for the pageant was "Celebrating Diversity through Cultural Competency." Rather predictably, these tweets appealed to the multicultural ethos of the Miss America pageant, citing Davuluri's win as evidence of the US nation's embrace of ethnically diverse ideals of "American beauty."

In the days that followed, South Asian American writers and bloggers weighed in as well, many arguing that Davuluri's Indian features productively challenged "euro-centric ideals of beauty" and contributed to "a broadening understanding of Americanness in a space that has historically taken a fairly narrow view of what qualifies as an acceptably American appearance and background" (qtd. in Hafiz). Other South Asian Americans, who were more critical of the sexist structure of beauty pageants, sidelined the issue of Davuluri's beauty and focused on the cyber-racism that it incited. The writer Sanjena Sathian, for example, argued that even though Davuluri is neither Arab nor Muslim, even "if she were, people still have no right to racism" (qtd. in Hafiz). Others countered the racist backlash by heralding Davuluri's achievement as yet another example of South Asian American "model minority" success and hard work. The journalist Sandip Roy jokingly referred to Davuluri's beauty-pageant win as further evidence of a "South Asian stealth take-over of America—1) Subways 2) Motels 3) 7–11's 4) Taxis 5) Tech Support 6) Spelling Bees 7) ER's 8) #Miss America." Yet even as Davuluri's Miss America title adds to the list of ways that South Asians are visible in the US public sphere, it also remains distinct within the South Asian model minority narrative. As Ruchika Tulshyan, who wrote an article for *Forbes* magazine on Davuluri's historic win and the controversy surrounding it, observed, "I wouldn't be writing this if Nina had won a spelling bee or mathematics competition." Implicit within Tulshyan's comment is that, unlike South Asian educational, entrepreneurial, and professional-managerial success stories that reinforce popular repre-sentations of South Asians as highly successful minorities capable of achieving the American dream and yet as peripheral to dominant US national culture, and unlike even the culturally degraded labor of South Asian service-sector work that positions South Asians as undesirable and unskilled racial minorities, the crowning of an Indian woman as Miss America suggests that South Asian success in the cultural domain of beauty poses, at least for some people, a threat to American cultural identity. At the very least, it reveals an as yet unexplored facet of what the Latino writer Richard Rodriguez has called the "browning of America" (xiii). What Tulshyan's comment reveals, in other words, is that despite being a seemingly superficial aspect of mass culture, beauty matters: it has the power to galvanize sentiment and incite passions about race, national identity, and cultural belonging.

The debates that erupted over Davuluri's Miss America win bring to the forefront one of *Fashioning Diaspora*'s central concerns: the capacity for Indian feminine beauty to animate the social. The backlash against and fascination with Davuluri had to do with how her beauty catalyzed debates about South Asian racial formation, citizenship, and belonging within the dominant US public sphere. *Fashioning Diaspora* builds on and expands the scope of these debates about beauty and belonging, focusing on Indian beauty's socially animating capacities within diasporic cultural production. One of this book's main objectives is to show how diasporic subjects engage with and respond to various encounters with subjects, objects, and practices of Indian beauty and fashion and how such encounters produce embodied practices of citizenship and belonging.

A second, related concern of *Fashioning Diaspora* played out in a different but simultaneous debate around Davuluri's Miss America win that was taking place within both Indian subcontinental and South Asian American communities and that situated Davuluri's beauty within a transnational frame of analysis. Whereas some Indian nationals saw the US racist backlash against Davuluri as an example of American cultural backwardness, others used it to claim Davuluri as a diasporic daughter of the Indian nation. India's leading newspaper, the *Times of India*, for example, responded to the racist tweets with the front-page headline, "Racist Remarks Sour Indian Girl's Miss America Moment" (qtd. in S. Roy). In another *Times* article celebrating Davuluri's historic victory for Indians, the journalist Chidanand Rajghatta erroneously cited India as Davuluri's "country of origin" (Davuluri was born in the United States, though she was raised in India by her grandparents during her early childhood years). He even went so far as to argue that it was Davuluri's Indianness that "breathed new life" into the Miss America pageant, an American institution whose popularity has been flagging over the past two decades but received the highest ratings in nine years for the 2013 competition. Davuluri also received numerous requests from Indian officials for public appearances in India. Indians' desire to claim Davuluri—and the Indianness that she represented—as their own undoubtedly had to do with India's own recent cultural history as an epicenter of global beauty and fashion. This is a history that, by all accounts, began with the crowning of two Miss India pageant queens, Sushmita Sen and Aishwarya Rai, as Miss Universe and Miss World, respectively, in the 1990s. Sen's and Rai's titles, along with the liberalization of India's economy in 1991, helped to globalize and professionalize the Indian fashion and beauty industries, a phenomenon that I discuss in more detail later in this introduction and in chapter 2. These conversations within Indian and diasporic publics thus linked Davuluri's beauty to the globalization of Indian beauty on the subcontinent.

Yet even as some Indian media hailed Davuluri as an example of the ever-expanding model minority success of Indians abroad, other Indian and diasporic media analysts argued that Davuluri would not have had even a glimmer of a hope of winning the title of Miss *India*—precisely the title that Rai and Sen secured before going on to win international pageants—because she would have been considered too dark-skinned. These writers almost universally invoked the global success of fair-skinned

Indian beauty—such as that embodied by Rai and Sen—as the national standard against which Davuluri's ethnically Indian beauty simply failed to measure up. (These observations take on an ironic hue in light of Davuluri's claims that Rai is also one of her role models.) South Asian Americans, for their part, agreed with their Indian counterparts on this point; but some took the claiming of Davuluri as an "Indian girl" (rather than an American one) as an occasion to then vituperate Indians for promoting a fair-skinned beauty ideal. Asha Rangappa, the associate dean of Yale Law School, observed that while the racist backlash against Davuluri and its pushback by South Asian and non–South Asian Americans as well as subcontinental Indians was intended to "shame" America by revealing the racist underbelly of a liberal democratic nation, such public shaming actually "misses what ought to be the real shame target—India. After all, despite being a country of almost a billion people, India has left it to America to crown the first Indian beauty queen who looks . . . well, Indian." Rangappa here implies that the Indian light-skinned beauty ideal effectively denies dark skin as a more realistic and democratic Indian ideal.[1] Rangappa thus counters Indians' finger-pointing at the US racist backlash against Davuluri's brownness with her own finger-pointing at India's colorism against the majority of its dark-skinned citizens.

What I find noteworthy about these conversations between and among Indian and diasporic publics is the way that Davuluri's beauty invites an engagement with definitions of Indianness (and not just the Americanness that her win "officially" represents). Her beauty both dissolves and at the same time delineates a distinction between the categories Indian and Indian American, between nation and diaspora: Davuluri's beauty is an Indian accomplishment and yet insufficient to the task of representing Indian beauty; it is definitively diasporic and yet in need of Indian beauty as either its foil or counterpart; and if we take seriously Rangappa's point about skin color, diasporic beauty is more authentically Indian than Indian beauty itself. This constellation of discourses about Indian beauty reveals its transnational dimensions—the way that it occupies a symbolic field that travels between diaspora and nation and the "tense and tender ties"[2] through which these itineraries of beauty subtend one another, diverge, and converge. These differing opinions about how to frame Davuluri's success within the cultural domain of beauty thus highlight a second concern of this book—the way that diasporic beauty is marked by, apprehended within, and engages with transnational flows of Indian beauty.

Rather than understand Davuluri's winning beauty as an isolated or exceptional event, I treat it here as a symptom and a provocation, a point of entry into a broader examination of the links between beauty, fashion, femininity, race, diaspora, and the social. *Fashioning Diaspora* maps how transnational itineraries of Indian beauty and fashion shape South Asian American[3] cultural identities and racialized belonging, from the 1990s to the end of the first decade of the twenty-first century. The liberalization of India's economy in 1991 led to the increasing availability of US popular culture in Indian markets through the advent of Indian satellite television and other transnational media, as well as to the growing popularity of Indian cultural forms—namely, in music, food, and fashion—within the US national imaginary. This period is also marked by the Indian state's courting of the transnational capital of elite (and more specifically Hindu) non-resident Indians (NRIs) living and working in the United States, many of whom had migrated to the United States as professional and managerial labor migrants under the Immigration and Nationality Act of 1965 and who subsequently achieved middle- and upper-class status. Finally, some of the period I examine is a geopolitical moment defined by the historical periodization "post-9/11," during which "allegiances to the nation-state of India are unwittingly or often deliberately rearticulated through allegiances to the United States," especially as these allegiances require the exclusion of Muslim populations from both US and Indian global modernities (Puar, *Terrorist* 173). During this time, I argue, Indian beauty and fashion have operated as technologies of neoliberal governance, optimized for the cultivation of gendered forms of neoliberal selfhood and for the satisfaction of neoliberal consumer desires, nationally and transnationally.[4]

Fashioning Diaspora also puts pressure on these neoliberal rationalities of the self and the social by deploying transnational feminist critique as its method of examining beauty's force at the level of bodily intensities, capacities, and propensities as it circulates across various diasporic cultural texts. Transnational feminist analysis is a method that typically takes as its object of study the act of migration and the crossing of borders as distinctly gendered processes. However, I adapt this approach to focus not so much on the subjects and processes of migration—though I do attend to these—and more on the operations of beauty within these processes. I foreground how beauty, sometimes through and sometimes despite its associations with neoliberal desires and belonging, also animates the material realities of "race, migration, and political economy" and interrogates "globalism, empire, and the nation-state" (Butler and Desai 2).[5] That is, I deploy transnational feminist critique as a reading practice that allows me to examine how transnational flows of Indian beauty produce racialized and diasporic subjectivities and affiliations and how diasporic subjects at times transform these everyday performances, practices, and goods of Indian beauty and fashion in the process. Rather than designating a predetermined and discrete set of objects or practices, I use the term "Indian beauty" as a conceptual shorthand for a dynamic network of bodies, desires, events, performances, clothing and adornment practices, and commodities that are negotiated within a specific set of conjunctures in diaspora. Though this book focuses on diasporic cultural forms produced within the United States, it also attends to the way that other diasporic national sites, such as Britain and East Africa, actively shape and energize the transnational flows of Indian beauty that it maps. It thus follows Rajini Srikanth's persuasive argument that "the South Asian American experience is one of diaspora" (2).

Instead of attempting to offer a genealogy of the concept of "beauty" (a highly contested term and a difficult, if not impossible, endeavor), it is more useful to understand beauty as occupying various domains of the social in the diasporic cultural production that I examine. Beauty in this book refers to a mode of aesthetic judgment and a diasporic mode of embodiment—a physical attribute either earned by or conferred on the diasporic subject (in which Indian bodies are seen as possessing beauty or in which the physical attribute of beauty is defined as Indian), sometimes with the goal of producing aesthetic pleasure; and a style or performance of racialized femininity. These modes of judgment and embodiment are at times linked to the way that beauty operates as a form of aesthetic and sexual capital—the possession of beauty as a way to gain access to privilege or prestige. At other times, beauty operates as a form of labor and care—both the labor of self-beautification and the labor and care of beautifying an(other) or others. My purpose in describing beauty as occupying this heterogeneous social field is to emphasize that beauty, while it circulates within other networks of social power and social inequality, is not reducible to them. In an examination of the booming beauty industry in globalizing Brazil, Alexander Edmonds observes that "it is precisely the gap between aesthetic and other scales of social position that makes attractiveness such an essential form of value and all-too-often-imaginary vehicle of ascent for those blocked from more formal routes of social mobility" (20). Beauty, in other words, does not merely replicate other social structures or stand as an "effect" of these structures; beauty has its own internal logic and organization, one that structures the very domain of the social for many racialized diasporic subjects. Thus, although when Tulshyan notes that Davuluri's success in beauty is unlike other South Asian American accomplishments she does not mean so complex a rendering of beauty's social field as I have outlined here, her comment does locate beauty's particularity within this social field, its distinction as a form of prestige within the South Asian American community.

Closely tethered to the social life of beauty is fashion, a separate but related domain of the social that the second half of *Fashioning Diaspora* examines as part of mapping diasporic belonging. By "fashion," I mean both the creative input and economic processes that are required to translate the raw material of clothing into the symbolic meaning of style (fashionability) and the habits of dress and attire that inform everyday practices of self and identity (sartoriality). This conceptualization of fashion somewhat departs from the way that many fashion studies scholars theorize fashion. These scholars tend to view fashion and clothing as two distinct and nonoverlapping domains of culture. For these scholars, clothing is material (it is most often understood as the raw material of fashion) and fashion is immaterial (it is a constructed set of beliefs about the social value and function of clothing that exceeds its use value).[6] In an overview of the field of fashion studies, *Fashion-ology*, Yuniya Kawamura argues that "a form of dress or a way of using [clothing] is not 'in fashion' until it has been adopted and used by a large proportion of people in a society" (1). Kawamura's distinction between clothing and fashion is connected to her larger project of defining fashion as a system that is the product of a collective belief in clothes-as-fashion. Fashion, in this view, is not just about a fashion designer's individual creative genius but about a larger social apparatus of design, production, distribution, diffusion, reception, and consumption, all of which comprise the "social nature of fashion" (1).

While I am careful to distinguish between the dominant fashion system, which is part of a larger social apparatus of clothing-as-fashion, and clothing in the chapters that make up the second part of the book (chapters 3, 4, and 5), when I talk about fashion in this book, I refer to both fashion and clothing for at least two reasons. First, what counts as fashion in terms of design and consumer markets historically has excluded non-Western attire, which is often distinguished from fashion through the use of terms such as "dress," "clothing," "garments," and "garb." Moreover, the very distinction between clothing and fashion is, after all, also a symptom and marker of modernity—those subjects and cultures that can be fashionable are those marked as having the capacity to enter into a national or global modern. In India, like in other colonized nations, fashion was central to the colonial modernizing project (see Tarlo). (Indeed, in chapter 3, I examine how a contemporary diasporic young-adult novel represents colonial ideals of modern Indian womanhood in relation to the consumption of British-made fashions.) Though the dominant fashion system does much work to distinguish between the fashionable and the merely sartorial, the visual artists whom I examine in chapter 4, for example, complicate this distinction by, in part, revealing the racial, gendered, sexual, and colonial economies at work in producing it. These artists represent the bindi as a marker of both an eroticized and culturally backward Indian femininity in tension with the Western fascination with the bindi during the Indo-chic Western style trend of the 1990s. I show how diasporic artists redefine the "social nature" of fashion by making visible the social structures that transform clothing into fashion and by radically experimenting with the materiality of Indian fashion *and* clothing. In doing so, I argue that they create new forms of diasporic feminine embodiment that exceed the gendered and sexualized normativities and orientalisms of fashion.

While fashion and beauty circulate within distinct regimes of value—who or what is considered beautiful need not be considered fashionable, and vice versa[7]—there is at times slippage between the terms. Thus, while the first half of the book focuses on beauty and the second half on fashion, it is nevertheless the case that sometimes these two domains of culture seep into and solicit each other. This crosshatching happens when style makes beauty legible on the body, such as in chapter 1, when a fashion makeover allows the Indian migrant woman to "pass" as an American beauty, and again in chapter 2, when Western attire marks the upwardly mobile diasporic woman's Bollywood beauty. When I discuss the social structures and socializing capacities of beauty and fashion within diasporic cultural production, I primarily use the term "beauty" as shorthand throughout the rest of the introduction. I do this in part because of the relationality of these terms that I have just outlined and in part to avoid repetitious phrasing. The term "beauty," then, encompasses a range of material expressions including fashion (both sartoriality and style).

It is worth stating at the outset that my aim in *Fashioning Diaspora* is not to perform an extended analysis of representations of Indian beauty in transnational mass media—the Indian beauty queen, the Indian fashion model, the Indian fashion designer, the marketing and use of skin-lightening creams, or fashion magazines. Such objects and figures constitute perhaps the most visible evidence of the transnational circulation of cultural economies of Indian beauty.[8] Nor is *Fashioning Diaspora* an ethnography of these economies—this is not a study of South Asian American fashion designers, models, or beauty queens or of the beauty and fashion industries per se. This book certainly nods to and even occasionally pursues these economies (the fashion and beauty industries) and the figures (models, Bollywood starlets, fashion designers) that occupy its ranks, but it also expands the concept of "Indian beauty" beyond these economies and figures. If Indian beauty structures the domain of the social for diasporic subjects, then it is also the case that beauty takes on a variety of social forms in *Fashioning Diaspora*.

"Indian beauty" finds expression—and distortion—in diasporic cultural forms that themselves cannot be fully disaggregated from cultural economies of beauty: diasporic literary fiction that invokes the beauty and desirability of the diasporic Indian woman, which are symptomatic of a modernizing India and a growing diasporic bourgeoisie; young-adult fiction that accompanies objects of diasporic material culture such as a "politically conscious," Indian, anticolonial, freedom-fighting girl fashion doll; a short story about a Miss India USA beauty pageant; a young-adult, ethnic, "chick-lit" novel about an Indian American girl's desires to become a fashion journalist; and visual and performance art that critically engages with sartorially iconic and politically charged markers of Indian fashion such as the bindi and the sari. As even this brief description of the social forms of beauty reveals, I privilege diasporic Indian *femininity* as the gendered territory of beauty—femininity, in other words, is where beauty *lives* across the archive of diasporic texts that I assemble here. Though "beauty," "fashion," and "femininity" certainly are not equivalent terms, the social fields of diasporic beauty that I examine maintain strong attachments to feminine subjects (the immigrant and NRI woman; second-generation girls; the Indian American beauty queen) and to feminized objects of fashion (bindis and saris). There are several reasons for this. First, fashion and beauty are conventionally feminized domains of culture—their associations with the private (versus the public), culture (versus economy), and consumerism (versus politics) marks their "frivolous and casual" (rather than serious and intentional) nature (Tu 9). Recent and emerging scholarship on fashion and beauty reveals that femininity is at the heart of these investigations, whether it is studies of fashion models, the fashion industry, plastic-surgery practices, or cosmetics.[9]

Second, because I am interested in understanding how Indian beauty and fashion are negotiated in a South Asian American diasporic context, any engagement with diasporic Indian beauty invites an engagement with the figure of the beautiful Indian woman that has emerged as emblematic of India's entry into global modernity. As I have already mentioned, the liberalization of India's economy in the early 1990s coincided with the rise of the Indian beauty queen onto the international pageant scene, inaugurating images of beautiful Indian women as emblematic of India's global economic reach. Such concurrence is not incidental, as female beauty "often emerges as a key site of the modern—as lure, moral threat, or even liberation" (Edmonds 30). Indeed, within late-twentieth-century and early-twenty-first-century contexts of global mass media, the Indian woman's construction as beautiful and fashionable has had a central role to play in the definition of India as a globally modern postcolonial nation. The figure of the global Indian beauty queen has been central to definitions of "new" Indian womanhood, a newness marked by a "potential for professionalism in the workplace and through [the new Indian woman's] adherence to an essentialized notion of Indianness" (Radhakrishnan 49). The outward projection of this image to the Western world could be found on the covers of three major US magazines from 1999 to 2006. *National Geographic*, *Time*, and *Newsweek* all featured "beautiful" and fashionable Indian and diasporic Indian women—emblematic of the new Indian, female, professional, consumer citizen-subject—on their covers to represent India's emergence into a new global economy. *National Geographic* presented two very different Indian women on the cover of its 1999 "millennium supplement" on "global culture"; one is dressed in a gold-brocaded sari and gold jewelry, and she smiles approvingly at an Indian fashion model dressed in a black-vinyl body suit and gazing boldly into the camera. The juxtaposition of these two contrasting images of Indian femininity captures in visual terms one of the central stories featured within the millennial supplement: India's rapid entry into global modernity. Seven years later, in 2006, *Newsweek* and *Time* followed *National Geographic*'s lead by featuring on their covers beautiful Indian women as representative of a global Indianness (in the case of the *Time* image, of India's booming transnational IT industry). In these instances, however, it was the faces and bodies of *diasporic* Indian women—those living outside the subcontinent—that were harnessed to globality. *Newsweek*'s cover featured the Indian American actress, model, and television host Padma Lakshmi in a loosely tied sari with her hands clasped together in *namaste* (an Indian cultural greeting), underneath the caption, "The New India" (6 Mar.). The ornamented face of the UCLA Indian American business student and classical Indian dancer Gunjan Thiagarajah graced the cover of the *Time* issue, accompanied by the caption "India, Inc." (26 June). In both of these mass media, photogenic, diasporic Indian women represent the globally modern Indian nation, displayed as global corporate brand.[10]

These feminized representations of Indianness in some ways hark back to earlier nationalist ideologies that positioned the Indian woman at the center of anticolonial nationalist discourse in the nineteenth century. In this discourse, the middle-class Indian woman's "essential" spirituality within the home—one that was opposed to Indian men's susceptibility to the necessary but "corrupt" material and rational social order outside the home—became central to anticolonial and postcolonial conceptualizations of modern nationalism (see Chatterjee). *Fashioning Diaspora* zeroes in on the particular uses of beauty in shaping both this inward and outward projection of Indian womanhood, inquiring into the way that this traditional-but-modern notion of Indian femininity is recycled, revised, and reassembled within the diasporic imagination.

Third, while beauty and fashion as feminized cultures are typically framed as reflecting the twin oppressions of patriarchy and profit—they "keep male dominance intact" (Woolf 3), and they drive consumption and exploit labor—it is also possible to imagine beauty and fashion, by virtue of the feminized economies in which they circulate, as allowing for an agential femininity, one that embodies and can express "diverse aspirations for self-transformation, social mobility, and sexual pleasure and power" (Edmonds 30). If diasporic Indian beauty lives, as I say, in femininity, then *Fashioning Diaspora* shows that these are social domains that locate diasporic femininity as, more often than not, challenging dominant nationalist and diasporic ideologies of gender and sexuality. Within these ideologies, Indian femininity merely "represents" an Indian national global modern tied to historically male domains (the public sphere, techno-scientific labor, and social progress) that is then reproduced in diaspora. As Gayatri Gopinath has argued, the very concept of diaspora is most often rooted in narratives that privilege "bonds of relationality between men" and in ways that "invariably displac[e] or elid[e] female diasporic subjects" (*Impossible* 5). Gopinath points specifically to the "prosperous, Hindu, heterosexual, NRI businessman" (10) who is at the heart of Indian nationalist conceptualizations of diaspora, so that even when diasporic narratives represent women, they often do so in nationalistic terms, as "the borders and boundaries of communal identities" of the nation (9).

Gopinath's characterization of diaspora's genealogies of heteromasculinism is useful for my purposes because it points to how, even when Indian femininity is used to represent Indian global modernity and despite the existence of a critical mass of cultural production by and about diasporic women, such representations may ultimately do little to disrupt the reproduction of capitalist heteropatriarchies in national and diasporic public cultures. I forward the analytic of "fashioning diaspora" to bring into view diasporic female subjects—and, more importantly, diasporic femininity—as central to narratives of South Asian diaspora and racial formation. This is not to make an essentializing claim that the social domain of beauty somehow inheres in the concept of "diasporic femininity" or that all diasporic women are folded into its social logic (again, beauty, fashion, and femininity are not equivalent terms). But it is to say that beauty offers one way—and, given the proliferation of images of Indian beauty across global mass media that mark the Indian global modernizing project, perhaps one of the most visible ways—to illuminate how femininity produces racialized subjectivities and diasporic affiliations that have remained below the threshold of dominant male-centered narratives of diaspora.[11] Put another way, "fashioning diaspora" gives vitality to mass-media images of Indian/diasporic femininity by recognizing that these are not merely images but also embodied and desiring *subjects*, bodies with flesh and bones.

The concept of "fashioning diaspora" makes two overlapping interventions into existing discourses about nation and diaspora. First, it takes seriously that representations of Indian feminine beauty have, however problematically, come to stand in for—dare I say, even to supplant—the figure of the "new" Indian woman that has come to represent India's entry into global modernity, such that the consumer practices and forms of neoliberal capitalist mobility that produce this figure have trained their focus on her relation to and apprehension within beauty. Whereas Indian beauty might thus be said to merely represent a range of other forms of neoliberal selfhood and national identifications that constitute new Indian womanhood, *Fashioning Diaspora* examines beauty as an important, timely, and severely underexamined one. It also recognizes that this particular articulation of Indian femininity has social lives beyond the Indian nation-state. Its attachments to mobility, pleasure, desire, consumption, labor, and commodification are part of neoliberal subject formation and practices of belonging in the diaspora, and at times these attachments redound on neoliberal practices of belonging within the Indian nation.

The story of diasporic embodiment and belonging that I tell is not just about women and girls, though these subjects do occupy the greater part of the book's critical attention. Even as beauty resides within and attaches to ethnically Indian feminine subjects and feminized objects, its socializing force exceeds the habitus of diasporic female subjects to operate on a range of diasporic and, in some cases, nondiasporic subjects. As I will show, encounters with Indian feminine beauty and objects of fashion in the cultural production that I examine point to possibilities for affiliations between and among diasporic women and girls—including undocumented migrants and sexual minorities, mothers and daughters, but also white women, South Asian immigrant male service-sector workers, and middle-class South Asian men. In mapping beauty's capacities to produce diverse and heterogeneous forms of embodiment, affiliation, and attachment, my aim is not to construct a coherent story about diaspora. Rather, in using beauty as an analytic for examining diasporic life-worlds, I conceive of fashioning diaspora as a "practice of diaspora," a way of identifying diasporic embodiment, affiliations, and attachments that can still account for the "constitutive differences" (Edwards 11) of diasporic racial formations—differences of nationality, gender, class, generation, citizenship status, sexuality, and region. Stuart Hall conceives of this concept of diaspora-as-practice as an "articulation," a "'complex structure' in which things are related, as much through their differences as through their similarities" ("Race" 33). The idea of Indian beauty as a practice of diasporic articulation—one that, even as it is rooted in diasporic femininity, operates on a diverse range of bodies and subjects—allows us to see how beauty produces multiple spatial scales of social belonging, affiliations across multiple forms of difference, and multiple forms of embodiment that are not reducible to a single kind of diasporic subject or a unified way of imagining diaspora.

Reassembling Beauty's Neoliberal Attachments

What do the social domains of Indian beauty in South Asian American diasporic cultural production look like? What forms of attachment, affiliation, and embodiment do they produce? Across what forms of difference? How and why is it Indian beauty that provides the occasion for these attachments? To get at these questions, it is first necessary to address the way that beauty generally and Indian beauty specifically most often circulate within neoliberal political rationalities and reproduce the neoliberal values and ethos of the new global economy. Wendy Brown defines neoliberalism as more than an economic process or policy that designates the retreat of the welfare state from providing social services for its citizens and the privatization of state forms of care. Neoliberalism, according to Brown, is a form of governmentality, a political rationality that reaches beyond the state and the economy so that "all dimensions of human life are cast in terms of a market rationality" (40). Beauty fits easily into the market rationalities of neoliberalism. Whether understood as physical attributes, commodities, or creative industries, beauty traffics in beliefs about the market logic of liberal democracy (e.g., the democratic "right" to consume and accumulate beauty commodities as part of consumer citizenship) and social transcendence and self-transformation through the accumulation of objects of beauty. Beauty thus traffics in a "lifestyle politics of neoliberalism, which emphasizes rational consumption, privatized modes of self-care and self-management, and the optimization of individuals' health, wealth, and happiness" through an unregulated global market (Pham, "Blog" 16). Beauty, it would seem, is tailor-made for neoliberalism.

Indeed, whether explicitly or implicitly, fashion and beauty cultures have been at the center of many convergences between consumer cultures and definitions of democratic citizenship within 1990s Indian neoliberalism. Whether defined in and through the terms of middle-class Indian women's increased consumer spending on products to enhance their physical appearance, the increased availability of full-service beauty salons and skin-lightening products and procedures, or aspirations to fashion design and modeling as career choices for urban girls and women, Indian beauty is connected to neoliberal practices of citizenship.[12] More recently, we are witnessing the influence of India's beauty boom and the global visibility of Indian beauty taking on new forms and formats within national and diasporic media. Bollywood films such as Madhur Bhandarkar's biopic *Fashion* (2008), featuring the 2000 Miss World title holder Priyanka Chopra, chronicles the rise and fall of an Indian supermodel—allegedly based on the real-life rise and fall of the Indian supermodel Gitanjali Nagpal—who becomes an overnight success as a lingerie model but quickly enters a downward spiral of sexual affairs, drugs, and alcohol, only to realize the error of her ways in time to walk the Paris runway during Paris Fashion Week. The popularity of skin lightening among middle-class urban men has been the subject of another Bhandakar film, *Traffic Signal* (2007), and a national and diasporic outcry erupted in 2012 over an Indian television ad for Clean and White Intimate Wash, a product that promotes the virtues of "vagina brightening" or lightening among young, upwardly mobile Indian women. Rupal Oza describes what she calls "the making of neoliberal

India" as involving the arrival of the Indian beauty queen onto the international pageant scene and a concomitant "beauty boom" that gave rise to expanding global markets for Indian beauty products and services.

Indian fashions, too, have become highly visible in the form of coveted commodities within the global fashion industry. Even before the rise of global cities such as Bangalore, Mumbai, and Delhi made India a global fashion destination and the site of a new creative economy of fashion industrialists, Indian-inspired fashions, known as Indo-chic, took the global fashion industry by storm in the 1990s. Indo-chic later came to define the fashion landscape of India as well, as Indian fashion designers found that they could use this style aesthetic to cultivate a sense of cosmopolitanism among elite and urban Indian consumers. Defined as the marketing and consuming of Indian-inspired style commodities during the 1990s through the first decade of the new millennium, Indo-chic marks a new phase and form of orientalism, distinct from and yet continuous with its colonial-era predecessor, that can be found in late-twentieth- and early-twenty-first-century popular forms, such as fashion, music, and media, that have proliferated under late global capital.[13]

The increased production and consumption of women's lifestyle magazines on the subcontinent in the late 1990s prompted the production of similar magazines, such as *Anokhi*, *Nirali*, *Sapna*, and *Nirvana*, for South Asian American women at the beginning of the new millennium. (*Nirvana* was discontinued in 2004 but bore the same overall visual aesthetic of India's best-selling women's beauty magazine, *Femina*, which began publication in 1959.[14]) In addition to providing South Asian diasporic women with the latest fashion and beauty buzz on the subcontinent, these magazines regularly feature profiles on South Asian American models who are entering the US fashion industry, such as Sonia Dara, who became the first Indian American female model to grace the cover of the *Sports Illustrated* swimsuit issue in 2012, and the Indian American model Melanie Kannokada, who became the face of the global skin-care line Bare Essentials in 2010. And we can now add to this list Nina Davuluri, Miss America 2014.

Such Indian and diasporic media forms and figures of Indian beauty are themselves symptomatic of the convergence of Indian and US neoliberalisms. Indian beauty, in the diasporic context, is not just a result of Indian neoliberalisms but intersects with neoliberal practices of citizenship in the United States, which stress liberal individualism through professional achievement and participation in the global marketplace. As Bakirathi Mani has observed, the hegemonic narrative of South

Asian American identity as defined by upwardly mobile and professionally skilled legal immigrants is one that is produced out of and in turn reinforces neoliberal formulations of US multicultural citizenship, a way of "managing racial and class difference within the state" even as its "color-blind society purports to move beyond race" (*Aspiring* 6). Multicultural citizenship is a practice of neoliberal belonging that allows South Asians in the United States to continue to think of themselves as model minorities, a racial formation rooted in an ideology of liberal autonomy and individual achievement that belies the actual class heterogeneity of South Asian Americans as an immigrant group. The model minority narrative of South Asians as hardworking, successful, and upwardly mobile dovetails with the emergence of neoliberal citizenship practices on the subcontinent. As Mani argues, "the flexible operations of multiculturalism and its alliance with narratives of upward mobility [among South Asians in the United States] reveal unexpected linkages between domestic ideologies of nationhood and transnational practices of citizenship" (6), as elite diasporic subjects, like their elite subcontinental counterparts, participate in transnational circuits of capitalist accumulation and consumption. It becomes easy to see how diasporic beauty cultures traffic in the neoliberal ethos of social transcendence, liberal individualism, and class mobility that has become central to hegemonic definitions of both Indian and South Asian American belonging. Within a framework of intersecting Indian and US neoliberalisms, Indian and diasporic articulations of beauty can allow South Asian American consumer identities and practices to be recruited into the neoliberal logic of the nation-state—and vice versa—because they participate in "the proliferation of market-based notions of individual autonomy" (Mani, *Aspiring* 7).[15] Such intersections are what allow, for example, Davuluri—a subject on whom the official conferral of beauty constructs her as a model minority subject—to become a diasporic daughter of the Indian nation despite having very few material links to the homeland (and despite her less-than-ideal Indian beauty).

In the chapters that follow, I focus on diasporic negotiations of Indian beauty, which have remained virtually unexplored within feminist scholarship on beauty, fashion, race, and globalization,[16] examining the strength of beauty's neoliberal attachments. As should by now be clear, within a neoliberal framework, beauty produces a social field that is structured not by collectivity or collaboration—socialities that have been integral to theorizing Asian American and diasporic racial formations—but rather by greater individualization as beauty circulates as forms of individual fitness under capitalism. Upon first glance, then, beauty seems antithetical—perhaps even hostile—to these more politicized ways of thinking about the social. Within consumer cultures, beauty is most frequently understood as a commodity and thus as a dematerialized aesthetic object or disembodied aesthetic practice. Even as an object of philosophical inquiry, as in liberal humanistic discourse that claims it as a transcendent, universal social good, beauty generally appears devoid of historicity and materiality.[17] Beauty, in short, "seems to offer itself as a quintessential object of fetishization" (Cheng, "Wounded" 202). Given the centrality of femininity and racial difference to genealogies of the fetish, popular understandings of racialized feminine beauty tend merely to reinforce their fetishistic associations with objectification and commodification. Beautiful women of color or non-Western women are either a much-needed corrective to white, Euro-American-centric models of beauty, making these women "better" fetishes than their white female counterparts, or their racialized beauty is particularly tragic evidence of the fetishization of feminine beauty.[18] Even if we concede that cultural or racial differences influence standards of beauty, such a concession does little to displace the question of what or who is considered beautiful. While definitions of beauty might remain elusive (what makes a person or thing beautiful remains to some extent highly subjective even though there are certainly historically agreed-on conventions, even when it is relegated to the domain of aesthetic inquiry) and thus frustratingly immaterial, beauty operates as a regime of value with material effects. Put crudely, even if many of us might argue over what beauty is, just as many of us would be hard-pressed to deny that there are certain forms of power to be gained from possessing it and even certain forms of power to be lost from lacking it. Feminist inquiries into beauty have deemed beauty either punitive (beauty as undemocratic, elitist, and sexist) or recuperative (beauty as salutary and democratizing). My aim in this book is neither to punish nor to celebrate beauty, since both of these approaches can remain caught within or reproduce the very capitalist heteropatriarchal frameworks that they seek to contest. Rather, my aim is to show that the practices associated with beauty are socializing in the way that they make possible new racialized subject formations, affiliations, and forms of diasporic belonging.[19]

My hope is that the concept of fashioning diaspora can help us to think differently both about beauty and fashion as domains of the social and about diasporic articulations of belonging. I thus aim to shed light on two interrelated processes. First, I hope to show how and under what conditions beauty produces diasporic embodiments and affiliations that put pressure on and even fracture the coherence of neoliberal practices of belonging. Second, in animating the social domain of beauty in diasporic cultural forms, I hope to help us to think differently about beauty, not simply as dematerialized, overly commodified cultural practices that work seamlessly in the interests of globalizing capital but as social domains that can be radically material and that articulate South Asian American racial formations and cultural identities through embodied practices of citizenship and belonging. These forms of the social challenge existing frameworks for theorizing diasporic belonging, insofar as nation-as-homeland sustains the "imaginary coherence" of diaspora (Hall, "Cultural" 224). Rather, in this book, it is the social domains of Indian beauty that provide the occasion—the material substrate even—for diasporic articulations of belonging, rather than the strength of material or political ties to India.

This is not to say that beauty is simply an imaginary construct. Indeed, it is to say precisely the opposite: that diasporic beauty possesses a materiality that in turn has real effects: producing culturally "inauthentic" modes of diasporic embodiment and generating attachments that are incomplete, partial, and emergent. Such forms of embodiment and affiliation draw attention to diaspora not as constituted by a coherent cultural identity but as a concept that recognizes how migration and settlement produce a diasporic culture marked by "heterogeneity and diversity" (Hall, "Identity" 235). Nor is it to say that India is merely a phantasmatic region in the cultural texts that I examine; indeed, in every chapter of this book, India is a very real place—a diasporic homeland, an NRI tourist destination, a place of out-migration, a site of outsourced global labor, a place that inspires global fashion. Yet beyond India as a material site, it is the "idea of India"[20]—an India feminized through Indian beauty's materiality and through material objects and goods of Indian fashion—that captures the diasporic and, in some cases, even the nondiasporic imagination. One of the gambles that this book takes, then, is to showcase what affiliations, intimacies, and embodiments emerge when we prioritize Indian beauty as a material and affective force over identity as a representational politics in analyzing South Asian American cultural forms. As it turns out, beauty is a force that generates partial, incomplete, and emergent national and transnational attachments, and intraracial, interracial, transclass, and feminist and queer generational affiliations and embodiments.

Materiality, Affect, Assemblage

So how is the social domain of beauty—the contours of which I have just outlined—distinct from what we have come to recognize as the figures and objects that constitute a cultural economy of Indian beauty—beauty queens, fashion models, fashion designers, skin-lightening creams, and so on? How can we—and is it possible to—map its expanse, not to mention its "heterogeneity and diversity"? *Fashioning Diaspora* engages recent scholarship in feminist cultural studies that has turned to the concept of assemblage as a way of tracking smaller-scale shifts in economy, culture, and politics that have remained unattended to within studies of contemporary globalization. By "assemblage," I mean an aggregation marked by the radical difference, and even seeming incommensurability, of its components. In contrast to conventional accounts of globalization that most often rely on the principles of equivalence and homogeneity to examine large-scale structural and social transformations, the concept of assemblage privileges principles of "connection and heterogeneity" that illuminate shifts in magnitude, intensity, scale, and duration within transnational flows of culture (Deleuze and Guattari 7).[21] These smaller-scale shifts draw attention to "new material, collective, and discursive relationships" that otherwise elude capture within grand narratives of global structural transformation (Ong and Collier 4). Understanding beauty as an assemblage shifts our attention away from ideological critiques of the Indian fashion and beauty industries such as beauty pageants, cosmetics, and women's beauty magazines, which have been primarily concerned with shifting standards of beauty (what beauty *is*), and toward animating where and how beauty organizes and constellates various social actors within its material force (what beauty *does*). As a way of conceptualizing beauty as the result of multiple determinations that are not reducible to a single logic, the analytic of an assemblage is better equipped to explore the cultural work that beauty does within contemporary diasporic cultural forms. Beauty in this book thus possesses a multiplicity of form and scale, "attun[ing] to movements, intensities, emotions, energies, affectivities, and textures as they inhabit events, spatiality, and corporealities" within diasporic culture (Puar, *Terrorist* 215).

These difficult-to-capture habitations of beauty demand more expansive frameworks for analyzing beauty as a mode of aesthetic judgment, a form of labor, a form of care, public performances of femininity, and the gendered embodiments of fashion. They demand also, I argue, a *slowing down* of our reading practices in order to apprehend it. Assemblages often lend themselves to a hyperkinetic and expansive method of mapping and diagramming. This is a method that is clearly informed by the temporality of assemblages as always emergent, moving unpredictably along various lines of flight, so that it becomes the scholar's job to capture their diffuseness. But this book's approach to assemblage is slightly different. Rather than merely tracking tropes or metaphors of Indian beauty in ways that attend to beauty's diffuseness and ubiquity, each chapter of *Fashioning Diaspora* is focused on a single text, author, or sometimes genre of cultural production in order to capture the magnitudes, intensities, scales, and durations of beauty's force. This slowed-down method of diagraming sometimes involves lingering on the seemingly minor or fleeting presence of beauty in these texts so that we might catch glimpses of its capacities to illuminate the uneven textures and emergent possibilities of diasporic belonging. In tracing the habitations of beauty and the moments and places that beauty asserts its socializing force, beauty-as-assemblage lends itself to the concept of diaspora as a practice or articulation—a "complex structure" defined through difference and heterogeneity. Such a concept of diaspora allows for theorizing diaspora not just through and as identity politics. It also allows us to conceive of identity and belonging as unfixed becomings, as "an encounter, an event, an accident," as "multi-causal, multi-directional, liminal," and as "a process" by attending to the particularities of the social force of Indian beauty within various scenes of its emergence (Puar, "I Would"). For example, in chapter 3, we will see how a young woman's feelings of exclusion from hegemonic definitions of diasporic community at a Miss India USA pageant condition an alternative economy of beauty and pageantry that allows her to form fleeting bonds with the pageant's South Asian male staff.

Before describing the social field of fashion and beauty that assemblage allows me to map, I offer a word on archive. Conceptualizing assemblage demands gathering texts together in which beauty animates and is animated by a social field and then tracking its social force. Thus, the objects that I have assembled in this book are those in which I found Indian beauty doing a particular kind of cultural work and working in a range of ways on various social actors. I include literary, visual, and performance-based texts produced by South Asian American women. Within all of them, fashion and beauty are explicit or implicit narrative, visual, and performatory concerns. And all are of varying feminist persuasions, a politics on which I elaborate within each chapter. But there are also important differences among them. Some of these texts and authors are canonical texts of South Asian American fiction (Bharati Mukherjee, Jhumpa Lahiri, and Chitra Divakaruni). Others are "minor" literary texts of South Asian American fiction, authored by women who are much less well known within South Asian American literary studies (Pallavi Dixit and Kavita Daswani). Since fashion, like beauty, most often circulates within a distinctly visual register, I also look to visual production and live performance that take up South Asian fashions, such as experimental feminist visual media by Swati Khurana and Prema Murthy, which meditate on the bindi, and a one-woman live performance about the sari by Shailja Patel. Most of these cultural producers are first-generation immigrants, with the exception of Dixit, who is second generation. Some of these texts, such as fiction by Mukherjee and Lahiri, were produced or are set just before or right after the implementation of neoliberal market reforms on the subcontinent; others were produced and are set firmly within entrenched neoliberal market rationalities within South Asia and the United States.

If women and girls have been historically neglected as subjects of diaspora, then this book shows how beauty structures their diasporic life-worlds. All of the texts that I examine concern the efforts of diasporic women and girls to negotiate the social. And like all archives, the texts that make up this one have been whittled down from a much more vast range of cultural production through which I sifted, searching for if, where, and how practices and objects of Indian beauty "came alive." In some cases, like in the fiction by canonical South Asian American writers, diasporic engagements with beauty were already familiar to me. But the inclusion of others required perusing online bibliographies of literary and visual cultures, surfing the websites of visual-arts collectives, festivals, and documentary films, and looking through diasporic women's lifestyle magazines. And like all archives, many texts did not make the cut. Sometimes even when artworks purported to be about beauty—such as when an Indian fashion object (e.g., a sari, a turban, or a bindi) or the word "beauty," or terms closely linked to it, were featured in the title or the cover of an artwork or novel—beauty was nowhere to be found within the actual text itself (evidence, once again, of the symbolic power of beauty but its also sometimes frustrating lack of material density). Thus, even though images, articles, and ads on Indian beauty that were featured in diasporic women's magazines piqued my interest, they did not frequently provide me with the kind of insight into the social domains of beauty that I found in the texts that I have gathered here. This is not to discount the deeply influential nature of mass culture in shaping diasporic public culture—indeed, these magazines sometimes allowed me to make productive connections between popular conversations about diasporic fashion and beauty cultures and the representations of beauty and fashion that I was exploring in literature, visual art, and performance.

While both beauty and fashion most often circulate within explicitly visual economies, the first half of the book examines primarily diasporic literature as animating beauty's social field. The diasporic visual and performance cultures that I explore in the last two chapters of the book—experimental video, digital media, and live performance—visualize the embodied practices and affects of wearing, handling, and exchanging material objects and goods of fashion that remain beyond the threshold of the visible and the tactile within the dominant fashion system.[22] I approach diasporic visual and performance art's various engagements with South Asian fashion as furnishing a form of what the Asian American art historian Margo Machida calls "expressive capital," a "repertoire of collective responses to [society's] moment and place in the world" (6–7). This is a "moment and place" that begins in the 1990s and continues into the present, when the more or less persistent desire for Indo-chic—Indian-inspired clothes, accessories, fabrics, and textiles—became a way of symbolically resolving social contradictions wrought by late-capitalist globalization: Asianness could be made culturally desirable even when it was "politically suspect" (i.e., after 9/11); it could signal to American consumers both a premodern past free from the pressures of accumulating wealth under late-capitalist globalization as well as a hypermodern present that represented the potential gains of globalization.[23] The opening of Asian markets—particularly those of India, China, and Southeast Asia over the decade of the 1990s—made Asia a dominant presence in the global economy. Though diasporic visual and performance art draw on fashion as a repertoire through which to examine the relationship between culture, globalization, and diaspora, not all of the visual texts that I discuss place Indo-chic at the center of this relationship; nor does Indo-chic always appear as these artworks' explicit subject matter. Nonetheless, the use of South Asian fashions in diasporic expressive forms is variously informed by, gains particular traction within, and redefines the racial, gender, and sexual politics of Indo-chic.

By invoking Machida's notion of collectivity as an organizing logic for the arrangement of texts in this latter part of the book, I do not mean to imply that diasporic visual cultures exhibit an aesthetic or political unity across their engagements with South Asian fashion. It is precisely the heterogeneity of these artists' aesthetic strategies, media forms, and political commitments that makes intelligible the varied and diffuse embodiments and affiliations that fashion generates across these artworks. Instead, I draw on Machida's use of the term "collective" to designate a common interest in South Asian sartorial forms as a "repertoire," or shifting inventory, of dress through which visual and performance artists capture the material histories, affective circuits, and embodied practices of diaspora.[24] The way that clothing and accessories are worn, combined, passed down, cared for—in short, what these artists do with fashion and the cultural work that fashion does in these artworks— allows us to glimpse fashion's capacity to generate feminist and queer diasporic embodiments and affects. These include feminist and queer femininities, the flat affects of bridal adornment, and cross-generational feminist rage.

As is perhaps by now clear, *Fashioning Diaspora*'s archive puts pressure on the predominantly social scientific approaches that have characterized recent examinations of cultural economies of beauty in nonwhite and non-Western contexts, a disciplinary field that might loosely be called critical beauty and fashion studies. Attention to the material practices that are involved in making and consuming beauty detail not only how nonwhite and non-Western populations have largely been excluded from colloquial and academic conversations about beauty (a simple cry for inclusion). More importantly, this body of work attends to the way that beauty is part of modern subject formation, racial formation, and citizenship practices within these contexts.[25] While sociological studies of beauty tend to claim it as an empirically observable part of everyday life imbued with racial meaning, in directing attention to literary, visual, and theatrically performed engagements with beauty, *Fashioning Diaspora* understands beauty as structuring racial formation and diasporic sensibilities in ways that may elude capture within the "ethnographic field." Though beauty cultures may certainly be observable beyond the neoliberal will to social transcendence and self-transformation in the field, cultural production "aestheticizes and theorizes the social relations and material conditions" of diasporic racial formations in ways that may not be empirically observable (Chuh 28). Cultural production, unlike sociological studies of fashion and beauty—and, for that matter, unlike sociological studies of race and ethnicity—is in a sense less tightly constrained by theories of racial formation in which the state plays a central role. These frameworks posit a "coherent and conscious racial subject" in ways that may be less attentive to "desires, anxieties, memories, and dispositions that lie below the threshold of rational consciousness" and that a decidedly aesthetic representational mode, one that is always situated in relation to social structures, can help to uncover (Koshy, "Why" 1545).

Moreover, beauty-as-assemblage allows me to track, when relevant, between the representational worlds of what the postcolonial feminist scholar Rajeswari Sunder Rajan has called "real and imagined" women. For Sunder Rajan, "'real' women cannot lie outside the 'imagined' constructs in and through which 'women' emerge as subjects" (10). The hermeneutic of women as "real and imagined" allows Sunder Rajan to showcase the epistemological pitfalls of either naturalizing a universal humanist subject or presuming a poststructuralist feminist critique of the "death of the subject" in feminist analyses of marginalized populations. For me, the critical payoff of Sunder Rajan's intervention into feminist knowledge production is that it enables me to show that at times cultural production and cultural producer can help to illuminate each other within the social field of beauty. At the end of chapter 2, for example, I turn to popular media representations of Jhumpa Lahiri's own ethnic beauty in order to show how the force of beauty that emerges across Lahiri's fiction is also a force that captures *her*—Lahiri's beauty shapes her literary celebrity and the way that her fiction is received by various reading publics. Similarly, in chapter 4, the visual artists Swati Khurana and Prema Murthy use video and digital self-portraiture as an aesthetic through which to stage their critiques of Indo-chic fashion and of sartorial authenticity. In these artworks, Khurana and Murthy take up the practice of wearing the bindi both as fashionable accessory and as an everyday article of clothing. For Khurana and Murthy, "real" Indian women do not lie beyond the realm of representation; the real inheres in their various acts of (self-)representation.

Finally, understanding beauty as an assemblage demands attending to the materialities and affectivities of beauty in diaspora. Beauty is material in two senses: it animates material histories and realities of migration, race, gender, class, and sexuality; and it also has material effects—it produces embodiments and affiliations that would otherwise remain unintelligible within a diasporic imaginary and when framed solely within neoliberal market rationalities. It allows us to examine beauty and fashion as constituted by a range of social forms, which I described earlier—physical attribute, labor, capital, a material object of bodily adornment and comportment, and so on. Sometimes the materiality of beauty—especially in chapters 1, 4, and 5—is defined in and through its capacities to materialize histories of colonial, postcolonial, racial, and gendered violence. In chapter 1, the immigrant protagonist's exceptional beauty both mediates her encounter with a body marked as "violent" by the postcolonial Indian state—the Sikh male "terrorist"—and is itself a form of embodiment that threatens her violability as an undocumented immigrant. In chapter 4, the bindi's appearance as everyday fashion brings into visibility histories of gang violence against South Asian immigrant communities that must remain repressed in order for the bindi to circulate as Indo-chic style. And in chapter 5, the sari is used in ways that visualize subjugated histories of colonial and postcolonial violence against South Asian and black African women.

Attending to the materialities of beauty across diasporic cultural production also involves attending to the representation of its *affects*.[26] I understand affect as the opening up of the body through sensory stimuli to affiliations it otherwise would not be primed to make.[27] Beauty's affects—estrangement, identification, abjection, fear, desire, and rage, among others—are themselves material in that they are the bodily, psychic, social, and spatial effects of beauty. Affect is, to quote Sara Ahmed, "economic": "Affect does not reside positively in the sign or commodity, but is produced as an effect of its circulation. . . . Emotions circulate or are distributed across a social as well as psychic field" (*Cultural* 45). This definition of affect and emotion allows us to think of affects not as forms of individual expression but as part of the social and socializing force of beauty and fashion.[28] The affects of beauty and fashion are material insofar as they operate on, in, and through bodies such that they remain open to social attachments and embodiments of various kinds.

Encounters with Indian feminine beauty, as I will show, generate incomplete, emergent, and ephemeral forms of affiliation and belonging across multiple spatial scales: national, transnational, and global, as well as nonheteronormative and feminist modes of embodiment that challenge dominant national and diasporic definitions of cultural identity. Indian beauty emerges as a performance of femininity that is attached to national and transnational mobility, even as it precludes full belonging within the US or Indian nations (chapter 1). It also appears as a style of diasporic femininity that generates cross-gender and cross-racial modes of identification that point to desires (even if unrealized) for cosmopolitan belonging (chapter 2). Indian beauty is also central to social constructions of diasporic girlhood, demonstrating how the performance of diasporic femininity at an ethnic beauty pageant creates affiliations across class, generational, and citizenship divides, and how colonial fashions shape diasporic nationalism, while the global fashion industry produces ethnic affiliations through the globalization of feminized labor (chapter 3). A popular commodity of Indo-chic fashion—the bindi—is transformed from a dematerialized style icon into a radically material practice of feminist and nonheteronormative racialized embodiment (chapter 4). And a quintessential garment of Indian femininity—the sari—is reappropriated as a material technology of historical retrieval that destabilizes the cultural coherence of a diasporic Indian identity through queer generational attachments and through affiliations across racial difference (chapter 5).

Seeing beauty-as-assemblage also enables us to track beauty's *limits* as part of its socializing capacities—the places or moments in which it *fails* to materialize as a mode of embodiment, performance, practice, or attribute. In recuperative Western philosophical and feminist treatments of beauty, which are rarely, if ever, attentive to questions of racial difference, much less to the intersections of race, gender, and sexuality, an attachment to beauty "might dangerously contribute to an annihilation of its antithesis, ugliness, as a prerequisite" (M. Nguyen 364).[29] In this book, beauty is in close proximity to the very qualities to which beauty in such treatments is typically rendered antithetical or annihilative. This includes not only ugliness but also an array of closely aligned qualities: plainness, ordinariness, unstylishness, unsightliness, and the like. In the chapters that follow, these qualities sometimes emerge as beauty's conceptual antinomies, closely tethered—even bound—to beauty's aspirational or obligatory force. Where there is beauty, these precarious antinomies are never very far. Beyond merely indicating the uneven distribution of beauty, in which the absence of beauty threatens to foreclose on sociality—a foreclosure that must always retroactively point to the redemption of beauty for any realization of the social—they can work to draw a person or a thing, beautiful or otherwise, in relation to others.

I locate these as politically and socially productive failures. I call these failures productive first because they offer a political critique, however implicitly, of the links between beauty as a gendered regime of bodily discipline and the instrumentalization of these regimes of disciplinarity for driving a global capitalist economy. Such failure occurs, for example, when an Indian male subject desires but fails to secure the sexual capital of the NRI woman as a form of transnational mobility in Jhumpa Lahiri's short story "Interpreter of Maladies." More importantly, though, these failures are productive in the sense that I locate in them a sociality that can only emerge *through* beauty's material presence in the first place. As I examine in chapter 3, even as a Miss India USA pageant contestant's failure to measure up to the pageant's definitions of idealized diasporic femininity produces her feelings of exclusion from middle-class definitions of diasporic community, such feelings of failure become the conditions of possibility for diasporic affiliations across class lines that in turn produce an alternative scene of beauty and pageantry. Following Judith Halberstam's recent argument that the practice of failure can "exploit the unpredictability of [capitalist, patriarchal, etc.] ideology and its indeterminate qualities" (89), I argue that beauty's failures generate modes of sociality that emerge from within such ideological unpredictability and indeterminacy. That is, if beauty fails to materialize as promise, aspiration, obligation, or commodity, then it also materializes particular kinds of affiliation from within such failures. The concept of beauty-qua-assemblage can thus help to assess and even to undiscipline beauty's attachments to neoliberal practices of US and Indian national identity—beauty as commodities that secure self-advantage or social privilege or as a mode of bodily discipline and regimentation that generates ever greater forms of autonomy—and move toward an understanding of beauty as a deeply, if unevenly, socializing force.

In illuminating Indian beauty's materiality and affectivity, this book attends closely to beauty's capacity to captivate, its force as a set of affective fields or "territories of feeling" within the consumer spaces of contemporary capitalism (Thrift, "Understanding" 292). For, as mentioned earlier, even though I do not pay sustained attention to commodities of beauty that might be more directly apprehended within these spaces, such as cosmetics or fashion magazines or fashion models,[30] it would be rather disingenuous not to acknowledge the way that the diasporic literary and visual texts under investigation here are by now as much a part of diasporic *consumer* culture as they are a part of diasporic public culture. Whether as persons or things, the "diasporic beauty" forms that I examine in this book generate an affective field that is commoditized, in the sense that they exist within texts that circulate as part of market-driven popular culture or in the sense that beauty within a given text or set of texts is particularly susceptible to the machinations of capitalist consumption. Nigel Thrift, for example, describes the way that glamour, particularly the glamorous personas of celebrities, "amplifies interest and yearning" among consumers such that these affects rival or might even be considered an integral part of a commodity's use value (305). Following Thrift's observations about how commodity aesthetics are increasingly geared toward generating a shared experience of aesthetic pleasure among consumers, we might say that in mapping beauty's capacities for captivation, this book does (and in some ways must) traffic in *commoditized* affects.

Yet could we also imagine the social field of beauty as producing forms of *political* animatedness? If so, what kinds of racialized, gendered, classed, and national bodies contain the capacity to be animated in these ways? The literary scholar Lauren Berlant's notion of the juxtapolitical offers a productive opening into thinking about beauty's materiality and affectivity within racialized and feminized contexts of South Asian diasporic consumer and public cultures that I discuss in this book. Berlant argues that nineteenth- and twentieth-century American mass "women's culture"—popular novels, films, and advertisements—produced a market domain of female consumers that exists "in proximity to the political" but that is not, properly speaking, "addressed to the political register" (*Female* x, 3). This public of loosely connected female consumers is juxtapolitical in the sense that their common historical experience and aspiration toward normative femininity and its concomitant promise of love, romance, and marriage reveal a disenchantment with and lack of investment in (nation-state) politics, if only because historically subordinated populations, in this case "women," have had restricted access to it.[31] A shared affective investment in the sentimental plot of romantic love—and a shared complaint about its various disappointments—operates as a kind of emotional relief from the political.

To the extent that beauty is a normatively feminine convention that most often circulates within and as "apolitical" and "feminized" consumer culture, many of the forms of sociality that beauty makes intelligible in this book might in some cases be understood as juxtapolitical.[32] But whereas for Berlant the social aggregate of consumer affects cohere, however loosely, within what she calls "intimate publics" (*Female* viii), the forms of sociality that I map through beauty are much too nascent or incomplete to produce anything like a public, even as they might occur within the domain of public culture. The juxtapolitical terrain of beauty's affects in this book is instead constituted by a "momentary recognition of possibility" of affinities, attachments, and affiliations (Staiger et al. 4). Affect is most often counterposed to the faculties of rational thought and action and consigned to the primitive (bodily) passions possessed and exercised by those who are most affected by these historical structures—women, girls, the enslaved, the colonized, the diasporic. Transnational feminist and queer studies of race and diaspora have thus begun to invest in the political possibilities of affect as central to the apprehension of these structures, particularly within aesthetic representational forms.

Much of this work has focused on the examination of experimental or avant-garde art that is organized almost exclusively by the affects of racial and ethnic melancholia, loss, and trauma.[33] I am also interested in what happens when we expand our mapping of racialized and diasporic affects within the life of texts that are viewed as overly ludic or as lacking the gravitas of these experimental forms or within experimental forms that engage seemingly frivolous objects of fashion and beauty—those, in short, that might be considered too "apolitical," "feminized," or commodified for intellectual rehabilitation within studies of race and diaspora.

As will become clearer in the pages that follow, the forms of belonging that beauty's affects make intelligible—even as they variously challenge the neoliberal market rationalities and capitalist heteropatriarchies of the new global economy—are not always convertible to a politics that we might recognize in the modes of social transformation, transgression of social norms, or revolutionary action. Mapping the juxtapolitical register of beauty revises and disrupts a narrative of resistance that has become a dominant way of framing Asian American studies. The framework of resistance risks imposing certain political unities onto identity categories that are otherwise fractured by class, nationality, religious, gender, generational, linguistic, and sexual differentiation. It also risks overlooking the way that Asian American racial formations often collude with the assimilative, multicultural logic of the state, rather than adhering to the oppositional consciousness of movements for racial equality, even when Asian immigrants are stereotyped and excluded by the state as "perpetual foreigners."[34] Because resistance frames Asian American scholars' commitments to antiracist and anticapitalist politics, scholars in the field also tend to read Asian American *cultural production* through the framework of resistance, a tendency that "constrains the ways in which we understand the dynamic production, consumption, and circulation of popular culture" (Mani, *Aspiring* 12). At the same time, as the Asian American cultural critic Lisa Lowe reminds us, "some of the most powerful [cultural] practices may not always be the explicitly oppositional ones, may not be understood by contemporaries and may be less overt and recognizable than others" (69). Keeping in mind both cautions about our collective desires for resistance and the places where it can be found, my aim is to demonstrate how assemblages of beauty generate modes of sociality and political relationality in which subjects must confront their *uneven* access to social and economic capital and *contingent* and *partial* claims to formal and cultural citizenship.

Outline of the Book

In the first part of *Fashioning Diaspora*—chapters 1 and 2—I examine beauty as a form of physical attractiveness that materializes the failed promises of national and transnational belonging for diasporic Indian women, postcolonial Indian men, and white American women. In chapter 1, I focus on the exceptional beauty of the eponymous Indian heroine in Bharati Mukherjee's seminal novel of the Indian American "immigrant experience," *Jasmine* (1989). Jasmine's beauty operates as an assemblage by ceaselessly generating both the promise and limits of national belonging throughout her migrations. Jasmine's beauty—which takes the form of a series of makeovers—is deterritorializing in that it offers Jasmine temporary release from a set of socially marginalized positions within the Indian and US nations, and it is also territorializing in that it simultaneously forces her to remain tethered to these positions. I show how Jasmine's beauty at once seeks to manage *and* threatens to expose her social positions as a rural postcolonial Indian, working-class, and undocumented immigrant subject, a set of marginalized subjectivities that much postcolonial feminist scholarship on the novel has overlooked. Jasmine's exceptional beauty exposes the terms of national belonging within a not yet fully liberalized Indian nation and within a multicultural yet anti-immigrant US nation. The chapter then argues that Jasmine's desire to be "plain" expresses an alternative form of national belonging, though provisional and unrealized, within the novel's political imagination. Unlike beauty's mutating attachments to either social valorization or social denigration, plainness is a form of cultural citizenship that raises the possibility of rendering material histories of racial difference ordinary—rather than socially valorized or denigrated—within the US nation.

Chapter 2 examines how Indian beauty's socializing capacities expand outward beyond the multiply marginalized female diasporic subject and beyond the territorial reach of the nation in the South Asian American writer Jhumpa Lahiri's short-fiction collection *Interpreter of Maladies* (1999). In this chapter, beauty is a form of glamour, sophistication, and bourgeois charm that operates on non-Indian, nonfemale bodies in a transnational context. In Lahiri's fiction, beauty is an attribute of the upwardly mobile, cosmopolitan, Indian female body and dovetails with the advent of neoliberal citizenship practices in India in the 1990s. In Lahiri's stories, feminine beauty generates affects that illuminate and critique transnational mobility as a form of liberal cosmopolitanism and thus constitute Lahiri's feminist cosmopolitics. Within both India and America, white American women and postcolonial and immigrant Indian men encounter an Indian female glamour and sophistication that incite and thwart desires for transnational belonging. These desires revise what Berlant has described as prosthetic femininity (*Female* 109), a desire to wear a particular brand of femininity as one's own, and what the cultural anthropologist Aihwa Ong has called "flexible citizenship," a form of transnational belonging that involves elite diasporic subjects' use of transnational links in order to accumulate economic and political power within a global arena. Lahiri's fiction points to the failures of these neoliberal modes of transnational belonging but remains equally critical of national attachments, engaging this mode of cosmopolitan feminine embodiment in order to "provincialize" a dominant Hindu national culture in diaspora. The chapter concludes with a consideration of how Lahiri's own celebrated beauty, reflected in mass-media images and in popular and critical commentary surrounding her literary celebrity, paradoxically makes intelligible and threatens to reterritorialize her feminist cosmopolitical stance toward beauty as a form of global agency within her fiction.

In the second part of the book—chapters 3, 4, and 5—I examine how the beauty assemblage unfolds across a lesser-known archive of literary and artistic production in order to map the capacities of Indian beauty to produce emergent forms of diasporic belonging. In chapter 3, Indian female beauty finds expression as a set of performances and consumer practices among diasporic female youth that forge new possibilities for diasporic citizenship. The first part of the chapter shows that a short story about the Miss India USA pageant, Pallavi Dixit's "Pageant" (2009), reimagines Indian beauty and pageantry beyond an idealized diasporic Indian femininity and as part of an affective economy that generates affiliations between a middle-class pageant contestant and quasi-legal South Asian male service-sector workers who are employed as members of the pageant's waitstaff. The chapter then extends the practice of diasporic citizenship to the marketing and fictional narrative of an Indian American Girl doll, Neela Sen, an anticolonialist, revolutionary, girl freedom fighter. I pay special attention to the girl protagonist Neela's negotiations of colonial-era fashions in shaping her anticolonial feminist consciousness and to the way that the politics of clothing in the fictional account, *Neela*, overlap with and diverge from American Girl's overall multicultural mission of politicizing girlhood through consumer culture. Fashion, I argue, is central to the novel's interlocking political projects of diasporic consumer feminism, diasporic nationalism, and anti-imperialism. The chapter concludes with an examination of Kavita Daswani's young-adult "chick lit" novel *Indie Girl* (2007), in which a young Indian American woman aspires to be part of a creative class of global fashion industrialists. I show that Indie develops a diasporic racial consciousness when she learns that her membership in this class is crucially tied to fraught intimacies with her local ethnic community and to the lives of Indian women who are part of a global garment industry.

In the visual and performance art that I examine in chapters 4 and 5, diasporic feminist artists repurpose and remediate South Asian fashions, namely, the bindi and the sari, during the height of Indo-chic as a dominant global fashion aesthetic. In shifting attention away from fashion's material production, which has been the focus of much feminist scholarship on Indian fashion and fashionability, these artists nonetheless remain concerned with the materiality of these style objects in generating distinctly feminist modes of embodiment. In chapter 4, I examine how two media artists, Swati Khurana and Prema Murthy, self-consciously cite the circulation of fashion within the realm of the visual. Yet they also experiment with radical forms of materiality that dislodge the bindi from its status as mere style commodity and imagine a response to Indo-chic's orientalist appropriations in ways that move beyond a recourse to cultural authenticity and that produce culturally inappropriable, feminist modes of diasporic feminine embodiment. In chapter 5, I examine the ways that the Kenyan Indian American poet and performance artist Shailja Patel's narrative- and performance-based sartorial engagements with a quintessential Indian female garment—the sari—reveal the potentialities of clothing to materialize cross-racial and nonheteronormative generational attachments.

The story of diasporic beauty that I tell here is a necessarily partial and incomplete one. Invariably, texts will have escaped my notice, and this is a risk that is itself symptomatic of the complex and paradoxical nature of beauty, the way that it is everywhere and yet difficult to pin down and to animate as a social domain. Sometimes, beauty might be almost imperceptible, fleeting, or seemingly inconsequential within the representational world of a text or set of texts that I discuss—it might come alive in a look, an article of clothing put on and then discarded, a conversation, a gait, a gesture, a material object that flashes onto the scene and then disappears. In prioritizing these "beautiful forms" within the life of a text or set of texts, I foreground their capacity to make intelligible bodies, subjects, and populations, such as women, girls, service-sector and fashion-industry workers, postcolonial subjects, and sexual minorities. I also attend to the intimacies, affiliations, and embodiments that they make possible, such as transclass, cross-gender, interracial, cross-generational, and nonheteronormative attachments. These are subjects, populations, and social relations that have remained largely unseen and unattended to in studies of diaspora. Even when the cultural texts that I examine are not explicitly "about" beauty or even when the subjects within these texts are positioned only tenuously within or fully outside the register of beauty or the dominant fashion system, beauty is nonetheless "observable within certain social relationships and moments" across these texts (Edmonds 20). This book shows that beauty is a material and affective force that structures the diasporic social imaginary, one that reworks some of its most established narratives and opens up emerging ones. Its mapping of diaspora through assemblages of beauty and fashion offers a conceptual lens through which to rethink feminized cultures such as beauty and fashion as politically degraded or denigrated and as instead vital to our understanding of diasporic racial formation within a new global economy. While this project limits itself to a transnational feminist analysis of beauty in South Asian American cultural production, my hope is that its approach to beauty can allow for a richer understanding of previously neglected or as yet emerging archives of diasporic cultural production that foreground beauty as everyday practices of racial formation, sociality, and belonging.

1 /   Excepting Beauty and Negotiating Nationhood in Bharati Mukherjee's *Jasmine*

Does beauty come under the jurisdiction of the nation-state?
—WAI CHEE DIMOCK (107)

Halfway through *Jasmine* (1989), Bharati Mukherjee's seminal immigrant novel about becoming American, the eponymous "illegal" immigrant heroine stumbles upon an underground beauty economy—the importing and sorting of Indian women's hair. Jasmine watches as her guardian, Professorji, measures and sorts switches of rural Indian village women's hair in a restaurant basement in the South Asian immigrant "ghetto" of Flushing, New York:

> The hair came in great bundles from the middlemen in villages as small as Hasnapur [Jasmine's home village] all over India. . . . Every weekday Professorji sat from eight o'clock till six on a kitchen ladder-stool in a room he rented in the basement of the Khyber Bar BQ measuring and labeling the length and thickness of each separate hair. Junk hair he sold to wigmakers. Fine hair to instrument makers. Eventually, scientific instruments and the US Defense Department. It was no exaggeration to say that the security of the free world, in some small way, depended on the hair of Indian village women. (153)

Exportable as an ingredient for either feminine beauty products (wigs) or for technologies of US national security, Indian women's hair is a commodity that circulates within both a dominant US economy and an Indian economy about to enter into market neoliberalism during the final years of the Cold War.[1] Synecdoches of Indian village women's bodies, the bundles of hair figure as racialized and gendered fetishes in the transnational trafficking of bodies and goods. Professorji points to this transnational economy's vital dependence on Indian village women's allegedly more "naturally" beautiful hair. He tells Jasmine that Indian women's hair is free of "shampoos, gels, dyes, and permanents" and contains a "virginity and innocence" (153) that American women's hair lacks.

Professorji's fetishistic valorization of Indian women's hair as pure, natural, and therefore more valuable than American women's hair uncannily prefigures the construction of female consumer citizens within a globalizing Indian fashion and beauty industry, as I discussed briefly in the introduction. *Jasmine* was published just two years before Indian economic reform policies inaugurated the unimpeded flow of transnational goods and capital in 1991, which impelled the transnationalization of the beauty and fashion industries on the subcontinent. The scene of underground Indian beauty in Mukherjee's novel certainly anticipates this beauty boom. But it also lays bare the attenuated forms of gendered violence that underwrite it, as Indian women's beautiful hair is depicted as part of an illicit global hair trade. This hair trade is now a legitimate multibillion-dollar industry and has been the subject of such recent documentary films as Raffaele Brunetti and Marco Leopardi's *Hair India* (2008) and Jeff Stilson's *Good Hair* (2009). These films document the increasing global demand for Indian women's hair—collected mostly from rural villages such as Jasmine's own Hasnapur—due to the entry of large multinational beauty brands into India and the increasing demand for weaves and extensions among the upper middle classes in India and Europe and the United States.[2]

Yet when seen through Jasmine's eyes, this economy of Indian female beauty does not hail a transnational consumer citizenry, as do the mass-media images of beautiful Indian women that I discussed in the introduction. Captured in the switches of hair, Indian female beauty is instead a material object of an emerging global hair trade that constellates transnational histories of racialization, labor, gender exploitation, and migration. These histories redound upon Jasmine as an undocumented South Asian immigrant subject. Professorji invites Jasmine—as a "former" Indian village woman—to sell her hair to him so that he can purchase for her a forged green card that would allow her to seek employment and to "feel safe" (148) in the highly policed immigrant space of Flushing. Such a promise of safety and security, however, contains an ironic twist. On the one hand, the prospect of selling her hair offers Jasmine a way of securing legal (resident alien) and economic status within the US nation during the anti-immigrant fervor of the late 1980s.[3] On the other hand, Jasmine's observations about the use of Indian women's hair in the making of "scientific instruments" for the US Defense Department point to her recognition that Indian hair also helps to secure US national borders against undocumented immigrants like her—and even documented immigrants like Professorji—whose labor, body, and body parts are required for such securitization. Jasmine's beautiful hair might thus afford her a provisional feeling of freedom; but it also could be used as the raw material for the imperial nation-state's biopolitical surveillance. This scene's valorization of Indian female beauty thus amasses a set of tensions and contradictions around Jasmine's migration, mobility, and citizenship.

In the rest of this chapter, I examine how Jasmine's physical beauty operates as an assemblage across her migrations within India and the United States. Jasmine's beauty is a deterritorializing force that offers her temporary release from a set of socially marginalized positions within both the Indian and US nations—her rurality, migrant labor, and illegality. And it is also territorializing, in the way that it forces Jasmine to remain ineluctably bound to these positions by materializing, or threatening to materialize, the histories that produce them. Despite the publication of *Jasmine* more than a decade before Indian beauty queens were to be heralded as some of the most beautiful women in the world and before Indian female beauty and fashion were to explode within global markets, *Jasmine* maps the material histories that produce Indian female beauty as emblematic of Indian global modernity and the way that this beauty allows Jasmine to manage the material realities of national and diasporic migration.

Jasmine charts the eponymous heroine's migrations across India and the United States and the multiple identities—Jyoti, Jasmine, Jazzy, Jassy, and Jane—that she acquires within each of these migrations. Jasmine leaves her native village of Hasnapur to move to the city of Jullundhar, India, where, after escalating communal violence claims her husband's life, she secures illegal documents, hops a plane, and is smuggled aboard a cargo ship and across the US border in South Florida. From there, she migrates to the South Asian ghetto of Flushing, New York, to Manhattan, where she falls in love with her white male employer, and finally to the "American heartland" of rural Baden, Iowa, where she marries a farmer and becomes pregnant with his child.

Because *Jasmine* is so often framed as an exemplary text of the post-1965 Indian American "immigrant experience," I argue that Indian female beauty must be understood as a crucial part of that exemplarity and a reframing of that experience. Despite a veritable explosion in South Asian American literary production within the past two decades, *Jasmine* continues to occupy a central place on the syllabi of college courses on Asian American, South Asian American, immigrant, and postcolonial literatures (Carter-Sanborn 575). *Jasmine's* contentious canonicity within these various fields of literary study has much to do with the way the novel is most often read and taught: as a straightforward narrative of progress from tradition to modernity, third world to first world, oppression to liberation. Feminist literary critics in particular have tended to read Jasmine's migrations—and the new names that Jasmine acquires along the way—as mapping her journey from foreign subject to one who exuberantly celebrates "becoming American." Sandhya Shukla has observed that Mukherjee "has in some sense become representative of Indianness to Americans" in part because she "constructs a sense of Indianness with clear gestures towards the possibilities of becoming American" (165, 161). As a result, the novel has also been accused of divesting diasporic Indianness of any ties to the subcontinent. Speaking more explicitly of the novel's US nationalistic endorsements, Patricia Chu has characterized *Jasmine* as a "female immigrant version of the American Horatio Alger myth" (130). Postcolonial feminist critics such as Inderpal Grewal, Rajini Srikanth, and Susan Koshy, among others, further link the novel's assimilative and US nationalistic investments to its heteropatriarchal narrative of white male rescue, focusing on Jasmine's sexual relationships with white men. These critics see these investments as absolving the novel (and Mukherjee) of having to address histories of both progressive feminist politics in India and the structural inequalities of race in the United States.

Rather than contesting these feminist critiques of Mukherjee's novel outright, I nuance and unsettle feminist claims that *Jasmine* is an Indian immigrant narrative of American exceptionalism—a nationalist narrative in which US populations understand the United States as a uniquely free and democratic nation founded on the ideals of personal liberty. I do this through a careful examination of Jasmine's beauty as a form of racial and gendered exceptionalism. Such forms of bodily exceptionalism, I argue, animate a set of crises and contradictions around the South Asian female immigrant subject's Indian and US national belonging. From Jasmine's childhood days in Hasnapur, when she is named the most beautiful of nine daughters, to her movie-star looks in Jullundhar to her "jazzy" femininity in Florida and New York, her good looks clearly mark her as somehow special. Jasmine's exceptional beauty within both India and the United States in one sense attests to the transnational formation of the model minority stereotype, in which the US state heralds so-called model South Asian immigrant subjects as ethnic-minority exemplars of its liberal ideals of freedom and progress. These immigrants' so-called Asian values of hard work and capitalist achievement are then leveraged to secure the truth of such ideals.[4] Model minority discourses of post-1965 South Asian immigration to the United States construct these allegedly economically and culturally exceptional Asian immigrants as more easily absorbed into the liberal logic of multicultural inclusion[5] and, concomitantly, as aiding and abetting in the historical erasure of racial inequalities in the constitution of the nation and in promoting it as a racial democracy.[6] Yet, as we see in the scene with the switches of Indian hair, Jasmine's confrontation with her beauty is also inextricably linked to the social inequities that constitute her rurality, racialized labor, and illegality. The encounter with beauty is therefore also one that repeatedly fractures the coherence of South Asian model minority discourses and the liberal fantasies of national inclusion that support them.[7]

A transnational feminist examination of Jasmine's beauty provides a radical reframing of the South Asian immigrant "experience" as one that is not as rooted in a model minority narrative of upward mobility as it may first appear. I show that Jasmine's beauty generates much of the text's narrative momentum by constantly unfolding across her socially marginalized positions (rural postcolonial, migrant laborer, "illegal alien") within the nation, animating both the promise and limits of Indian and American national belonging. That is, Jasmine's beauty operates not vertically to secure her progressive belonging to the US nation but rhizomatically, forcing her to confront a range of social inequities that follow her with various intensities and duration across her Indian and US migrations. Moreover, I show that in its attachments to forms of national inclusion and exclusion, Indian female beauty in *Jasmine* complicates liberal humanistic discourses about beauty, in which beauty is regarded solely as a redemptive force that facilitates social inclusion through its alignment with democratic ideals such as empowerment, rights, and freedom. Such liberal democratic ideals themselves traffic in a fetishistic logic of beauty in which the conferral or possession of it has depended on the historical erasure and denial of the realities of race and nationality, among other axes of social difference.[8]

We see in Jasmine's apprehension of (her) racialized femininity within the transnational beauty economy of Indian hair, for example, a much more complicated logic. Beauty does not promise Jasmine the ability to transcend the historical and material conditions of her position as a rural, migrant, and undocumented South Asian subject as a way of claiming belonging within the nation. Rather, beauty refuses any facile disavowal or transcendence of her racial and national difference and thus of her excessive foreignness/nonwhiteness. In the underground economy of Indian hair, Jasmine's beauty is materially linked to her precarious status within the US nation as a racialized immigrant subject. Contained within Jasmine's beauty is the promise of national inclusion through beauty's exchange value—selling her hair to purchase a green card. But as an ingredient for the Defense Department, beautiful Indian hair is used to secure US borders against immigrant subjects like Jasmine, marking Jasmine's potential exclusion from the nation. Jasmine's beauty allows her to see herself as at once a model minority—a racialized embodiment of liberal democratic ideals of freedom and progress through the achievement of legal and economic status—*and* as a racial problem that the xenophobic US state must manage. In the face of the impossibility of legal citizenship, Jasmine recognizes that selling her hair offers her the tenuous promise of cultural citizenship.[9]

Beauty's Borders: Rurality and Metro-Modernity

If Jasmine's potential insertion into the transnational economy of Indian hair locates her precarious position within the US nation, then it does so by implicitly outing her identity as a former Indian village woman within this economy. Even before Jasmine arrives in the United States, her beauty allows her to manage her rurality within India in order to conform to the Indian nation's emerging vision of itself as globally modern. At the same time, Jasmine's "metro-modern" femininity illuminates the unevenness of the Indian state's modernizing project as well as her ambivalence about her place within that project. This project included the forced management and withdrawal of state services to rural populations; these populations were both violently subject to and figured outside the vicissitudes of state-sponsored modernization.

Unlike in Flushing, in Hasnapur and Jullundhar, Jasmine's femininity discloses an illicit trade economy that is emerging aboveground as part of Indian modernization. Earlier in the novel, Jasmine, in a former incarnation as fourteen-year-old Jyoti, travels from her "feudal" village of Hasnapur to a movie house in the "modern" city of Jullundhar to meet her future husband, Prakash, an English-speaking, Punjabi engineer whom Jasmine calls a "modern man, a city man" (76). Before leaving Hasnapur, Jyoti consciously dresses for "effect" to secure her place in the bourgeois marriage market. In doing so, she is keenly aware of her facial disfigurement, acquired from rebelling against domestic seclusion by playing outdoors. Near the beginning of the novel, young Jyoti falls and cuts her head on a twig sticking out of a bundle of firewood, much to the horror of her older sisters, who, with their unmarred "butter smooth arms," tell her, "Now your face is scarred for life! How will the family ever find you a husband?" (5). Also "scabrous armed from leaves and thorns," Jyoti attempts to distract from her tainted appearance by dressing "movie-starrish": "Effect must be calculated. I braided my hair three different ways. From my mother's rusted-out trunk, I extracted one of her few Lahore saris, a pale peach embroidered all over with gold leaves. I added Pitaji's [my father's] dark glasses. . . . At the last minute I stuck a jasmine wreath in my hair" (70). Jasmine's attempts at self-beautification and "calculated effect" are part of her desire to modernize herself so that she can appear as a feminine complement to Prakash's understanding of himself as the new modern, urban, middle-class man.

Jasmine's metro-modern self-makeover ostensibly erases all signs of rurality in her comportment and countenance. Yet her self-transformation also indexes a blurring of the Indian nation-state's distinctions between the rural and the urban as Jasmine can measure the success of her gendered performance of modernity only through an object that ambiguously marks the border between the two spheres. As she dresses to produce the look of metro-modern femininity before her journey to Jullundhar, Jasmine checks her appearance in a "rearview rectangle that Arvind-prar [her brother] had twisted off a UN jeep he'd found rusting in the demilitarized zone near the border": "At the bottom of the mirror were some English words I didn't exactly understand . . . OBJECTS IN MIRROR ARE CLOSER THAN THEY APPEAR" (71). The surface irony of her reflected gaze remains in the fact that while Jasmine apprehends her newly beautified self as an object, one that through her successful performance of bourgeois femininity gets her "closer" to Jullundhar, Prakash, and modernity, the object "closer than it appears" must also be Jasmine's palimpsestic facial scarring, betraying the intended "effect" of a metropolitan femininity. Moreover, her metro-modern appearance is "reflected back" to her through the severed part of an object that marks the uneven topography of India's modernizing project: a rusted UN jeep retrieved from the demilitarized zone of the Punjab. The jeep serves as a reminder of antistate movements in the Punjab during the early 1980s in which the Khalsa Lions sought a separatist Sikh state (Khalistan) and of state violence under Indira Gandhi's state-sponsored modernizing campaign in the mid-1970s. Known as the Emergency, the campaign suspended civil liberties while attempting to modernize the nation by implementing population control through, among other measures, forced sterilization in rural and working-class communities. The UN jeep mirror's refraction of Jasmine's palimpsestic wounds therefore metaphorizes the modernizing project of India as a cosmetic one that attempted to rid the country of its unseemly rural, subaltern others. As Jasmine later reflects, "I put on the dark sunglasses to *look* movie-starrish" (72, my emphasis). Like the Indian nation-state's modernizing campaigns, Jasmine's modern, metropolitan "look" remains a primarily perfunctory cosmetology.

The vestigial presence of the UN jeep also locates modern Jullundhar well within the boundaries of "feudal" Hasnapur. Bordering the village of Hasnapur, the demilitarized zone (DMZ) is also arguably a future export processing zone, or EPZ. Jasmine earlier observes that "in villages close enough to the border, smuggling was not an unacceptable profession" (49). National borders, as sites of state and antistate violence, double as sites for the illicit trading of electronics that must be serviced as part of the state's modernizing project. In the novel, these are often the same goods made over into technologies of religious and communal violence, such as bombs and small explosives. Prakash's job as an engineer in Jullundhar depends on electronic goods smuggled across village border towns such as Hasnapur, annexing these towns into the Indian state's emerging vision of itself as a modern nation. Thus, Jasmine's ability to see her facial scars in the jeep's mirror also alludes to the violent reach of the nation-state: the disfiguring vicissitudes of state-sponsored modernization are "closer than they appear." As Jasmine drives with Prakash into the countryside on their leisure Sundays, she observes the violent contradictions of a nation poised to open its borders to foreign investment: "Beggars with broken bodies shoved alms bowls at suited men in automobiles. Shacks sprouted like toadstools around high-rise office buildings. Camels loped past satellite dishes" (80). The DMZ/EPZ is a border zone along which a history of economic disparity and military and communal violence is only fetishistically covered over by its purported modernization.

Even as Jasmine feels pressed to enter into the state's modernizing project as a "new kind of city woman" by concealing facial disfigurations resulting from her tomboyish play (77), such self-beautification delimits her role in this allegedly more modern Indian space: she becomes

Prakash's aesthetic accouterment. Jasmine notices that Prakash treats her very much like the electronic equipment that he repairs. The VCRs, radios, and televisions are illicit "high-status goods" that are often conspicuously displayed from tenement windows as the symbolic wealth of an emerging bourgeois elite: "He liked to show me off. . . . He said, 'You are small and sweet and heady, my Jasmine.' . . . Jyoti, Jasmine, I shuttled between identities" (77). Jasmine's performance of bourgeois femininity secures her place within the Indian state's modernizing regime, but her feeling of shuttling between rural and urban identifications betrays an uncertainty about this very performance. Communalist violence—a Sikh "terrorist" bombing in the Punjab, a sign of India's uneven modernization that claims Prakash's life—only reinforces her ambivalence about state modernization, prompting her to (illegally) migrate to the United States. Once in the United States, Jasmine's beauty allows her to aspire to and to claim model minority status and thus to manage yet a different set of crises around her illegality and her legibility as an embodiment of racialized immigrant labor.

Beauty's Labors: Legality, Care Work, and the Racial Management of Shame and Fear

Many postcolonial and diasporic feminist readings of *Jasmine* have suggested that Jasmine leaves India in order to secure a place within the (white) American mainstream through a process of liberal feminist self-reinvention. However, when mapped through beauty's deterritorializing and reterritorializing force, Jasmine's US migrations reveal, more precisely, her racial self-management. Such self-management is a response to the social constraints of a multicultural US nation in which racial differences are both celebrated and policed and, as Rey Chow has argued, where the very categories of race and ethnicity remain tied to the commodification of (undervalued) labor.[10] Within these historical and material constraints, Jasmine's racial self-management-through-beauty operates within the vicissitudes of what Chow has described as "coercive mimeticism," a process by which "those who are marginal to mainstream Western culture are . . . expected to objectify themselves in accordance with the already seen," to appear, to themselves and to dominant culture, as ethnics (107).

Though feminist critics rightly have remained critical of Jasmine's liberal self-making, opting out of such self-management altogether would be a rather difficult and costly prospect for this rural, undocumented, and working-class subject. Jasmine's beauty promises to mitigate the multiple risks of economic and political insecurity. In what follows, I show that, to the extent that Jasmine's attribution and performance of beauty enable her model minority racialization, they do so by allowing her a "sense of legitimacy and security" under the constraints of capitalist liberalism (Chow 110). Once in the United States, Jasmine's comeliness distinguishes her from other immigrant subjects and communities of color—such as her guardian, Professorji, and the Flushing community of South Asian immigrants with whom she resides, as well as the Caribbean "day mummies" in Manhattan and the Guatemalan Kanjobal Indian migrant field and domestic laborers with whom Jasmine works and socializes. These populations are racialized through their participation in undervalued forms of migrant and working-class labor that ostensibly prohibit their assimilation into dominant national culture. For Jasmine, though, beauty holds out the promise of assimilation, such that assimilation becomes the social reward for the immigrant woman's beauty. Still, even as Jasmine's beauty conditions and secures her will to assimilate through liberal self-making, it also paradoxically impels complex and even violent confrontations with her status as an undocumented immigrant and, concomitantly, with her embodiment as racialized immigrant labor. Jasmine negotiates the everyday material realities of her illegality and working-class labor through her feminine attractiveness. Such negotiations, rather than allowing her to lay claim to the US nation as a legal, upwardly mobile subject, ultimately mark her as inassimilable and expose the very material histories of race, nation, and labor that she seeks to conceal.

Upon Jasmine's arrival in the United States, she is raped by Half-Face, a cargo-ship captain who smuggles Jasmine, who is part of a population of "refugees, mercenaries and guest workers" (100), across the US border in Florida. Jasmine had hoped to open an electronics store in the United States with Prakash. The rape marks Jasmine's body, both in terms of sexual violence and self-mutilation: she slices her tongue—an act of self-purification—just before murdering Half-Face and fleeing the scene. Yet the encounter with Half-Face also results in the threat of another bodily disfiguration. Prior to raping her, Half-Face perceives that Jasmine is "afraid" of his threat to "rub scars all over [her] pretty little face" (113). Half-Face's perception of Jasmine's fear of facial deformation—rather than of her fear of being raped—suggests that for Jasmine a loss of beauty might be a more severe form of racial injury than sexual violence is. Half-Face's threat of scarring Jasmine's face also contains within it the possible recognition that Jasmine's face already *is* scarred—the very scar that she earlier attempts to conceal in order to become a metro-modern Indian woman. In threatening physical ugliness, Half-Face threatens to exacerbate and multiply an existing facial deformation. Ugliness could potentially prohibit Jasmine from using her beauty to mitigate the racial denigration that she faces as an undocumented immigrant: whereas Jasmine's status as an undocumented migrant prevents her from appealing to the US state as a victim of sexual violence, physical beauty, as we have already seen, holds out the promise of other forms of social power.

That the moment of Jasmine's arrival in the United States is marked by an encounter with (a loss of) physical beauty is significant for the way that it resonates with and at the same time revises nineteenth-century eugenics and anti-immigration discourses that frequently cast the immigrant body as an inherently disabled body. The disability studies scholar Douglas Baynton has shown that social "fitness was equated with beauty and ugliness with disability" within nineteenth-century eugenics discourse and that proponents of anti-immigrant legislation often used what they perceived to be immigrants' "visible abnormalities" to disqualify them from entering the nation (28). Immigration inspectors set apart for examination "visibly disabled people"—as well as those whose ethnic appearance was assumed to signal bodily abnormality—upon arrival at New York City's Ellis Island (28). Baynton here points to a slippage not only between perceived physical and mental abnormalities—to appear physically abnormal was, according to eugenicist logic, to indicate mental deficiencies as well—but also between "visibly disabled" people and an ethnic appearance that deemed immigrants physically and mentally unfit for US entry.

Jasmine, unlike her nineteenth-century immigrant predecessors whose ethnic appearance might have marked them as socially unfit bodies, is of course recognized as "pretty." It is Half-Face, so called because he "had lost an eye and ear and most of his cheek in a paddy field in Vietnam" (104), who is quite literally disfigured from the violence of war. Yet insofar as Half-Face threatens facial scarring as a form of bodily contagion that he can "rub" off of himself and onto Jasmine and insofar as disability within histories of anti-immigration discourse is assigned to immigrant bodies that are deemed to be socially "unfit," the threat of facial disfigurement is to the beautiful Jasmine akin to the threat of being made to possess a physical disability. Though not tied to historically state-mandated forms of physical and mental fitness, beauty is a form of social fitness that would allow her to mitigate the other social inequalities that she might face *as* an undocumented subject, one who remains aware that she is unprotected by the very state into which she seeks entry. Certainly, Jasmine's pretty face still cannot shield her from her susceptibility to racialized and gendered violence (including being raped by Half-Face). But Half-Face's perception of Jasmine's fear of being physically disfigured anticipates the way that, later in the novel, Jasmine's beauty (her valuable hair) actually does allow her to manage her undocumented status.

Though Half-Face points to the potential social value of Jasmine's beauty in the face of her illegality, beauty later becomes a sign of her devalued labor as a migrant subject. Shortly after Jasmine is raped, Lillian Gordon, a philanthropic white Quaker woman, rescues Jasmine, trains her to be hired out as a "domestic" and a "picker" (134), and remakes the destitute Jasmine into "Jazzy." After ordering Jasmine to take off her bloodstained salwar kameez, Lillian has her change into "Peter Pan collars, maxi skirts, T-shirts with washed-out pictures, sweaters, cords, and loafers" and instructs her on how to "walk American" (132). When Jasmine "successfully" complies, Lillian pays her two dollars and congratulates her by saying, "You pass, Jazzy" (133). The makeover centers less on Lillian's desire for Jasmine to be made into a beautiful subject (since she presumably already is). Rather, mirroring the aesthetic of riffing and improvisation that are central to the musical and dance forms of jazz (which the name "Jazzy" itself riffs on), the makeover demands the performance of a feminine attitude, gait, and style that Jasmine understands as a quintessentially American form of embodiment. Jasmine's ability to perform these gendered improvisations secures her bodily exceptionality in comparison to other racialized immigrants whose brownness makes them particularly susceptible to state surveillance. Lillian tells Jasmine that because of her makeover, she "passes" as "American" in contrast to the other "dark people *like* [Jasmine]" whom "[the INS] pick up" (133, my emphasis).[11] Given that discourses of passing in the United States are historically embedded in the stories of light-skinned or mixed-race African Americans, what does it mean for Jasmine to pass as American in contrast to those dark bodies that are *like*, rather than unlike, hers?[12] How or to what extent does her "jazziness" afford her an approximation to Americanness in the face of her immigrant brownness?

Such questions of passable brownness and citizenship become particularly pressing within the anti-immigrant legislation that frames *Jasmine*'s publication. Jasmine was published during large-scale immigration reform laws such as the 1986 Immigration Reform and Control

Act (IRCA), which supposedly redressed the so-called open-door Asian immigration policy of the Immigration and Nationality Act of 1965. Acts such as the IRCA levied fines against employers for hiring undocumented immigrants and required employers to attest to their employees' immigration status, in addition to ratifying other forms of immigrant surveillance. Jasmine is aware of the particular danger that her "delicate status" (136) as an undocumented migrant poses to her during this time: she characterizes herself as among a cast of "refugees and mercenaries, and guest workers" illegally entering the United States on the Gulf Shuttle (100); she watches INS raids on the television (27); and she later discovers that Lillian is jailed for "harboring undocumenteds" (136) in her home.

In telling Jasmine that her performance of jazziness allows her to pass as American, Lillian revitalizes a discourse of passing as white within the early-twentieth-century context of state-sponsored segregation law through a discourse of passing as brown within the context of 1980s anti-immigration law. In making over Jasmine into an alluring (and therefore passable) form of brownness, Lillian solicits the aesthetic of racial mixing, or mélange. As the literary critic Anne Cheng has argued, mélange allows women of color to pass as beautiful within predominantly white spaces or under the constraints of white ideals of feminine beauty by "denouncing yet revealing [racialized] difference" ("Wounded" 207). The racial indeterminacy of the biracial body is particularly useful in considering how Jasmine's made-over appearance affords her the ability to remain undetected by the state. South Asians such as Jasmine have occupied a racially ambiguous position within a longer history of US racial formations. Eluding definitive racial categorization as black, white, or Asian over the course of the twentieth century, South Asians have been understood as possessing a kind of racial indeterminacy.[13]

The aesthetic of mélange promises to dispel the threat of recognizable and undesirable brownness, such as that of undocumented migrant laborers like the Kanjobal Indians whom, along with Jasmine, Lillian also trains to be pickers and domestics. Lillian reminds Jasmine, "Now remember, if you walk and talk American, they'll think you were *born* here. Most Americans can't imagine anything else" (134–35, my emphasis). Given histories of South Asian American racial indeterminacy, the aesthetic of mélange is more clearly linked to the biracial or racially mixed black body, since blackness is rarely questioned as "natural-born" Americanness.[14] The makeover that makes Jasmine "look like" a light-skinned black woman allows her to approximate white ideals of aesthetically pleasing (read: nonimmigrant) brownness.[15] After Jasmine performs her jazziness at a shopping mall, Lillian asserts, "You don't strike me as a picker or a domestic" (134), and Jasmine admits to having "worked hard on the walk and deportment" (133). Here, Jasmine's "hard work" at approximating mixed-race black feminine "deportment" disrupts Lillian's view of Jasmine as an embodiment of racialized labor; her "jazzy" femininity exceeds the putative legibility (or the demand for legibility) of legal citizenship.

If as a form of racialized labor Jasmine's performance of jazziness allows her to "look like" a citizen-subject, then it is also a form of labor that redounds upon *Lillian's* citizenship as well. In teaching Jasmine how to be jazzy, Lillian establishes herself as a citizen who operates outside the dominant xenophobic logic of the US state. By "harboring undocumenteds" (136) and training them to be pickers and domestics, Lillian traffics in a form of feminist humanitarianism that defies the state's racist management of immigrant bodies. The teaching of undocumented immigrant women to have usable skills directly violates immigration reform laws such as the IRCA, which promised to "curb undocumented immigration through employer sanctions and increased surveillance of work authorization forms" (Schlund-Vials 127). In rescuing Jasmine *from* the particular forms of racialized labor to which the Kanjobal women are consigned, ostensibly because they do not fall under beauty's regimes of exceptionalism, Lillian rescues Jasmine *to* beauty. In a discussion of US imperial feminist rhetoric that framed veiled Muslim women in the Arab world as in need of "rescue" after the events of 9/11, the cultural anthropologist Lila Abu-Lughod explains, "When you save someone, you are implying that you are saving her *to* something. What violences are entailed in this transformation, and what presumptions are being made about the superiority of that to which you are saving her?" (788–89). In Lillian's estimation, Jasmine's makeover and her "jazzy" appearance as an American-born citizen promise her "a democratic future of movement, choice, and independence, where beauty is imagined to live" (M. Nguyen 367). Jasmine's makeover is an act of humanitarian care that allows Lillian to imagine herself as providing Jasmine with precisely this kind of democratic future, despite Jasmine's lack of formal citizenship.

Lillian becomes a humanitarian citizen through her act of beautifying Jasmine, even as such an act is in direct violation of US laws governing immigrant populations. The kind of feminist humanitarianism that Lillian's makeover enables resembles the way that Western-based feminist nongovernmental organizations (NGOs), such as Beauty Without

Borders, have begun linking the business and practice of beauty to the project of social justice in developing countries ravaged by war and social unrest. The feminist scholar Mimi Nguyen describes the way that such humanitarian projects wield a discourse of democracy through beauty, for example, by helping women in post-9/11 war-ravaged Afghanistan to set up beauty schools and teaching them about modern techniques for applying makeup and cutting and styling hair. Such projects are based in an understanding of beauty as a universal social good that can help to empower women, who are the most vulnerable victims of state and imperial violence. Such forms of self-empowerment function as a form of "humanitarian imperialism" (M. Nguyen), a form of imperialism that reproduces what the postcolonial feminist scholar Ella Shohat, riffing on Gayatri Spivak's construction of "white men . . . saving brown women from brown men" (297), has characterized as white women rescuing brown women from brown men (Shohat and Stam 85). Whereas in Nguyen's analysis of feminist NGOs such as Beauty Without Borders, Western feminists become imperialist humanitarian subjects by using beauty to optimize life for Afghani women whose lives have been ravaged by US imperialist projects in Afghanistan, in Mukherjee's novel, Lillian's makeover of Jasmine is a form of imperialist humanitarianism in the way that it allows Lillian to use beauty as a way of optimizing (Jasmine's) life under the gaze of a xenophobic US state.

Though beauty as a form of care need not advance such forms of liberal rescue (and we will see an example of this in chapter 2), Lillian's makeover of Jasmine does in fact operate in this way. We later learn that Lillian's daughter, Kate, is writing a book about Lillian called *An American Kind of Saint: The Lillian Gordon Story* (137), based on Lillian's work with undocumented women. Given that Lillian's humanitarianism is clearly *un*-American insofar as it is in defiance of immigration law, the biography's title is of course ironic. Yet the naming of Lillian's sainthood as "American" is nonetheless significant for the way that it highlights the imperialist rhetoric inherent in such forms of liberal rescue (who can provide it, who can receive it, under what conditions, etc.). Lillian's makeover of Jasmine into Jazzy is part of a larger community of care that Lillian sees herself as providing undocumented, noncitizen subjects such as pickers and domestics, who fall outside the care of the state. In her makeover of Jasmine into Jazzy, Lillian is both a feminist humanitarian citizen in defiance of IRCA legislation and, at the same time, complicit with a narrative of US exceptionalism through her promotion of beauty as a form of ideal citizenship (natural-born Americanness).

The wearing of jazziness that results from Lillian's makeover of Jasmine also prompts Jasmine's recognition that the racialization of "good" national subjects entirely depends on the racialization of "bad" national subjects and even, as will become clearer later in Jasmine's encounter with the figure of the "Sikh terrorist," bad *non*national subjects. Jasmine later nuances this tension between the simply foreign and the dangerous by concluding, "Educated people are interested in differences; they assume that I'm different from them but exempted from being one of 'them,' the knife-wielding undocumenteds hiding in basements webbing furniture" (33). Moreover, as a form of passable brownness, jazziness demands a historical forgetting of Jasmine's racial traumas as a migrant subject, such as her rape by Half-Face and her subsequent self-mutilation. In telling Jasmine, "Let the past make you wary. . . . But do not let it deform you" (131), Lillian constructs the act of remembering these material histories of racial violence as itself self-deforming, rather than recognizing how the command to forget such violence is another kind of self-abnegation. Jasmine understands that her jazziness is bound to a sociality that is conditioned by her relationship to Lillian as her employee, and she longs for an alternate form of relationality. As Jasmine lives and works with the Kanjobal Indian women, she is temporarily included in their "locked, companionable world" and, in feeling "nostalgic" for it, violates Lillian's eschewal of nostalgia as an act of self-deformation ("do not let it deform you"; 134). As Jazzy, she is denied entry into that companionable world, disclosing the uneven and arbitrary racialization of migrant subjects in the United States. Jazziness thus forecloses on—even as it produces the desire for—the possibility for Jasmine to occupy a social terrain outside a value economy of aesthetically appealing brownness.

Moreover, Lillian's act of rescuing Jasmine from the xenophobic gaze of the state and to the presumably more liberal gaze of beauty actually does little to guarantee democratic belonging for Jasmine. Almost as soon as Lillian carves out a model for Jasmine's brownness that allows her to "pass as American," Jasmine's Indian beauty catalyzes feelings of immigrant shame and becomes reterritorialized into undesirable immigrant brownness. After Jasmine safely secures passage to New York City as a result of her ability to "walk and talk American," she successfully locates her husband's friend Professorji and a larger community of Indian immigrants in Flushing and ends up living with them. Upon discovering Professorji sorting switches of Indian women's hair in the basement of the Khyber Barbecue, Jasmine exposes the way that, despite his training as an engineer in India, his participation in a transnational beauty economy marks his downward mobility in the United States. Professorji's job as a sorter of hair evinces a shift in the US state's demand for unskilled South Asian immigrant labor that began during the late 1980s and that replaced the wave of largely professional-managerial labor of the 1960s and 1970s. Jasmine observes that Professorji is "upset that [she] found him; found him out": "He suspected that I'd deliberately shamed him. . . . Now [his wife] would get suspicious if I didn't talk about the university and his labs and all his assistants" (152). Professorji attempts to manage his shame by insisting to Jasmine that he is still a scientist, and he holds up a long black hair from his tray as "proof": "No synthetic material has the human hair's tensile strength. How to gauge humidity without strands? Like this beautiful one. How to read the weather?" (152). Professorji's inauthentic status as a model minority subject—a "man of science"—depends, paradoxically, on his ability to calibrate and promote Indian beauty's authenticity. In turn, Jasmine recognizes that to sell her "authentically" beautiful hair in exchange for forged immigration documents would mean being bound to an affective economy of immigrant shame. Jasmine watches as a hired "master forger" of immigration documents writes out for her "a fake bill of sale" for her "future hair when it was twenty-four inches, for three thousand dollars": "[Professorji] was buying my silence for his shame, and I felt the shame as well" (153). In agreeing to sell her future hair, Jasmine shares with Professorji feelings of shame around their mutual and mutually constituted acts of self-forgery—Professorji's passing status as a man of science and her passing citizenship: "and I felt the shame as well." Jasmine's admission to feeling shame "as well" suggests that despite both her and Professorji's attempts to avoid it, shame already suffuses and circulates within the underground economy of Indian women's hair. In order to escape these feelings of shame, Jasmine flees the scene with the master forger's "fake bill of sale" but never capitalizes on it. She pays Professorji back with money she earns as an au pair in Manhattan. Jasmine thus rejects both the valorizing and shaming force of beauty through the equal exchange of money for money rather than hair.

Curiously, this moment in *Jasmine* finds rather divergent expression in the work of another South Asian American novelist, Meena Alexander's *Manhattan Music* (1997). Alexander's novel is worth mentioning here not only because Alexander, like Mukherjee, is part of a South Asian American women's literary canon, but also because *Manhattan Music* mediates the process of "becoming American" through a negotiation with beauty. Whereas Jasmine's shame results from the way that her beauty offers her the promise of legal alien status (Indian hair for a green card), Sandhya feels shame when her existing status as a legal alien forces her to see herself as insufficiently beautiful, when her Indianness, in other words, is a sign of her *lack* of physical beauty. When Sandhya receives her green card, she experiences a crisis around her beauty. The conferral of permanent residence status incites in Sandhya a desire for another kind of body, one marked by the guarantees of legal citizenship. She muses,

> Supposing she were to swallow the green card, ingest that plastic, would it pour through her flesh, a curious alchemy that would make her all right in the new world? . . . What if she could peel off her brown skin, dye her hair blonde, turn her body into a pale Caucasian thing . . . ? Stepping carefully onto the sidewalk she pondered the version of beauty that she had gleaned from the old movies that had made their way to Hyderabad [a city in South India]—Marilyn Monroe, though she was far too sexy to emulate. . . . Someone like Michelle Pfeiffer would be better, her filmi body curved just right as she flung her blonde hair over her cheek, held tight to her purse, lifted up her stockinged ankle, showed off her heels. (Alexander, *Manhattan* 7)

For Sandhya to "peel off her brown skin," "dye her hair blonde," and possess a "pale Caucasian" body would, she believes, guarantee her legibility as a citizen body. Such a desire is marked by the recognition that the "legal alien" status conferred on her through the possession of a green card cannot, as she says, make her "all right in the new world." Indeed, the green card serves only to make her more aware of the racial discrimination that she faces as a noncitizen subject. Alexander has noted that this moment in *Manhattan Music*, which is inspired by her own experience receiving a green card during collective acts of racial violence against South Asians in New York City in the 1990s (about which I will have more to say in chapter 4), references the way that many South Asians at that time wished to "be freed of their skin, but of course you can't do that" (*Words* 88). Sandhya wants to pass as a citizen-subject not through a recognizable and desirable form of brownness (mélange), as Jasmine does, but through the embodiment of white feminine Hollywood beauty and glamour. Rather than allowing Sandhya to feel secure in her Indian body as a legal immigrant, her green card incites feelings of racial self-loathing, so that her desire for whiteness is tied to a desire to ameliorate feelings of brown shame. Though *Jasmine* and *Manhattan*

Music are divergent in their representations of cultural citizenship, both speak powerfully to the way that feelings of immigrant belonging are mediated through beauty's shaming force.

Jasmine, for her part, seeks out a job in which she can dissociate herself from the feelings of brown shame that she associates with working-class South Asian immigrant labor. After writing to Lillian's daughter, Kate, who in addition to penning her mother's biography is also a photojournalist whose photos of migrant workers inspired Lillian to shelter and train them for domestic service, Jasmine secures a job as an au pair for an upper-middle-class Manhattanite couple, Wylie and Taylor Hayes. Yet Jasmine's well-practiced jazziness forever threatens to dissolve in this space of white, upper-middle-class wealth: as an au pair, she is an attenuated form of precisely that gendered racialized labor above which Lillian attempts to elevate her and that the Kanjobal are trained to perform: a "domestic." As the postcolonial critic Bruce Robbins has argued, the au pair is a kind of live-in guest whose labor value is not strictly subject to a wage economy, as is the domestic servant's. Yet within an international division of labor in which mostly women travel from former colony to metropole as part of a global care industry, the class distinction that might otherwise exist between the au pair and the domestic servant is rendered indeterminate. In this new world order, in which "gender and racial identities cannot be reduced to class terms," the "third world au pair" might be "an educated, relatively privileged figure or, on the contrary, a domestic servant forced to do the dirtiest, most isolating and most poorly remunerated job" (Robbins 108–9).

Jasmine anxiously negotiates this class indeterminacy of the transnational au pair through her understanding of beauty as part of a consumer economy. When the Hayeses hire Jasmine, they position her within the feminization of global domestic work and its production of demeaning racial stereotypes, telling her, "You're probably tired of Americans assuming that if you're from India or China or the Caribbean, you must be good with children. . . . Ancient American custom, dark-skinned mammies. Don't be flattered by it" (168, 169). The Hayeses display their multiculturalist sensitivity to ethno-national difference through self-deprecating, white liberal guilt for hiring Jasmine as a domestic worker. At the same time, their final reference to "dark-skinned mammies" collapses the geographic boundaries of a feminized domestic labor force, inserting Jasmine's Indianness into a history of black slave labor.[16] Their potential enjoining of Jasmine's "Indianness" to "blackness" here is notable, given the previous discussions of her "jazziness" as a black aesthetic.

But it is also notable because Jasmine is part of community of black female migrant workers. Jasmine communes with two other Caribbean "day mummies" in the building, one of whom likens her job to "slavery" and is motivated to unionize, while the other complains that she is not the "common person" that her job "cleaning up dirt, especially white folks' dirt," has made her (179).[17]

Jasmine repeatedly invokes her own class status as a "professional" in order to exempt herself from colonial and neocolonial histories of racialized labor to which the caregivers attach themselves: "Wylie . . . called me her 'caregiver.' . . . I was a professional, like a schoolteacher or a nurse. . . . I was professional" (175). As if to convince herself of the purchasing power that her status as a professional secures, Jasmine begins to consume indiscriminately: "First came a Japanese knife set. Then a radio-controlled Lamborghini. A cassette car stereo for the car I mean to buy someday. A triple-beveled, herringbone, 14-carat gold neck chain. . . . I was turning over my entire paycheck for things I couldn't use and didn't know how to stop" (186). Jasmine replaces commodification with compulsive consumption in an almost neurotic effort to dissociate from that history of racialized labor that she has been trained to perform and that she is so keen to disavow. Jasmine names her desire for equal participation in consumer capitalism. She confesses, "I fell in love with . . . graceful self-absorption. I wanted to become the person they [Taylor and Wylie] thought they saw: humorous, intelligent, refined, affectionate. Not illegal, not murderer, not widowed, raped, destitute, fearful" (171). Calling her desires for bourgeois femininity "self-absorption," Jasmine implicitly critiques the bourgeois consumerism of her employers, who enable her to consume compulsively. Taylor renames Jasmine "Jassy," which is only a slight variation of "Jazzy." Jasmine is now able to make herself over into Jassy—for example, by buying "spangled heels and silk chartreuse pants" (176)—as a result of her new purchasing power. Yet acts of self-making are made possible only through her participation in feminized global domestic service.

Jasmine's self-makeovers through her newly discovered purchasing power provide her a measure of social privilege, in that looking like a professional allows her to mitigate her racial inferiority as a domestic servant. Yet her encounter with the figure of the "Sikh terrorist" forces a productive undoing of this bourgeois femininity. The encounter impels Jasmine to confront the material histories of her racially denigrated position as an "illegal alien" and, in doing so, to confront her legibility as a terrifying body. The encounter between these figures—terrorist and undocumented migrant—reveals the coconstitution of a geopolitics of terror and a biopolitics of beauty. As Jasmine pushes the Hayeses' daughter, Duff, in a stroller through Central Park, Jasmine is terrified by her (perhaps imagined) sighting of Sukkhi, a Sikh who is fighting for the sovereign Sikh nation of Khalistan and who was Prakash's murderer in India. While Mukherjee's depiction of Sikh masculinities (here and elsewhere) is undeniably problematic in its reproduction of the stereotype of the Sikh terrorist, what is more interesting is the way its deployment throws into crisis Jasmine's self-management as a model minority South Asian.

On the one hand, Jasmine's exceptional beauty consistently codes her as racially and nationally distinct from the (implicitly male) "terrorist" or "enemy within" the Indian and US nations.[18] This carefully maintained distinction between "good" (model minority) and "bad" (terrorist) South Asian subjects functions along gendered lines; such a distinction overlaps with those forms of gendered exceptionalism that distinguish Jasmine from other racialized immigrant laborers such as the Kanjobal Indian migrant workers and the Caribbean "day mummies." Yet on the other hand, Jasmine's sighting of Sukkhi simultaneously reveals the way that these seemingly incommensurable migrant bodies actually shore up each other's abjection from the nation. When Jasmine thinks she spots Sukkhi in New York City working as a "dark skinned hot dog vendor," Taylor encourages her to report him to the authorities. Rather than risking being a "native informant," she responds by confessing her widowhood, fake documents, destitution, rape, and act of murder to Taylor, adding "I'm illegal here, [Sukkhi] knows that. I can't come out and challenge him, I'm very exposed" (189). The perceived appearance of Sukkhi threatens to expose Jasmine's production of her jazziness as a form of racial self-management: upwardly mobile, professional, and "not illegal." This moment of encounter certainly reinforces class and religious stratifications between upwardly mobile, professional-managerial, model minority South Asians and those downwardly mobile, working-class, "nonmodel" South Asians who exceed and thus threaten the coherence of this ideological formation. More significantly, however, it also evinces a model of *affiliation* that privileges "contingency and indeterminacy" through what the cultural studies scholar Jasbir Puar has described as "contagion." While conceding that "contagion" usually relates "to unwanted and afflicted bodies," Puar argues for a model of contagion in which "all bodies are mired in contagions: bodies infecting other bodies with sensation, vibration, irregularity, chaos, lines of flight that betray the expectation to loyalty, linearity, the demarcation of who's in and who's not. Contagions . . . conduct the effects of touch, smell, taste, hearing, and sight into shivers, sweat, blushes, heat, and pain, among many other sensations" (*Terrorist* 172). Contagion, in other words, allows for the transmission of affect, expressed by somatic, precognitive responses (shivers, sweat, blushes), which in turn gives way to affiliation. Upon recognizing/phantasmatically projecting the hot dog vendor as Sukkhi, Jasmine begins "shivering": "I wanted to talk, but my throat had sealed. I couldn't get my breath" (188). Jasmine's shivers and dysphasia are precognitive responses to the "dark skin" of the hot dog vendor, a body that exceeds proper regulation by the state; these responses symptomatize the "infection and transmission" of that excess.

As brown bodies unregulated by the state, Jasmine and Sukkhi bring each other to mutual crisis through the aggregation of working-class, immigrant, undocumented, and terrorist bodies in the urban metropolis.[19] Jasmine perceives/misrecognizes the vendor as Sukkhi/the terrorist while working as a "day mummy." After spotting Sukkhi, she muses aloud to herself, "'I'm alone all day, I'm out in the park—' I remembered Stuart [an economics professor at New York University who studies third-world poverty] having observed me for months, and suddenly I felt filthy, having been observed, tracked, by Sukhwinder" (189). Jasmine's seemingly non sequitur concatenation of Stuart's and Sukkhi's surveillance of her immigrant labor as inducing a feeling of "filth" attempts to manage linguistically the feeling of pervasive state surveillance of her racial excess. Jasmine's affective response registers not so much her fear of Sukkhi as the "stickiness" of fear (Puar, *Terrorist* 284), the fear impelled by her brown body (like Sukkhi's). In the encounter with Sukkhi, then, Jasmine's jazziness—the brown style and consumer goods of beauty that allow her to pass as American and a "professional"—no longer secure her gendered exceptionalism: as a racialized subject affectively charged with fear, she is marked as nonexceptional within—indeed, as affiliated with—those racialized metropolitan populations from which she has worked so hard to distinguish herself.

Beyond Beauty: Racialized Strangeness and Plainness

Surfacing as physical appearance, bodily comportment, or as consumerist femininity, beauty allows Jasmine to manage, however unsuccessfully, her racialization as an undocumented and working-class South Asian immigrant subject within various US metropolitan spaces.

In this final section, I turn to Jasmine's insertion into a racial economy of strangeness and plainness that operate beyond beauty's value economies. In the rural American "heartland" of Baden, Iowa, where she arrives after fleeing New York, Jasmine's elusive racialization as "strange" involves a different kind of racial fetishization and self-denial. Her subsequent desire to be racially "plain" aspires to redress beauty's failed promise of cultural citizenship by insisting on the material histories that constitute her racialization as South Asian.

Unlike in the metropolitan sites of Flushing and Manhattan, in rural Baden, Jasmine's racial difference lacks historical particularity and "ethnic referential density" (Koshy, "Geography" 145). Jasmine describes Baden as "a basic German community," such that even Danes and Swedes are racially distinct and negatively stereotyped as "the inscrutable Swedes" and "the sneaky Dutch" (11). Whereas in urban centers like New York, from which Jasmine migrates and where immigrants from western Europe maintain only symbolic ethnicities, in Baden, European identities function as ethnic categories with particular histories of and stereotypes about immigrant labor still attached to them.[20] When Jasmine arrives, Baden's small farms are giving way to big agribusiness and recreational tourism, and globalizing economic production has ushered in a new Asian labor force to service this economy. Bud Ripplemeyer, an Iowa farmer and Jasmine's future husband, has made several trips to China as part of a farming bank delegation that goes there to speculate on the Chinese soybean market. Bud is forced to join the delegation as large developers buy up land and buy out local farms, threatening them with bankruptcy. After visiting China, Bud decides to adopt Du, a teenage Vietnamese refugee from Hong Kong whose penchant for "recombinant electronics" (156) secures him a place within this emerging economy. Even before Bud's trips to China, Asia is a spectral presence in Baden, lurking in the Ripplemeyers' past participation in US imperialist aggression such as the Korean and Vietnam Wars, which implicitly shape "the fifty years of 'selfishness'" (14) that Bud feels after returning from China and that compels him to adopt Du. Despite an emerging awareness of Asianness, however, "farms are spread out too widely for significant shifts in racial-spatial composition to be observed," so that the denizens of Baden maintain a sanctioned ignorance about racial difference that perpetuates dominant scripts of whiteness (Mani, "Imagination" 38).

Whereas a fetishization of non-European racial difference might lead to the kind of benevolent and not-so-benevolent racism that Jasmine experiences in Flushing and Manhattan, in Baden, Jasmine's racialization occurs within a collective will not to know the specific contours of her racial difference: "The farmers are afraid to suggest I'm different. They've seen the aerograms I receive, the stranger lettering I can decipher. . . . In a pinch, they'll admit that I might look a little different, that I'm a 'dark-haired girl' in a naturally blond country. I have a 'darkish complexion'" (33). Later, Jasmine notes why Bud himself courts her: "because I am alien. I am darkness, mystery, inscrutability" (200). Interestingly, though, when she is seen with Du, Jasmine is folded into an emerging social fabric of Asianness. While accompanying Bud to adopt Du, for example, she notices "the [adoption] agency was charmed by the notion of Bud's 'Asian' wife, without inquiring too deeply" (14). Jasmine's various forms of interpellation as Asian by association, "alien," "dark," and "inscrutable" certainly belie a trenchant post–Cold War orientalism in Baden. But they also name a form racial difference that is, quite simply, unrecognizable within Baden's racial economies. Jasmine's "darkish complexion" does not fit into recognizable scripts of whiteness *or* Asianness—despite her brief references to claiming affiliation with Baden's new Chinese, Korean, and Vietnamese immigrants.

Yet the set of material conditions germane to Baden at this historical moment—a faltering rural economy, the racial hegemony of whiteness, and a growing population of Asian immigrants—allow for a provisional and contingent form of belonging that I call *stranger sociality*.[21] Jasmine is produced as a racially "strange" body through her different encounters with the farming community. While listening contently to Mother Ripplemeyer's stories of the Depression, connecting them to the water famines she faced as a young girl in Hasnapur, Jasmine muses, "I thought we could trade some world class poverty stories, . . . but mine make her uncomfortable. Not that she's hostile. It's like looking at the name in my passport and seeing 'Jyo'—at the beginning and deciding that her mouth is not destined to make those sounds" (16). Similarly, Jasmine notes that despite her sexual relationship with Bud, he "has never asked [her] about India; it scares him" (12). Here Jasmine's Indianness strains against the referential limits of nonwhiteness in Baden, even as Bud and Mother Ripplemeyer express awareness of these limits. Ethnic referentiality would require Bud and Mother Ripplemeyer to decide—rather than avoid deciding—whether Jasmine's Indianness should be understood as a form of threatening or nonthreatening nonwhiteness.

The town's reluctance to name Jasmine's racial or ethnic difference in a globalizing local economy registers their "possessive investment in whiteness" (Lipsitz). But Jasmine's interactions with the Ripplemeyers nonetheless reveal an intimacy based on her racial ambiguity. She notices that the house she lives in "looks small and ugly from the dirt road": "but every time I crunch into the driveway and park my old Rabbit between the rusting, abandoned machinery and the empty silo . . . [I think] that all of us Ripplemeyers . . . belong" (13). As a counterpoint to a global city such as New York, where her racial identity is properly named and nameable, Jasmine's sense of belonging in Baden is tied to her legibility as racially strange. While working as an au pair for the Hayes family, for example, Jasmine observes, "Taylor's friends in New York used to look at me and say, 'You're Iranian, right?' If I said no, then, 'Pakistani, Afghan or Punjabi?' They were strikingly accurate about most things, and always out to improve themselves" (33). Jasmine mocks the ways in which such concerns about the accuracy of ethnic identity is motivated by a white liberal "sensitivity" to racial difference. Though critical of Baden's burgeoning racism toward new Asian immigrants, Jasmine opts for the experience of nonspecific racial difference rather than such elitism. Jasmine's intimacies with Baden's farming community emerge not in spite of but because of her racial categorization as an ambiguous nonwhite.

Stranger intimacy is, ultimately, an untenable mode of belonging for Jasmine. Racialized strangeness allows her to bypass the labor of racial self-management within the various beauty economies that govern most of her migrations. Yet it also demands of Jasmine another kind of self-management since she must disavow or withhold revealing her South Asianness. Whereas Jasmine's beauty produces a set of crises around her national and racial position as a rural, undocumented, and migrant subject in Hasnapur, Flushing, and Manhattan, racialized strangeness requires Jasmine's racial self-denial as part of her crisis of belonging in Baden. A key scene in the novel, in which Jasmine and Bud have sex, forces Jasmine to confront this crisis. After Bud exclaims, "I have never seen anyone so beautiful" (36), Jasmine reflects that this declaration leaves her feeling "torn open like the hot dry soil, parched" (38). Given Bud's stated fear of India and Jasmine's Indianness, Bud's interpellation of Jasmine as beautiful leaves Jasmine feeling both seen and not seen. Her beauty thus produces a form of double-consciousness: she recognizes that in calling her "beautiful" Bud xenophobically perceives her racial difference and yet also disavows the material histories that constitute that difference. Bud's response to Jasmine's beauty is here metonymic of the way that Jasmine's sense of belonging in Baden requires precisely this kind of racial designation and obfuscation. Evoking images of rape,

Jasmine's references to feeling "torn open" and "parched" suggest that to be called beautiful requires acceding to the erasure of her racialization as South Asian.

Jasmine's racial ambiguity in Baden leaves her vulnerable to racial self-denial and therefore to being assimilated into whiteness. Seemingly fearful of granting Jasmine any kind of referential density, Bud interpellates Jasmine within a US-based iconography of white feminine and feminist glamour, precisely the kinds of white feminine embodiment that Alexander's protagonist, Sandhya, idealizes as an alternative to her immigrant brownness. Jasmine admits, "Bud calls me Jane. Me Bud, you Jane. . . . Calamity Jane. Jane as in Jane Russell, not Jane as in Plain Jane. My genuine foreignness frightens him." But, Jasmine goes on to claim, "Plain Jane is all I want to be" (26). Jasmine's desire to be plain rejects these glamorized, white American icons—the orientalizing Jane who rescues Tarzan; the nineteenth-century American Indian-killing vigilante; and the 1950s Hollywood starlet. Instead, it conjures Charlotte Brontë's nineteenth-century British heroine, Jane Eyre.

Jasmine's appeal to "plainness" in her allusion to Brontë's Plain Jane unsettles certain commensurabilities between female beauty and liberal democratic ideals of citizenship, particularly as they have been constructed within the genre of the Western female bildungsroman. Indeed, Jasmine's multiple migrations and name changes have led several critics to read *Jasmine* as a late-twentieth-century ethnic American rewriting of Brontë's nineteenth-century British classic novel of this genre.[22] Before arriving in Baden, Jasmine twice references Brontë's 1847 narrative, once when she is forced to abandon the novel during her English education in India because she finds the prose too difficult and once in comparing herself to Jane Eyre and Bud to Jane's eventual husband, Rochester (35, 236). Literary critical comparisons between *Jasmine* and *Jane Eyre* have focused extensively on Mukherjee's recasting of the third-world woman in Brontë's novel as a female agent in her own right, rather than as supplemental to the consolidation of the white, imperialist, female subject.

Yet what awaits further elaboration within this comparison is the way that both Jane and Jasmine negotiate their statuses as citizens through their relation to physical beauty. As paradigmatic of the nineteenth-century British novel of social uplift, *Jane Eyre* has been read as indexing the rise of the physically plain or unbeautiful subject—Plain Jane—as one deserving of rights as a citizen. The orphaned, destitute Jane repeatedly points out her lack of physical beauty as a way of reinforcing her democratic disposition. Yet the literary critic Douglas Mao has recently offered a corrective to this reading by arguing that *Jane Eyre* is really a story about the rise of Jane as a *beautiful* subject who must *shed* the material histories of her plainness—"bastardy, drunkenness, flight, poverty" (205)—before she is deemed worthy of her full rights as a citizen. The mid-nineteenth-century British novel posits an aspiration toward the beautiful as a state of ideal citizenship for the white, imperial, female subject Jane. Yet such aspirations are much more tenuous in a late-twentieth-century transnational American context for the racialized, undocumented, female subject of *Jasmine*. For Jasmine, the possession of physical beauty fails to guarantee the transcendence of such material histories in order to achieve the status of citizen-subject. The relation between female beauty and citizenship in *Jasmine* is thus much more fraught. Jasmine's desire to be "Plain Jane" revitalizes plainness not as a socially devalued subjective state to transcend, as in Brontë's novel, but as an ideal mode of feminine embodiment that demands recognition of and engagement with material histories of migrant racial difference. Jasmine's observation that her "genuine foreignness" precludes Bud's calling her Plain Jane suggests that her "foreignness" is incommensurable with being seen as plain—as her migrations make clear, her Indian brownness marks either her social valorization or denigration.

What remains unthinkable within Bud's (and by extension Baden's) racial logic, then, is the possibility of Jasmine's *racialized* plainness, defined through an unremarkable, unexceptional racialized corporeal presence. Jasmine's desire for plainness, I would argue, should be understood as resonating beyond Baden's borders and within and beyond the borders of the US nation. Baden's globalizing local economy, its concomitant shifting racial composition as a result of Asian immigration to the region, and its location as the site of Jasmine's retrospective narration allow for the "scale-jumping" force of Jasmine's appeal to plainness as one that subtends all of her migrations.[23] In the face of both denigrated (rural, terrorist, undocumented, resident alien) and valorized (modern, jazzy, upwardly mobile, model minority) forms of South Asianness, racialized plainness exceeds the liberal logic of national inclusion because it demands an engagement with material histories of difference.

In Jasmine's appeal to plainness she suggests that the very dialectic of beauty-plainness, such as that which structures the terms of liberal democratic ideals of citizenship in Brontë's novel, is informed by an ineluctable racial logic. Jasmine must constantly negotiate this racial logic across her various socially marginalized positions.[24] Thus, while Mukherjee's "Plain Jane" certainly cites Brontë's concerns with beauty and citizenship, *Jasmine* is not simply an ethnicized version of the canonical female bildungsroman in which either the beautiful *or* the plain subject is restored to her rights as a citizen. Instead, for Jasmine, beauty operates as an assemblage, a state of endless becoming that can guarantee at best only a passing form of citizenship. Jasmine admits at the beginning of the novel's retrospective narration, "in Baden, I am Jane. *Almost*" (12, my emphasis). *Almost*-Jane raises both the promise and the deferral of racialized plainness as an ideal form of cultural citizenship.

Racialized plainness ultimately exceeds the political imagination of Mukherjee's fictional narrative. Yet it nonetheless speaks to Mukherjee's broader critiques of liberal multicultural belonging in nonfiction essays and public speeches published during large-scale anti-immigration reform legislation at the end of the twentieth century. Mukherjee critiques liberal multiculturalism for failing to redress state-sanctioned xenophobia because its logic of inclusion is based on a collective aspiration to probationary whiteness that carries with it "the sinister, or at least misguided, implication that American culture has not been affected by the American-Indian, African-American, Latin-American, and Asian-American segments of its population" ("Beyond" 32). Mukherjee here acknowledges the centrality of racialized populations to the constitution of US national culture, and she later claims about her "literary agenda," "It does not end until I show that I (and hundreds of thousands of new immigrants like me) are, minute-by-minute, transforming America" ("Beyond" 34). When situated within these critiques of center-periphery models of national culture, racialized plainness articulates racial difference as germane to and thereby *unexceptional* within the national citizenry. In this respect, the kind of plainness for which Jasmine yearns shares some features with what Paul Gilroy, in the British national context, has described as an "ordinary, demotic multiculturalism" (99). Unlike liberal multiculturalism, which celebrates "cultural difference" as part of belonging in diversity in the face of state-sanctioned xenophobia and violence, demotic multiculturalism refers to "concrete oppositional work: political, aesthetic, cultural, scholarly" (99) that reduces "the exaggerated dimensions of racial difference to a liberating ordinaryness [*sic*]" (119).[25] By inciting multiple confrontations with Jasmine's rurality, illegality, and migrant labor, her beauty solicits those material histories that structure what might otherwise exist as merely celebratory forms of cultural difference, as well as those forms of state-sanctioned xenophobia that impede legal and cultural citizenship. While Jasmine's reference to plainness does not reflect—or stops short of imagining—the "concrete oppositional work" of Gilroy's demotic multiculturalism, her desire to be Plain Jane does by default rearticulate plainness as a yearning for "liberating ordinaryness" around those material histories.

As an alternative form of cultural citizenship that aspires toward rather *un*exceptional ways of inhabiting South Asian immigrant difference, racialized plainness in *Jasmine* can be framed as anticipating the ongoing spectacularization *and* demonization of certain South Asian immigrant bodies since 9/11 and since the US-led global "war on terror" in 2003. In the 1990s and the first decade of the new millennium, a renewed Indophilia within US national culture—exemplified by a "millennial" fascination with Bollywood aesthetics and idioms and Indo-chic fashionability—occurred alongside the increased surveillance, criminalization, and disappearance of South Asian, Muslim, and Arab men, a double-sided phenomenon that I explore more in chapter 4 and the epilogue. Prefiguring a historical moment in which forms of some South Asianness are subject to various forms of racial valorization and others to racial denigration, Jasmine's declaration "Plain Jane is all I want to be" raises a question that was later to resonate forcefully for racialized subjects under empire: who is allowed the luxury of plainness, where plainness is a staunchly racialized form of citizenship? Mukherjee's canonized late-twentieth-century South Asian American novel raises this question within a slightly earlier moment of post–Cold War anti-immigrant hysteria, one that should be understood as continuous with our current imperial moment of state-sponsored xenophobia and immigrant baiting.

By mapping Jasmine's beauty as a force that deterritorializes and reterritorializes the heroine's attachments to material histories of race and nation, in this chapter I have sought to complicate beauty's normative attachments to liberal modes of inclusion—assimilation, liberal multiculturalism, and the discourse of the South Asian model minority—that otherwise sustain a narrative of American exceptionalism. Through its shifting identifications with racial valorization and racial denigration, the Indian woman's beauty repeatedly marks the limits of racialized belonging in a multicultural and yet xenophobic immigrant nation. As a provisional response to those limits, Jasmine's desire for plainness pushes against such exceptionalizing modes of apprehending and inhabiting racial difference. By raising the possibility of rendering material histories of racial difference mundane and ordinary within the national citizenry, racialized plainness demands a release from the labor of national and racial self-management and thus a release from the very terms of liberal belonging under which beauty most often labors.

In chapter 2, I build on this chapter's examination of Indian female beauty as a state of gendered exceptionalism by turning to diasporic fiction produced during the height of India's beauty boom in the late 1990s. Demonstrating how Indian beauty operates as a form of sexual capital, I foreground the limits and possibilities for Indian female beauty to generate emergent cross-cultural, intraethnic, and interracial identifications and affiliations in a transnational context.

2 /   Prosthetic Femininity, Flexible Citizenship, and Feminist Cosmopolitics in the Fiction of Jhumpa Lahiri

In Jhumpa Lahiri's short story "The Treatment of Bibi Haldar," the title character, an unmarried, twenty-nine-year-old Indian woman who is prone to bouts of hysteria, spends her days recording the inventory of the "hennas, hair oils, pumices, and fairness creams" that are crammed along the three walls of her cousin's cosmetics shop in Calcutta (163). Considered a charity case because of her illness, Bibi "had never been taught to be a woman," and her lack of physical beauty is the starkest sign of her feminine failure (163). A group of married women who live in the same building with Bibi and who serve as the collective narrators of the story, describe Bibi as "not pretty": "Her shins were hairless and splayed with a generous number of pallid freckles," "her upper lip was thin, her teeth too small. Her gums protruded when she spoke" (163). Nonetheless, Bibi longs to participate in the feminine rituals of self-beautification that are associated with a soon-to-be bride. Bibi would "curl up" "amid the tins of talc and boxes of bobby pins" in Haldar's beauty shop and wail, "I will never dip my feet in milk. . . . My face will never be painted with sandalwood paste. Who will rub me with turmeric?" (160–61). In a tautological twist, a local doctor tells Bibi that marriage itself will provide the cure for her illness, so Bibi begins to invest earnestly in her personal appearance: "With some damaged merchandise from Haldar's shop she polished her toenails and softened her elbows. . . . She applied glycerin to smooth her lips, resisted sweets to reduce her measurements" (162).

Published at the end of the twentieth century as part of Lahiri's debut collection of short stories, *Interpreter of Maladies* (1999), "Treatment" speaks to the neoliberal market rationalities of beauty in a globalizing India. The beauty products and practices that Lahiri's story catalogues are part of the explosion of "creams and lotions, massage oil, bleaches, talcum powders, face washes, face packs, body oils, under-eye cream, and exfoliators" that began to proliferate in Indian urban centers in the 1990s and that now constitute a vast market segment of the Indian beauty industry (Parameswaran 71). Bibi's access to these commercialized beauty products rescues her from a life of isolation and destitution and improves her social standing (and, even more remarkably, her mental health) by making her a viable prospect on the marriage market. Yet the market rationalities of beauty—the compulsory heterosexuality of the marriage market and the beauty products that Bibi uses to enhance her feminine appearance—also give way to beauty as a homosocial practice of care. If beauty is a "treatment" or remedy for Bibi's social mistreatment, it is also a treatment that the townswomen administer as a collective act of social responsibility. Despite expressing relief and thanks among themselves that Bibi "was *not* our responsibility" (167, my emphasis), the community of Indian women who frequent Haldar's cosmetics shop, no longer content only to feed and talk to Bibi as a way of addressing her social neglect, take it upon themselves to beautify Bibi: "Some days, we combed out her hair, remembering now and then to change the part in her scalp so that it would not grow too broad. At her request we powdered the down over her lips and throat, penciled definition into her brows" (166–67).

In a further elaboration of the way that beauty as a neoliberal "technology of the self" that optimizes Bibi's chances on the marriage market (Foucault, *Technologies* 88) gives way to collective acts of care, the townswomen collectively exploit beauty as a commercial enterprise. When the beauty shop owner Haldar refuses to comply with arranging Bibi's marriage, as the doctor orders, and instead sequesters her to the storage room because he fears that her hysteria has infected his newborn child with an unbreakable fever, the townswomen boycott the beauty shop as a form of social protest: "To express our indignation we began to take our shopping elsewhere; this provided us with our only revenge. Over the weeks, the products on Haldar's shelves grew dusty. Labels faded and colognes turned rank" (169). The women's beauty boycott succeeds in driving Haldar out of business, and Haldar is forced to pack all of his unsold cosmetics into boxes and haul them into the storage room. Bibi is largely left to fend for herself financially (with the exception of three hundred rupees that Haldar leaves her in an envelope) and is later discovered pregnant by an unknown man. She tidies up the storage room and sells the leftover beauty inventory for half the price.

Bibi's entry into the business of beauty is emblematic of a contemporary shift toward beauty as a profession for Indian women outside the home. Anita Anand documents in *The Beauty Game* (2002), her book on middle-class Indian women's obsession with beauty in postliberalization India, how Indian economic liberalization policies enabled the lifting of duty rates on fast-moving consumer goods such as cosmetics, allowing multinational cosmetics brands to compete or enter into joint ventures with domestic brands. The increasing availability of these products contributed to the professionalization of beauty among middle-class women (Anand ch. 1). This beauty boom was also facilitated by the crowning of two Indian women, Aishwarya Rai and Sushmita Sen, as international beauty queens in the mid-1990s. Rai's and Sen's success on the global pageant scene inspired droves of rural and urban Indian women to try their hand at modeling and beauty pageants. Others were inspired to convert their homes into makeshift beauty parlors or to seek professional training that would allow them to open hair studios and pageant-grooming businesses. The establishment during this time of the Cosmetology Society of India (CSI), India's first governing body for beauty industrialists working in the fields of cosmetology, hair styling, and skin care, and the rise of Indian fashion designers, whose designs were being shown in fashion capitals such as London, Milan, and Paris before the advent of India Fashion Week in New Delhi in 2000, further drove the consumption of beauty products among the Indian middle classes (Anand).

By the end of Lahiri's story, beauty is a business that, like for many Indian women who made beauty into a profession, allows Bibi to become economically self-sufficient. However, Bibi's entry into the beauty business is not a narrative of individual entrepreneurial achievement, as it is for the beauty professionals in Anand's book. For it is only with the help of the townswomen who spread word of the cosmetics store and who remain committed to purchasing their cosmetics from Bibi that Bibi is able to establish herself as a beauty business owner: "From Bibi we purchased our soaps and kohl, our combs and powders, and when she sold the last of her merchandise, she went by taxi to the wholesale market, using her profits to restock the shelves. In this manner she ran a business in the storage room, and we did what we could to help" (172). The townswomen actively promote and support Bibi's beauty business, just as they actively boycott Haldar's earlier. Ultimately, beauty is part of growing consumer markets in a globalizing India, even as it animates practices of obligation and reciprocity among Indian women.

* * *

As one of two stories in Lahiri's short-story collection set in India, "Treatment" captures the way that the Indian beauty boom of the 1990s shapes the micropolitics of everyday life among urban Indian women. It shows how beauty as a market-driven industry operates in tandem with beauty as a form of affective labor and social responsibility within Indian neoliberalism. The rest of this chapter inquires further into beauty's capacity to produce intimacies from within and that yet also impinge on the structural logic of the market; it also illuminates intimacies that challenge the reproduction of compulsory heterosexuality when beauty travels beyond the borders of the Indian nation. In the rest of the stories that I examine—"Sexy," "Interpreter of Maladies," and "This Blessed House"—beauty is a physical attribute of the upwardly mobile, diasporic, Indian, female body; yet it operates on nonfeminine and non-Indian bodies as part of its socializing force. If in the previous chapter Indian female beauty both territorializes and deterritorializes a set of material histories that shape the female subject's Indian and American national belonging, in this chapter diasporic female beauty gives rise to desires for *transnational* belonging.

Interpreter of Maladies debuted at the end of a decade in which transnational media deemed Indian beauty queens the most beautiful women in the world and during an explosion of Indian fashion and beauty within global markets, which worked to transform the beautiful Indian woman into a global brand. Indian women became globally visible not only as icons of beauty but also, as books like Anand's make clear, as authorities on the subject (see, e.g., Vadhera). Such fetishization and cultural authority, as I discussed in the book's introduction, was fueled as much by US-based global media such as *Time, Newsweek,* and *National Geographic,* which harnessed the beautiful and fashionable Indian and Indian American woman to the branding of the Indian nation as globally modern, as by diasporic beauty and fashion media. Across these media, Indian women's beauty and fashionability signaled their access to transnational flows of capital and goods and the ability to travel across national borders with ease. Representations of Indian beauty in Lahiri's stories dovetail with beauty's role in shaping neoliberal citizenship practices among Indian women in the 1990s.

If mass-mediated images of beautiful Indian women cast them as mobile cosmopolitan subjects, then diasporic beauty in Lahiri's stories is central to what I call her feminist *cosmopolitical* project. Unlike liberal strains of cosmopolitanism that are defined by an "uncommitted bourgeois detachment" (Cheah 31) born out of capitalist mobility across national borders, cosmopolitics accounts for the way that the globalization of capital produces "(re)attachment, multiple attachment, or attachment at a distance" that cannot be contained by the territorial borders of the nation (Robbins 3). My understanding of Lahiri's cosmopolitics as distinctly feminist has less to do with the way in which her stories proffer an ideological critique of Indian feminine beauty; nor does it have to do with their representation of Indian feminist subjects. Rather, I locate Lahiri's feminist cosmopolitics in the way that Indian feminine beauty's affects illuminate and critique contemporary political and economic processes of globalization, migration, and travel and the way that these affects enable or foreclose certain cross-cultural, interracial, and intraracial intimacies that take place within these processes. Beauty's affects are central to Lahiri's feminist cosmopolitics in three distinct but overlapping ways. First, they are attached either to the fetishization of racial difference or to the fantasy of ethnic sameness—both privilege practices of mobility and flexibility as conditions of global belonging. Second, beauty's affective force in these stories highlights Lahiri's provincialization of the US and Indian nations—both nations remain at best spaces of partial and incomplete belonging for South Asian American, non–South Asian, and postcolonial Indian subjects. Third, these national and global attachments and detachments occur through the disarticulation of beauty from compulsory heterosexuality. Specifically, beauty produces feelings of estrangement, identification, and desire that foreclose on the possibility of hetero-romantic love as a dominant social form through which differences of race, culture, and nation are symbolically resolved.

Finally, by focusing on representations of beauty as part of Lahiri's feminist cosmopolitics, this chapter challenges dominant readings of Lahiri's fiction as at best a depoliticized rendering of ethnic difference that can be translated into "universal" narratives of human experience (see, e.g., Rajan and Sharma). Such readings frequently underwrite Lahiri's globally visible literary celebrity, a phenomenon secured by her winning of the Pulitzer Prize for fiction in 1999 for *Interpreter of Maladies*; the concomitant boom in Indian Writing in English (IWE) on the Indian subcontinent; and the renowned South Asian American director Mira Nair's widely popular film adaptation of Lahiri's debut novel,

The Namesake (2003), in 2006. Indeed, Lahiri is now a household name among both mainstream and minority reading publics in the United States and India. At the end of this chapter, I situate Lahiri's literary celebrity within the larger constellation of diasporic Indian beauty that I map across her short stories. Focusing on verbal and visual expressions of Lahiri's highly stylized beauty that circulated across transnational mass media in the decade following the publication of *Interpreter of Maladies*, I argue that the circulation of such images harness Lahiri to dominant representational schema of Indian beauty and can thus more fully attune us to the political stakes of Lahiri's feminist cosmopolitical engagement with beauty in her fiction.

Global Brands / Sexy Bodies

Lahiri's story "Sexy" tracks the extramarital affair between Miranda, a white American woman living in Boston, and Dev, a married, Bengali American man.[1] Fascinated by Dev's racial otherness, Miranda attempts throughout the story to try on accents of "Indianness." She attempts to Indianize her name (which Dev tells her resembles the Indian name Mira), to learn the Bengali alphabet, and to learn the Hindi words on the bottom of Indian restaurant menus that would allow her to express appreciation for Indian food. She also carefully studies and memorizes the map of Bengal on the cover of *The Economist* that Dev leaves in her apartment (97).

Though Miranda's Indophilia initially is tied to her sexual attraction to Dev, as the story progresses, it is increasingly mediated by Miranda's memories of and meditations on Indian women. In particular, she becomes curious about the physical appearance of Dev's wife, who has left for and then returns from a trip to India, where she has gone to visit her family, and who never actually appears within the story's dramatic action. When Miranda hesitantly asks Dev what his wife looks like, Dev replies that she physically resembles "an actress in Bombay named Madhuri Dixit" (98). Unbeknownst to Miranda, Dixit was a leading screen icon of 1990s Bollywood (or Hindi-language popular cinema) whose beauty and sensuality continues to remain iconic within Bollywood and across Indian and diasporic popular cultures more broadly.[2] In the subsequent scene, Miranda seeks out an Indian grocery store, where she watches a Bollywood song-and-dance sequence in which women "in harem pants [thrust] their hips in synchrony" (98). She gazes at the women on covers of Bollywood videos, with "skirts that sat low on the hips and tops that tied like bandanas between their breasts. They were beautiful, the way the women dancing on the beach were beautiful, with kohl-rimmed eyes and long black hair. She knew then that Madhuri Dixit was beautiful, too" (99). Miranda's three uses of the word "beautiful" are linked by a strongly implied syllogistic suturing of Dixit's unseen beauty to the unseen beauty of Dev's wife.

This suturing of these two bodies—Dev's wife and Dixit's—moves from implication to articulation later in the story, when Miranda recalls her memory of Dixit while in the Indian grocery. While Miranda is babysitting Rohin, her friend Laxmi's young nephew, Rohin calls her "sexy" as she models for him the dress that she has purchased in order to seduce Dev. Expressing surprise at the precocity of Rohin's reaction, Miranda asks him to define the word "sexy"—a word that Dev has used to describe Miranda earlier in the story (91). When Rohin responds, "it means loving someone that you don't know" (107), Miranda "felt Rohin's words under her skin, the same way she'd felt Dev's" (107–8). Even as she admits to having the same bodily sensations in response to Dev's and Rohin's description of her as sexy, Miranda's response to Rohin is in another way notably different. For here, the word is attached not to her memory of her romance with Dev but to her memory of the beauty of the Bollywood actress Madhuri Dixit and Dev's wife: "Instead of *going hot* [Miranda] *felt numb. It reminded her of the way she'd felt at the Indian grocery*, the moment she knew, without even looking at a picture, that Madhuri Dixit, whom Dev's wife resembled, was beautiful" (108, my emphasis). The word "sexy" produces for Miranda a reencounter with Indian beauty's affects.

Why does this repetition and definition of the word "sexy" elicit in Miranda the same feeling of numbness that Dixit's and Dev wife's *beauty* also elicits? And what place does this affective reencounter with beauty have within the narrative of the interracial romance? Why are beauty's affects part of Miranda's concomitant Indophilia? These questions exert considerable pressure on this scene, since shortly after hearing Rohin define and call her sexy, Miranda begins to fantasize about the deleterious effects of her affair on Dev's wife and plans to terminate it. Whereas it might be tempting and even plausible to interpret the end of the affair as simply a matter of Miranda's feelings of guilt,[3] this decision seems to have as much or more to do with Miranda's feelings of feminine failure. The revisited moment of Miranda's "feelings" at the Indian grocery is worth examining further precisely because it foregrounds Miranda's understanding of her "sexiness" as inextricable from Dixit (and, by extension, Dev's wife).

Specifically, this moment recalls sexiness as a particular kind of feminine embodiment that is bound to a liberal strain of cosmopolitanism, one that privileges travel and mobility, or what Bruce Robbins has called "feeling global." Miranda consistently perceives the way that globality, in terms of travel, mobility, and attachments beyond the nation, are mediated through Indianness. Dev's understanding of postcolonial geography and history, Rohin's precocious knowledge of world geography, Laxmi's diasporic family in Canada and Britain, and even Dev's wife's travels in India all work to consolidate Miranda's understanding of Indianness as marked by a worldly sensibility. Miranda is a transplant to Boston from an unnamed city in Michigan, where, we are told, "she knew no one" (89), and she, by contrast, is depicted as exceedingly provincial, a characteristic that is made embarrassingly apparent when initially she misunderstands Bengal as a religion instead of a region in India. Later, Dev is forced to bring her a map of Bengal in order to explain postcolonial geography to her because she "did not own an atlas or any other books with maps in them" (84). Miranda's instruction in worldliness occurs when Dev takes her to the Boston Mapparium. Standing on a transparent bridge so that she felt as though she "were standing in the center of the world," she examines the "glowing stained-glass panels" that encircle her. "The farthest [she] had ever been was to the Bahamas," and despite searching, she cannot pinpoint their location (91). It is at this precise moment in the Mapparium that Dev calls her "sexy," so that sexiness is here enjoined to the promise of Miranda's worldliness—the ability to bridge differences of race, culture, and nation that she believes she is pursuing in her affair with Dev. Yet upon later hearing Rohin call her "sexy," Miranda abandons the promise of her own cosmopolitan status vis-à-vis her romance with Dev and projects such globality onto *Dixit*'s body. In going "numb," Miranda sees herself as Rohin sees her: as someone who, in Rohin's words, Dev "loves" but "doesn't know," someone who, unlike Dev's wife or Dixit, is insufficiently beautiful, global, and Indian.

Miranda's feelings of numbness, which accompany her memory of Dixit's beauty, thus mark a crisis in her own white femininity: the encounter with Indian female beauty twice returns her to her less globally desirable, white American body. Miranda's whiteness is depicted as an aesthetically deficient mode of embodiment in the opening lines of the story, when Miranda is shopping at a department store cosmetics counter, where she meets Dev. Upon "assessing Miranda's complexion," the cosmetics saleswoman begins applying a heavy anti-wrinkle cream and then sweeps a "large brush . . . over her face," telling her, "This is blusher number Two. . . . Gives you some color" (86). That Miranda's face needs "some color" draws explicit attention to her white skin, a fact that Miranda is most certainly aware of during her encounter with Indian beauty. The literary critic Anne Cheng has argued that the apprehension of racialized feminine beauty incites in the viewer a subjective crisis of identification, regardless of the race or gender of the perceiver. Beauty's promise to obscure the pain of (historically undesirable) nonwhite racial difference—even as it solicits that difference as part of its perceptual logic—defines this crisis, as we saw in chapter 1. As part of the legibility of racial difference, the encounter with beauty also incites a judgment about that difference. Beauty is "a likely conduit for racial imagining [because] it engenders questions like: 'How am I like or not like her?' 'Could I have or be her, and what would that make me (racially and sexually)?'" ("Wounded" 208). Miranda's redoubled sensation of numbness is symptomatic of precisely this kind of psychic traversing. That is, if sexiness in "Sexy" is about "loving" someone that you do not know (Dev), it is also about something that remains subjugated and yet all the more recalcitrant within that erotic economy: *wanting to be* someone that you do not know (Dixit).

In returning Miranda to her white body, the feeling of numbness points to a desire to embody Dixit's style of racialized femininity, to wear her way of wearing her body. Put simply, Miranda seems to want a prosthetic body. I have in mind here the kind of prosthetic femininity that draws from the literary critic Lauren Berlant's formulation of the prosthetic body. In her analysis of how female bodies become national brands or trademarks in order to allow black and white women to participate in the early-twentieth-century US public sphere of commodity capitalism, Berlant argues that "one of the main ways a woman mimes the prophylaxis of citizenship is to do what we might call code-crossing. This involves borrowing the corporeal logic of an other, or a fantasy of that logic, and adopting it, as a prosthesis" (*Female* 140–41). Berlant reads the mutual gazing between the two mulatta women, Clare Kendry and Irene Redfield, in Nella Larsen's 1929 novel *Passing* as registering Irene's desire for a particular style of bourgeois, white femininity that Clare embodies, one that tends toward the "erotic, the sensational, which hyper-emphasizes the visual frame" (*Female* 108) and that allows Irene to suppress her juridically black body in negotiating the public sphere of the market.[4]

Certainly, Miranda's white skin—which is "pale as paper" and which makes her "striking" but "not pretty" (87)—does not and cannot for legal and historical reasons index the kind of surplus embodiment that always threatens to belie claims to national citizenship for mulatta women in Berlant's formulation of the prosthetic body.[5] Miranda's desire for the "fantasy of this [feminine] logic" (*Female* 132), in other words, is not compelled by the exigencies of formal or cultural citizenship within the US nation, since for her such forms of national belonging are naturalized by virtue of her whiteness. Rather, Miranda's fetishization of Indianness marks a desire to *escape* her white, American body—a body marked as provincial and uncosmopolitan—and to borrow the gendered and racialized feminine logics of Dixit's body, which would allow Miranda to see herself as a cosmopolitan subject. Whereas bourgeois, white femininity is a form of embodiment that promises national belonging for black and mulatta women who are historically foreclosed from fully accessing the early-twentieth-century US public sphere, the beautiful Indian female body holds out the promise of global belonging for the white, American woman whose whiteness, I am suggesting, binds her too tightly to the nation.

As Indian beauty's affects reinforce Miranda's provincialized national status, they simultaneously shore up Miranda's complicity with the diasporic female subject's cultural disenfranchisement within the United States. Well before Miranda's viewing of the song-and-dance sequence and the Bollywood video covers and just prior to learning of Dixit's resemblance to Dev's wife, Miranda recalls that, other than her coworker Laxmi and her lover, Dev, the only other Indians she knew were a family called the Dixits that lived in her neighborhood as a child growing up in Michigan. She remembers the Dixits as exceedingly unassimilated in their habits of dress, domesticity, and daily rituals and the ensuing forms of racism directed toward them, which she silently witnessed: "The mothers never invited Mrs. Dixit to join them around the [neighbor's] swimming pool. Waiting for the school bus with the Dixit children standing to one side, the other children would say 'The Dixits dig shit,' under their breath, and then burst into laughter" (95). Miranda recalls being invited to the "Dixit girl's" birthday party one year and then being frightened away by small markers of the Dixits' racial difference: food odors, clothing, and religious iconography. Miranda's xenophobia turns out to be form of racial trauma, since "for months afterwards, she'd been too frightened even to walk on the same side of the street as the Dixit's house, which she had to pass twice daily to get to the bus stop" (96). These memories of the Dixit girl resurface for Miranda upon hearing Dev describe his wife as resembling "an actress in Bombay named

Madhuri Dixit." Even before Miranda patronizes the Indian grocery looking for a film featuring Dixit, her initial response is to wonder if the Dixit girl, who had "been plain, wearing her hair in braids all through high school" and "the actress" Dixit "were related" (98).

In fantasizing about a blood relation between the plain Dixit girl and the Bollywood actress Madhuri Dixit, Miranda is able to suspend her anticipated knowledge of the latter's potential beauty. The fantasy of a blood relation between the two Dixits allows Miranda to believe, however momentarily and absurdly, that "Madhuri Dixit, whom Dev's wife resembled," is *not* beautiful, that Madhuri Dixit is, like the Dixit girl, plain. Miranda assumes that a shared nonwhite surname such as "Dixit" implies kinship based on blood ties rather than on a shared regional and communal ancestry on the subcontinent. Miranda's fantasy of equivalence between the two Dixits also reinforces the Dixit girl's "plainness" as tied to her sartorial choices and missteps, such as wearing "her hair in braids all through high school." Whereas plainness is a form of ideal racialized belonging for Jasmine in chapter 1, plainness here marks the South Asian female subject as culturally inassimilable. Even as Bollywood beauty seems to offer Miranda the promise of relief from the provinciality of her white, American body, this promise contains within it her memory of the Indian, female, ethnic subject's cultural disenfranchisement within the US nation, a form of exclusion based on the Dixit girl's perceived lack of fashionability—her plainness. The phantasmatic encounter with Madhuri Dixit's beauty binds Miranda's feelings of provinciality to her memory of the Dixit girl's inassimilability.

What requires still further elaboration within the scene of Miranda's encounter with Dixit's beauty is a second mode of feminine embodiment, one that exceeds Miranda's field of recognition. For Lahiri's South Asian, diasporic, and Bollywood-savvy audiences, Lahiri's choice to use Dixit as an embodiment of feminine beauty to which Miranda aspires is, I argue, far from arbitrary. For Dixit is not just "an actress in Bombay," as Dev tells Miranda, but an icon of 1990s Bollywood film whose star image is rooted in the historical emergence of her sexually assertive body on screen. To map the affective reverberations of this second form of embodiment is to take the risk of moving beyond the diegetic frame of Lahiri's story. But such a movement is in some ways inherent to the logic of beauty as an assemblage. If, as I suggested in this book's introduction, Indian beauty and style travel across "real" and "representational" registers and across multiple spatial scales, then Dixit's star image constitutes precisely such a line of flight within the assemblage, from diasporic fiction to Bollywood media.

Even the veiled reference to Dixit's sexual iconicity in Bollywood film deterritorializes the fictional world of "Sexy." For Bollywood audiences, the mere mention of Dixit's name is likely to recall a fully entrenched star image. During the 1990s, Dixit was the reigning female Bollywood star, and her sexually assertive body began to challenge new forms of gendered nationalism in which the sexually chaste Indian and diasporic woman's body came to stand in for the reproduction of the Indian nation. In particular, Dixit's controversial dance performance in the song-and-dance sequence "Choli Ke Peeche Kya Hai" (What Is Underneath Your Blouse?) from the film *Khal Nayak* (*The Villain*, 1993) emerged from within and amplified a series of "moral panics" in India around overt displays of female sexual expression on the Bollywood screen (S. Ghosh). The sequence came under particular fire from the Hindu Right, which deplored Dixit's performance as vulgar and sexually obscene. The religious backlash stemmed from the sequence's inversion of the typical heterosexual duet—the song is sung by two women who engage in erotic banter by entreating each other to be the ideal groom and bride. The Hindu Right also targeted the film's merging of two Bollywood female figures that, up until the 1990s, were hermeneutically differentiated— the Westernized vamp who embodied sexual agency and the chaste, virtuous, and "authentically Indian" heroine who embodied duty and honor. Dixit's role in the song-and-dance sequence in *Khal Nayak* and in subsequent films was crucial in reconciling these personae. The erotic autonomy signaled by Dixit's vampish sexiness exceeded the national injunctions of female chastity and conjugality that have so pervasively structured the conventions of the Bollywood romance genre.

Dixit's star image generated an audiovisual stream in which "sexiness" circulated as a new mode of Indian feminine embodiment. Her sexually assertive role in "Choli Ke Peeche" soon after inspired a proliferation of sexually charged soundtracks, many of which explicitly included the word "sexy" in the title and/or the lyrics: "Choli Ke Andar Kya Hai" (There Is a Secret under My Blouse) from *Khal Naaikaa* (*The She-Villain*, 1993), "Sexy, Sexy, Sexy, Mujhe Log Bole" (People Say I Am Sexy) from *Khuddar* (*The Self-Respecting One*, 1993), and "Meri Pant Bhi Sexy" (My Pants Are Sexy) from *Dulaara* (*The Loved One*, 1993), among others. Though India's Central Board of Film Censors changed the word "sexy" to "baby" in *Khuddar* and in other films and while state-owned television channels broadcasted these censored versions, satellite channels continued to show the uncensored "sexy" version, and the song-and-dance sequence circulated relatively unimpeded among diasporic audiences. The media stream generated by Dixit's performance in *Khuddar* made her a screen icon among South Asian and diasporic audiences. The lyrics of the song "Choli Ke Peeche" and the dancing between women became vehicles of "public pleasure and power" for middle-class urban Indian women, for urban Indian American women at India Day parades, and in queer and feminist South Asian public cultures. These populations variously "associate[d] sexual agency with these performances" (Mehta 9). As several queer and feminist scholars of Bollywood media have pointed out, Dixit's "sexy" body became a site on which to challenge the heteropatriarchal terms of national and diasporic belonging, particularly among Indian and diasporic women and sexual minorities.[6] As the title of Lahiri's story, "Sexy" alludes to a mode of feminine embodiment that defined Dixit's Bollywood star image and that challenged national and diasporic heteropatriarchal sexual norms. These minor histories of national and diasporic affective attachment to Dixit's Bollywood sexiness within the diegesis of "Sexy," however restricted to Lahiri's Bollywood-savvy audiences, circulate within Miranda's (failed) identifications with Dixit's/Dev wife's beauty. Even though contingently accessible, these affects are part of Lahiri's feminist cosmopolitical project in that they fail to cleave to the forms of identification and desire that allow Dixit's beauty to circulate within a strictly heterosexual economy of interracial romance or within heteropatriarchal definitions of national and diasporic public culture.

Beauty's Looks, Sexual Capital, and the Female NRI

If in "Sexy" the desire for Madhuri Dixit's star body stands in for the corporeal presence of the diasporic Indian woman, then Lahiri's story "Interpreter of Maladies" maps this desire for transnational mobility onto the *actual* body of the diasporic Indian woman. Bollywood media's influence on popular understandings of South Asian femininity continues to inform this shift from the prosthetic body to the real body, as the diasporic woman's body in Lahiri's story is figured as a hypostatization of the "Bollywood heroine." Whereas "Sexy" concerns the way that beauty's affects unsettle a dominant narrative of interracial domestic romance by pointing to a sublimated visual economy of *cross-racial* identification, "Interpreter" concerns the way that beauty unsettles transnational romance between Indian coethnics by pointing to a sublimated visual economy of *cross-gender* identification. This visual economy animates the failed aspirations of flexibility and mobility as practices of transnational belonging.

In "Interpreter," the Bollywood beauty of the female diasporic subject operates as a form of what the Asian American studies scholar Susan Koshy has called "sexual capital." Koshy defines sexual capital as

the aggregate of attributes that index desirability within the field of romantic or marital relationships in a given culture and thereby influence the life-chances and opportunities of an individual. Like the other forms of capital that Pierre Bourdieu calls social and cultural capital, sexual capital is linked but not reducible to economic capital . . . [and] highlights the impact of gender and sexuality on mobility. (*Sexual* 136)

I here repurpose Koshy's concept of sexual capital within US racial formations to refer to the way that the sexual desirability of the female diasporic subject mediates intraracial encounters and exchanges, complicates the binary of "domestication" and "sexual licentiousness," and operates beyond the territorial reach of the nation toward the complex entanglements of nation and diaspora. Thus, I examine transnational— rather than national—mobility as part of the privilege of possessing sexual capital. Specifically, I am interested in how the sexual capital of the Indian female nonresident Indian (NRI) Mina Das is central to the middle-class postcolonial Indian *male* subject Mr. Kapasi's desire for transnational mobility and capital as they come to define an emerging transnational class of Indian consumer citizens in the late 1970s and 1980s. If in "Sexy" Madhuri Dixit's phantasmatic beauty holds out the promise of sexual capital—the ability to travel across national borders with ease—in "Interpreter of Maladies" Mina Das embodies a sexual appeal that has undergone this conversion into (sexual) capital.

Told from the limited point of view of the postcolonial Indian national subject, "Interpreter" charts the burgeoning and then abruptly stalled transnational romance between Mr. Kapasi, an Indian tour guide, and Mina, his urbane Indian American client. Mina is traveling with her family to India from the United States to visit her and her husband's retired parents in the state of Orissa. Upon meeting the Das family, Mr. Kapasi describes them as "look[ing] Indian, but dress[ing] as foreigners did" (43–44) and perceives, with chagrin, their sense of superiority over him. Over the course of their tour, Mina learns that Mr. Kapasi's job as a tour guide is his secondary occupation and that his primary source of income is as a language translator for a doctor whose patients speak the nonvernacular language of Gujarati. Until this point disinterested in either the people or sites around her, Mina takes a sudden interest in Mr. Kapasi, telling him that she finds his primary job as a language translator "romantic" (57). As the intimacy between them builds, Mina, in a private moment with Mr. Kapasi during the tour, confesses a sexual secret. She tells him that unbeknown to her husband, one of her children is the offspring of a Punjabi man with whom she had an extramarital affair, a friend of her husband who visited her family while on a trip to the United States. The story climaxes when Mr. Kapasi refuses to absolve Mina of the "pain" of living with this secret, and Mina, flustered and frustrated by Mr. Kapasi's reaction, abandons him in the car to rejoin her family.

Despite barely talking to Mina, Mr. Kapasi interacts with her through a series of staccato, surreptitious, and refracted glances at her through the car's rearview mirror. These indirect acts of looking serve, among other things, to mark differences in the social class of national and diasporic Indians. Class difference between coethnics mediates much of the story's dramatic action. Though Mr. Kapasi is sexually attracted to Mina, he is aware that he is hired labor for the Das family; looking at or talking to Mina directly would therefore risk violating the class boundaries of employer-employee. As a middle-class Indian national subject with occupations as both a tour guide and a language translator, Mr. Kapasi cannot equally participate in the transnational circuits of capital that allow Mina, an upper-middle-class diasporic Indian, to travel to India and to hire Mr. Kapasi as her family's tour guide. Situated within the "closed" national economy of preliberalization India, Mr. Kapasi must work two jobs in order to pay for such luxury items as "the newer, bigger house, and the good schools and tutors, and the fine shoes and the television" (52) that he feels pressed to purchase for his family as part of an emerging transnational consumer citizenry marked by international travel, capitalist mobility, and conspicuous consumption. Mina's family, meanwhile, is part of a class of upwardly mobile diasporic South Asians that the Indian state began to recognize as NRIs, or nonresident Indians. Created primarily as a financial category in the 1970s to attract overseas investment in India, the NRI began to embody material and ideological investment for the Indian nation-state, producing new definitions of Indian citizenship that exceeded the territoriality of the state.[7] By the 1990s, the NRI allowed a selective diaspora (namely, from Canada, Britain, and the United States) to be recruited into the neoliberal logic of the Indian nation-state. Westernized and economically elite NRIs became paradigmatic "flexible citizens," subjects who use transnational links to "accumulate capital and social prestige in the global arena" (Ong,

Flexible 6).[8] By the 1990s, "the promise of dual citizenship, easier travelling, and increased investment possibilities were proffered as enticements to NRIs" (Desai 348).

Yet to stop our analysis of the interactions between Mrs. Das and Mr. Kapasi at an analysis of the uneven distribution of capital that separates diasporic flexible citizens from an emerging Indian middle class would be to miss how the gendered and sexualized dimensions of flexible citizenship structure the story's visual economy. It would, in short, miss the way that Mina's beauty and style are a form of diasporic sexual capital that is central to Mr. Kapasi's desire for flexible citizenship. Written in the 1990s, when both the Indian state and cultural industries such as Bollywood hailed the NRI as a cultural and political citizen, but set in the 1970s, when the NRI was primarily a financial category, "Interpreter" maps the way that Mina's Bollywood femininity operates as a form of sexual capital that promises flexible forms of travel, mobility, and consumption, which became increasingly definitive of an emergent transnational class of Indian consumer citizens.

Even as the rearview mirror's visual economy discloses and reinforces differences in middle-class identities between Indian coethnics, Mina's description of Mr. Kapasi's translator job as "romantic" also reveals how heterosexual desire structures this economy. For the first time in the story, "Mina's eyes met Mr. Kapasi's in the rearview mirror: pale, a bit small, their gaze fixed but drowsy" (50). In meeting Mr. Kapasi's gaze, Mina apprehends Mr. Kapasi as a social equal; her "fixed but drowsy" gaze indicates that he also piques her sexual interest. Yet Mr. Kapasi's use of the mirror also reveals a more complicated visual logic than one of compulsory heterosexuality can allow. As Mr. Kapasi begins "to check his reflection in the rearview mirror" and to "glance through the mirror at Mrs. Das" (53), his simultaneous anxiety over his appearance and his observations of Mina shift the visual economy of the story into the vicissitudes of what the feminist film theorist Kaja Silverman, in her work on marginalized male subjectivities in transnational cinema, has called "the look." Silverman defines the look as a mode of apprehension "under which we might idealize and so identify with bodies we would otherwise reject" as sites of identification (4). The look thus functions within a different visual logic than the objectifying gaze, especially for subjects such as the struggling middle-class Indian Mr. Kapasi who have limited access to the forms of social and cultural authority that the conventional gaze would require.

While references to Mina's "breasts" and "the golden brown hollow in her throat" (54) certainly point to Mr. Kapasi's sexual attraction to Mina, his other observations of her contain the more understated tone of appreciation or assessment. In earlier cataloguing of Mina's clothes, accessories, face, and body, for example, Mr. Kapasi "observes" the following: the "red-and-white checkered skirt that stopped above her knees, slip-on shoes with a square wooden heel, and a close-fitting blouse styled like a man's undershirt," which is "decorated at chest-level with a calico appliqué in the shape of a strawberry"; "the frosty pink fingernails painted to match her lips"; her "slightly plump" figure; "her hair, shorn only a little longer than her husband's" and "parted to one side"; "her large brown sunglasses with a pinkish tint to them"; and a "big straw bag" (46). Such observations ring more disinterestedly sartorial than erotic. This assessment is also, at times, shot through with disapproval, as in a later scene when Mr. Kapasi watches as Mina attends to her own self-beautification despite her daughter's pleas to paint her fingernails (49). As a stylish and beautiful subject, Mina vacillates between being the object of Mr. Kapasi's desire and the object of his critique and disillusionment.

In allowing for this vacillation, Lahiri also allows for the simultaneity of desire and identification. Mr. Kapasi's multiple assessments of Mina's physical appearance in the rearview mirror include the appearance of his own image alongside hers, so that they share the same visual frame, allowing for the possibility of cross-gender forms of identification. The temporal sequencing of these visual exchanges privileges identification over desire by temporarily suspending—or at least undercutting—the primary romance narrative. Just prior to his admiration of Mina's body and the assessment of her dress and style, Mr. Kapasi watches with interest as a tea-stall man at a rest stop serenades Mina with "a popular Hindi love song" and Mina walks back to the car, without "irritation or embarrassment," seemingly impervious to the man's declarations (46). As a tourist who is ethnically Indian and yet whose appearance and style mark her as "foreign," Mina embodies for the tea-stall man—and for Mr. Kapasi, who witnesses the serenade—a "diasporic consciousness," an awareness of first-world diasporicity as a position of privilege from which it is possible to claim authority over the "infantilized postcolonial nation-state" (Premnath 255). While her inability to understand the Hindi words of the serenade (or even that she is being serenaded) marks Mina's "foreignness" within the postcolonial nation, her Western style and appearance shore up her supranational status as a diasporic subject. The NRI increasingly came to define this supranational position of authority and privilege for the Indian state and within Bollywood films of the 1990s. Mina's mere visual presence conjures for the tea-stall man the genre of the Hindi, or Bollywood, love song, so that she is briefly inserted into Bollywood idioms.[9] The tea-stall man's "declarations" function as a performative, or a speech act: they insert himself and Mina into the hero/heroine roles of the song (and dance) sequence, the quintessential form of expressing romantic love in Bollywood films. The story associates Mina with Bollywood in other ways, too, such as when Mr. Kapasi watches her "fan herself with a Bombay film magazine written in English," a gesture that accompanies her sighing as "though she had been traveling her whole life without pause" (46–47).

Within the visual economy of the look, Mina's Bollywoodization operates as a form of sexual capital that would promise to recover Mr. Kapasi's deficit of cultural capital in his job as an "interpreter of maladies." Vernacular language translation secures him economic capital and, through Mina's reassessment of his job as "romantic," a measure of cultural capital insofar as Mina's romanticization assigns his job a value it previously did not possess. Yet what also transpires within Mr. Kapasi's witnessing of Mina's Bollywood hailing is his increasing preoccupation with the possibility of possessing, along with Mina, sexual capital. The particular form of sexual capital that Mr. Kapasi seems to want—and that Mina's interpellation as a Bollywood heroine invokes—is the illicit sexuality of the female NRI. In Bollywood films of the 1970s and 1980s, the wealth and Westernization of diasporic subjects were irreconcilable with an Indian national identity still bound, however tenuously, to the ideals of Nehruvian socialism. Bollywood "NRI films" of the 1990s, however, increasingly reconciled wealth and Westernization with a modern and cosmopolitan Indian sensibility. This shift within cultural representation "kept pace" with the state's economic and political policies, which recognized NRIs as political and economic partners with homeland Indians in building the future of the nation (Desai 348, 349). The figure of the female NRI, in particular, became central to these films' cultural reconciliation of wealth and Westernization with definitions of global Indianness. In some NRI films, the NRI woman's domestication within the trope of the arranged love marriage to the wealthy NRI man who returns as "the prodigal son who lovingly adores and maintains the motherland" (Desai 348) signals the compatibility of Westernization and wealth with global Indianness. In other films, the female diasporic subject is presented as susceptible to or as embodying a sexual illicitness that is associated with Westernization and that is frequently contrasted with the sexual decorum of the female homeland subject (Mishra; Uberoi; Mankekar). In both of these representations, however, it is the wealthy NRI businessman who most often experiences the privileges of transnational mobility between India and the diaspora; and it is the Indian woman, "whether NRI or from India," who does not have access to the same kinds of transnational mobility and who must "properly modulate tradition and modernity for the wayward NRI male" (Desai 353).

Mr. Kapasi's witnessing of Mina's Bollywood beauty revises this conventional formulation of the NRI Bollywood film. For in "Interpreter," it is not the economic capital of the NRI businessman but the diasporic sexual capital of the "wayward" NRI woman that holds out the promise of transnational mobility through a sexually illicit style of Bollywood femininity. Mina's Western style of dress, her "largely shaved, largely bare legs" (43), and her short hair suggest a mode of feminine embodiment that exceeds the (presumed) sexual decorum of either the "traditional" NRI or homeland woman in the Bollywood NRI film. Mina's flirtatious revaluation of Mr. Kapasi's job as romantic, her "drowsy" but "fixed" gaze at him in the rearview mirror, and her desire to engage Mr. Kapasi in intimate conversation further reinforce her perceived lack of sexual decorum. Such lack of decorum is later made explicit when she confesses to Mr. Kapasi that she has had an extramarital affair. Mina thus fails to conform to the "gender and sexual norms that are defined as traditional" in Bollywood films; instead, she embodies a sexuality that was "seen as problematic" for the Indian nation during this period (Desai 352). Mr. Kapasi witnesses in the tea-stall man's serenading of Mina-as-Bollywood-heroine the way that the body of the female diasporic subject serves as a projection of the nation's inadmissible desires. That is, even as she is marked by a sexually illicit mode of embodiment, this style of femininity is desirable, even if inadmissible, precisely because of its supranational quality.

I understand Mina's Bollywoodization as affectively priming Mr. Kapasi for his glances at her in the rearview mirror, where he sees in Mina-as-starlet a form of diasporic sexual capital that would relieve him of his own immobile middle-class national masculinity. For although vernacular language translation affords Mr. Kapasi increasingly the economic capital to aspire to consumer-citizen status within the nation, it also signals for him a loss of cultural capital (despite Mina's revaluation of it as "romantic"). For Mr. Kapasi, such forms of cultural capital inhere in the labor of *transnational*, over that of vernacular, translation: "He had dreamed of being an interpreter for diplomats and dignitaries, resolving conflicts between people and nations, settling disputes of which he alone could understand both sides. . . . The job [of vernacular language translation] was a sign of his *failings*" (51–52, my emphasis). Within the visual economy of the look, Mina's sexual capital promises to recover the deficit of cultural capital that he experiences in his job as an "interpreter of maladies."

Mina's Bollywoodization also deterritorializes the gendering of Indian beauty, as it affectively primes Mr. Kapasi for aspirational identifications with Indian *male beauty* as a form of sexual capital. Upon the Das family's arrival at their tourist destination, the Konarak temple, Mr. Kapasi turns his attention to the Indian male body by fixing his gaze on the "beauty" and "power" of the Surya, the Hindu sun god, on the temple's exterior (157). Though Mr. Kapasi's preoccupation with the Surya's beauty emerges from within a narrative of heterosexual romance, it also produces affective frictions within that narrative. The visual iconography of Konarak, along with temple carvings at Khajuraho, has been invoked in many postcolonial contexts to construct a narrative about modern sexual awakening from within an overarching narrative of premodern sexual repression.[10] The exterior of the Konarak temple is decorated with erotic visual iconography that draws from the legendary ancient Indian erotic text the *Kama Sutra*. The temple features "countless friezes of entwined naked bodies, making love in various positions, women clinging to the necks of men, their knees wrapped eternally around their lovers' thighs" (57). In Mina and Mr. Kapasi's shared gazing at the temple's erotic art, they participate in this narrative of Indian sexual modernity as the appreciation of its sexual iconography signals an impending sexual liaison. Yet an otherwise heterosexual romantic rendering of this scene is undercut by Mr. Kapasi's hope that Mina will also share in his recognition of the Surya's beauty and power, with which he is clearly enthralled (58). Despite initially wanting to "be alone with" Mina, Mr. Kapasi walks ahead of her

> to admire, as he always did, the three life-sized bronze avatars of Surya. . . . They wore elaborate headdresses, their languid, elongated eyes closed, their bare chests draped with carved chains and amulets. . . . The last statue, on the northern wall of the temple, was his favorite. This Surya had a tired expression, weary after a hard day of work. . . . Around his body were smaller sculptures of women in pairs, their hips thrust to one side. (58)

The Surya's "tired expression" clearly recalls Mr. Kapasi's references to the demands of his job as an interpreter of maladies, which he requires in order to aspire to consumer-citizen status within the nation. Yet the Surya's beauty, reinforced here through the pairs of women surrounding him in obeisance, also appears as an aspirational mode of identification that exceeds an Indian consumer identity and Mr. Kapasi's desire for Mina. For even as "he had an overwhelming urge to wrap his arms around [Mina], to freeze with her, even for an instant" as they gaze at the temple carvings, Mr. Kapasi also fantasizes that their embrace might be "witnessed by his favorite Surya" (59). Rather than objectifying Mina with this erotic economy, Mr. Kapasi's desire is that the Surya's witnessing of their embrace might legitimate his status as, essentially, Mina's erotic peer, her equal in his possession of sexual capital.

Mina's sexual capital becomes crucial to Mr. Kapasi's understanding of his own beauty and desirability. His knowledge of and comparisons to the Surya's beauty-as-power are forms of cultural authority that allow him to approximate Mina's power and privilege as a sexually desirable, supranational subject.[11] His erotic fantasy, after all, is not the "possession" of Mina but the possession of a photograph of Mina that she will mail to him and that he imagines keeping "tucked between the pages of his Russian grammar" (55); relatedly, his erotic nightmare is "the possibility of a lost letter, the photograph never reaching him, hovering somewhere in Orissa, close but ultimately unattainable" (56). In the place of his "dream" of being a language interpreter who could travel between nations, Mr. Kapasi fantasizes about the Surya's beauty: "Perhaps they would discuss [the Surya's beauty and power] further in their letters. He would explain things to her, things about India, and she would explain things to him, about America. *In its own way this correspondence would fulfill his dream, of serving as an interpreter between nations*" (59, my emphasis). While Indian male beauty cannot guarantee Mr. Kapasi literal mobility between nations—as would his forsaken career as a transnational language interpreter—it does "in its own way" allow him to imagine a position of sovereignty over his national status. If Mina possesses diasporic sexual capital, then for Mr. Kapasi Indian male beauty approximates this form of capital: as a projected embodiment of his own desirability and as a subject over which he has cultural authority, the Surya's beauty can provide him a prosthetic form of sexual capital. As such, male beauty offers him a way of claiming a symbolic place within an emergent flexible citizenry of transnational NRIs.

Yet this form of sexual capital ultimately eludes Mr. Kapasi. It operates instead as a form of what Berlant calls "cruel optimism." Berlant defines cruel optimism as "a relation of attachment to compromised conditions of possibility whose realization is discovered either to be *im*possible, sheer fantasy, or *too* possible, and toxic" ("Cruel" 94). Mina's sexual capital is exposed as a "compromised" and "toxic" condition of possibility for transnational mobility when the erotic energies of this scene are rerouted into an altogether different sexual scenario—the confession of Mina's affair. The confession betrays Mr. Kapasi's identification with Mina's sexual capital as a "sheer fantasy" and, even if possible as a relation of attachment, a "toxic" one because it reinforces rather than mitigates the uneven distribution of capital that structures class differences between coethnics. After confessing her affair to Mr. Kapasi, Mina asks him to then "suggest some kind of remedy" for the "pain" that she has endured from repressing her sexual secret for so many years (66). Mr. Kapasi, rather than obliging, "felt insulted that Mrs. Das should ask him to interpret her common, trivial little secret. She did not resemble the patients in the doctor's office, unable to sleep or breathe or urinate with ease, unable, above all, to give words to their pains" (66). Within a conventional reading of a burgeoning romance between Mr. Kapasi and Mina, which the story clearly invites, Mr. Kapasi's feelings of insult are symptoms of a tantrum-like jealousy—rather than her fantasies about a sexual present with Mr. Kapasi, the erotic friezes on the exterior of the Konarak temple prompt Mina's memories of her sexual past with another man. Or, perhaps even more simply, Mr. Kapasi's feelings of insult betray that his judgments about Mina's "pain" are in fact moral judgments about her sexual indiscretions.

Yet the force of Mina's exchange with Mr. Kapasi also clearly exceeds readings of personal jealousy or moral judgment. For Mr. Kapasi has already imagined Mina as a sexually illicit body—indeed, it is this very illicitness and lack of decorum that defines Mina's sexual capital in the first place. Furthermore, while Mina's confession may well shatter Mr. Kapasi's expectations of a tryst, his assessment of her confession as "common" and "trivial" expresses a critique both of Mina's false sense of injury—her nonresemblance to those whose "real" pain is inexpressible because of linguistic barriers—*and* of her liberal view that the affair demands confessing.[12] Whereas in the scene of Mina's Bollywood femininity, Mina's illicit sexuality signals a desirable form of transnational mobility, in the scene of Mina's sexual confession, Mina's sexuality is harnessed to negative and "trivial" affects of psychic "pain" (65), "guilt" (66), and "feeling terrible all the time" (65). The impact of Mina's confession on Mr. Kapasi has to do with the way it converts Mina's illicit sexuality—the very basis of her sexual capital—into a liability rather than an asset. After Mina confesses the affair, "the feeling [Mr. Kapasi] had toward her, that had made him check his reflection in the rearview mirror as they drove, evaporated a little" (65). In addition to depleting her sexual capital, the confession further devalues Mr. Kapasi's job as a language translator; Mina, who had earlier revalued it as a "romantic" job, here converts it back into a degraded (and even degrading) form of labor. For by entreating Mr. Kapasi to "suggest some kind of remedy" for the "pain" of keeping the affair a secret, Mina asks him to perform a service that is beyond his paid labor as a tour guide. Her request for him to "interpret" her sexual "malady" reinforces and further exploits class differences between coethnics that are produced through the uneven global expansion of and access to capital.

As a form of sexual capital, Mina's beauty points to the way a transnational class of NRIs accrues desirability within the Indian nation in ways that foreclose on practices of flexible citizenship among middle-class postcolonial Indian subjects. Despite the guarantees of political citizenship, then, Mr. Kapasi lacks the cultural and economic capital of the NRI, whose transnational mobility and purchasing power became central to both global and national definitions of Indianness at the end of the twentieth century. Mr. Kapasi's desire to access Mina's diasporic sexual capital in the face of his own struggle to maintain his consumer-citizen status is a mark of his lack of full belonging within the globalizing Indian nation. The failures of transnational mobility to produce supranational attachments for the Indian male national subject constitute Lahiri's feminist cosmopolitical engagements with Indian beauty. At the same time, Mr. Kapasi's desire to be seen and recognized as possessing the male equivalent of Mina's beauty raises the possibility of *emergent* diasporic intimacies. That is, even in the face of beauty's disappointments and failures, such desires for beauty might be forged beyond normatively sexual and gendered codes and beyond the uneven distribution of capital that condition flexible forms of transnationality.

Bourgeois Style, Home Décor, and Provincializing the Hindu Nation

Whereas diasporic femininity forecloses on desires for transnational mobility in "Interpreter of Maladies," in this section I consider diasporic beauty's affects as performing a related form of productive failure as part of Lahiri's cosmopolitical literary project: provincializing dominant Hindu national culture in defining diasporic settlement.[13] In the story

"This Blessed House," the feminine beauty and charm of the middle-class Indian American female subject challenges the reproduction of long-distance religious nationalisms in the US diaspora. As many feminist scholars of diaspora have noted, the body of the diasporic woman shores up the heterosexual, bourgeois, Hindu, male subject as the unmarked figure at the center of both community and state discourses of diaspora.[14] By turning to an examination of the diasporic woman's sexual capital in "This Blessed House," this section shows how the body of the diasporic woman unsettles hetero-masculinist attachments to a Hindu middle-class identity as part of diasporic bourgeois settlement.

In the opening scene of "This Blessed House," Sanjeev, an Indian American engineer, watches, simultaneously fascinated and repulsed, as his wife, Twinkle, an Indian American graduate student, arranges a row of Christian curios on their fireplace mantel: "a 3-D postcard of St. Francis done in four colors, . . . a wooden cross key chain, . . . a framed paint by number of three wise men, . . . a tile trivet depicting a blond, unbearded Jesus, . . . [and] a small plastic snow dome containing a miniature Nativity scene" (137). Twinkle's gradual excavation, collection, and display of these trinkets increasingly irks Sanjeev, leading him to devalue them as "silly," as they seem to "lack a sense of sacredness": "These objects meant something to Twinkle, but they meant nothing to him. They irritated him" (138). Sanjeev's irritation at the objects, which Twinkle calls "pretty" and "spectacular" (137, 139) in order to justify their domestic display, redoubles as his irritation at Twinkle for what he perceives is her diminishing "good taste" in matters of bourgeois domesticity (138).

The story climaxes when Twinkle, with the help of an entourage of housewarming-party guests, discovers the "final" fetish in the attic of their home: a massive silver bust of Christ. The bust's appearance among the Christian curios marks a sudden shift in Sanjeev's attitude toward them: "Its expression was confident, as if assured of its devotees, the unyielding lips sensuous and full. He hated its immensity" but also "its flawless, polished surface, and its undeniable value. . . . Unlike the other things they'd found, this contained dignity, solemnity, beauty even" (157). Sanjeev's conflicted recognition of and aversion to the bust's aesthetic self-assurance and its economic value slips, rather inexplicably, into an analogous fantasy about Twinkle's desirability. He predicts that "each time they had guests Twinkle would explain how she had found it [the bust of Christ], and they would admire *her* as they listened" (157, my emphasis). Twinkle's very name references in grammatical form the ability of her mere presence to solicit, like the bust, throngs of admirers at parties and social gatherings. Twinkle's ability to attract such admiration and adoration in "Blessed" animates the latent stresses and failures of Sanjeev's male immigrant embourgeoisement. Earlier in the story, Sanjeev studies his own appearance, one that he contrasts with Twinkle's captivating beauty:

> In the mirror of the medicine cabinet he inspected his long eyelashes—like a girl's, Twinkle liked to tease. Though he was of average build, his cheeks had a plumpness to them; this, along with his eyelashes, detracted, he feared, from what he hoped was a distinguished profile. He was of average height as well. . . . For this reason it irritated him when Twinkle insisted on wearing high heels. (140)

Sanjeev's irritability toward Twinkle is here routed through his anxiety about the plenitude of male performativity, his hope that he will pass as masculine enough when in public with Twinkle. Yet when read against his fantasy about his guests' admiration of the "undeniable value" and beauty of the statue/Twinkle, this passage also expresses a competition with an iterative femininity, as Sanjeev's "long eyelashes" and "plump cheeks" threaten to dissolve against Twinkle's more legible feminine performance in "high heels."

Like Mr. Kapasi's physical assessment of Mina in "Interpreter," Sanjeev's assessment of his feminized appearance references a strange mix of admiration of and competition with Twinkle's femininity. Yet whereas for Mr. Kapasi, Mina's sexual capital promises the approximation of transnational mobility, for Sanjeev, Twinkle's sexual capital thwarts his attempts to master the everyday practices of domesticity that define middle-class settlement in the diaspora.[15] The anxiety that Sanjeev feels over his home's order and appearance is a direct reflection of his success as a quintessential model minority subject. An MIT graduate who secures a prestigious position at an engineering firm, Sanjeev "had recently learned that he was being considered for the position of vice president. At thirty-three he had a secretary of his own and a dozen people working under his supervision who gladly supplied him with any information he needed" (138). Told by his mother that he has "enough money in the bank to raise three families" and that he now needs a "wife to look after and love," Sanjeev muses that "now he had one, a pretty one, from a suitably high caste, who would soon have a master's degree" (148). Indeed, for legal, professionally skilled, elite South Asian immigrants such as Sanjeev and Twinkle, who were allowed to immigrate under the family reunification provisions of the Immigration Act of 1965, the heterosexual household unit is the site within which "the immigrant bourgeoisie guards what it perceives to be the nation's cultural essence against contamination by dominant Western values" (Bhattacharjee 38).

If the space of house is a valorized site for the collective project of preserving national culture in the diaspora, then Twinkle becomes both the object and the subject of the couple's successful embourgeoisement within the home. While Sanjeev "had found the house on his own before leaving for [his] wedding, for a good price, in a neighborhood with a fine school system," it is Twinkle who takes charge of and receives praise for its interior decoration (145), and her feminine charm earns her increasing ground in constructing this idealized domestic space. Rather than issuing a masculinist or misogynist pronouncement to "butch up," the irritability that mediates Sanjeev's feelings toward Twinkle's femininity culminates in the rather heavily metaphorized gesture of extending himself into and surrendering to Twinkle's performance of bourgeois femininity: pressing "to his ribs" the bust of Christ, whose "sensuous" and "full" lips are, at this point, the simulacra of his wife's feminine features, Sanjeev "follows [Twinkle]," and the story ends (157). Sanjeev's gesture expresses the pedagogy of Twinkle's bourgeois and heretofore disavowed "good taste."

As Twinkle's feminine charm and good taste allow her to accrue social prestige as an upwardly mobile diasporic subject, these characteristics also work to decenter a dominant Hindu male identity within Indian American narratives of diaspora, in which the prosperous Hindu NRI male becomes the representative figure of diaspora.[16] At one point, Sanjeev is forced to explain to a housewarming-party guest who is unable to reconcile the couple's Indianness with their display of Christian curios that "there are Christians in India" (151). Yet lest his guest assume that he and Twinkle are Christian Indians, he quickly adds, "but we're not [Christian]" (151), a phrase he finds himself uttering "for the fortieth time" that evening (152). By both displaying a knowledge of religious diversity in India and yet repeatedly clarifying his own non-Christian affiliations to his house guest, Sanjeev betrays his concern that Twinkle's obsession with collecting and displaying Christian curios is somehow at odds with the couple's "Indianness."

Sanjeev clearly feels pressed to maintain nominal Hinduness as a sign of his middle-class immigrant life, which he feels the Christian decorations threaten to call into question. He assumes Twinkle's willing participation in maintaining this nominally religious affiliation and is frustrated when she does not oblige. Reflecting on Twinkle's fascination with the

Christian curios, Sanjeev muses, "She was like that, excited and delighted by little things. . . . It was a quality he did not understand. It made him feel stupid, as if the world contained hidden wonders he could not anticipate, or see. He looked at her face, . . . the eyes untroubled, the pleasing features unfirm, as if they still had to settle into some sort of permanent expression" (142). Twinkle's "pleasing" features reflect for Sanjeev a bourgeois sensibility that remains beyond his own immigrant embourgeoisement, despite his elite education and professional success. Though he is initially resistant to Twinkle's penchant for Christian curios, Sanjeev is here envious of her feminine beauty, charm, and bourgeois taste. Unlike him, she has the ability to see beauty and value in religious objects that he perceives as entirely incongruous with both their Indianness and their middle-class status. Twinkle's aesthetic self-assurance, both in her appearance and in her taste in displaying the Christian curios as home décor, allows her to remain "untroubled" by diasporic imperatives to reproduce a Hindu cultural identity. Twinkle's understanding of the Christian curios' potential to increase her bourgeois sense of style—though certainly signs of diasporic class privilege—can also be understood as her performance of emotional and political relief from the social reproduction of diasporic cultural and religious nationalisms.

Lahiri, the Cosmopolitan Beauty

We follow the transnational itineraries of lustrous star images because they bind us so firmly to hegemonic aspirations . . . that [smooth] over inequities that emerge from the restructuring of global capital.—BISHNUPRIYA GHOSH (GLOBAL 140)

I have been arguing that Lahiri's feminist cosmopolitical literary project is one that becomes intelligible through a focus on the affective capacities of diasporic beauty. These affects are generated from within an encounter with the beauty and desirability of the diasporic Indian woman, whether imagined (as in the case of Dixit / Dev's wife's) or real (as in the case of Mina and Twinkle). By way of conclusion, I extend this affective relay between what Rajeswari Sunder Rajan calls "real and imagined women" to an examination of the relationship between media representations of Lahiri's own ethnic beauty and the fictional representations of diasporic beauty that I have mapped in this chapter.[17] Sunder Rajan argues that "'real' women cannot lie outside the 'imagined' constructs in and through which 'women' emerge as subjects" (10). Adapting her observations about the role of representation in shaping subjectivities, I argue something of the inverse—that media representations of Lahiri's beauty allow beauty's affects to acquire greater political traction within her literary feminist cosmopolitical project. If beauty operates as an assemblage—if it is mappable through an aggregation marked by differences in scale, duration, and magnitude—then the construction of Lahiri's public image is part of this aggregation; the force of beauty that emerges across Lahiri's fiction is also a force that captures *her*. Lahiri's public image is replete with visual and verbal expressions of her highly stylized beauty and fashionability across transnational mass media. I examine the precise nature of such expressions and how they inform popular and scholarly reading publics' dominant reception of Lahiri's fiction as a genre of "cosmopolitan lite," in which her narratives are understood as transcending differences of race, nation, and culture. Such dominant readings, while they speak to the various ways in which Indian beauty is constructed as a commodity fetish, are at the same time inassimilable to the feminist cosmopolitics that I locate within her fictional representations of diasporic beauty's affects.

In the decade or more following the publication of *Interpreter of Maladies*, Lahiri's public image became increasingly harnessed to two predominant forms of media control.[18] The first was the repetition and standardization of certain "graphic inscriptions" that circulated—and continue to circulate—as part of Lahiri's public image. Such graphic traces are clearly invested in producing the author's glamorous beauty as a way of "intensifying aesthetic pleasure" for consuming publics (B. Ghosh, *Global* 147). The second is a more or less standardized popular reading of Lahiri's fiction as emblematic of "universal" themes of human experience, such as intergenerational and romantic conflict that render ethnic difference either inconsequential or nonthreatening to such themes. Though these appear to be distinct and even incommensurate forms of media control, Lahiri's beauty in these market-driven images does much to shore up depoliticized renderings of ethnic difference in her fiction.

Lahiri's star image became susceptible to repetition and standardization only after the publication of her debut novel, *The Namesake* (2003), when her literary celebrity had been fully secured by her winning of the Pulitzer just four years earlier. Early public images of Lahiri circulated primarily as part of online newspapers and literary and news magazines that reported on the author's seemingly sudden emergence onto the literary scene. Consisting mostly of thumbnail headshots, these images could be easily embedded into the article text and appeared primarily as a photographic authorial signature. Even slightly more stylized visual signatures that appeared within these media, such as Lahiri's publicity photograph for *Interpreter of Maladies* (see fig. 2.1), did not clearly harness beauty to

FIGURE 2.1. Author publicity photo
for *Interpreter of Maladies*, 1999.
(Photograph by Jerry Bauer)

this signature, as much as they did raw talent. This photo is a black-and-white headshot of Lahiri dressed in a turtleneck, shot in the confines of her Brooklyn home. In it, her eyes are turned away from the camera, staring off into the distance, suggesting a literary future yet unknown; in the background, we can make out an Indian batik print of an elephant, an orientalist visual cue that alerts us to the author's Indian origin.

But since Lahiri's debut novel, her public image has been harnessed with increasing frequency and scale to visual and verbal expressions of her beauty across a range of global mass-media platforms—highbrow literary magazines with a global distribution, mainstream global news media, literary and fashion blogs, and international fashion magazines. The "glam shots" of the author on the book jackets of *The Namesake* (2003) and her most recent collection of short stories, *Unaccustomed Earth* (2008), are among the most frequently recirculated visual images of Lahiri across these media platforms (see figs. 2.2 and 2.3). These photographs repeat certain graphic traces—a fully frontal gaze, piercing eyes, unsmiling lips, hair pulled back, exposed neck—that construct Lahiri as both sexual commodity and fragile beauty. These graphic traces acquire a "symbolic density" as they circulate across media platforms

FIGURE 2.2. Author publicity photo for *The Namesake*, 2003. (Photograph by Jerry Bauer)

FIGURE 2.3. Author publicity photo for *Unaccustomed Earth*, 2007. (Photograph by Elena Seibert)

over time (B. Ghosh, *Global* 152). They are reproduced in snapshots of Lahiri at celebrity public events, photo shoots of Lahiri lounging in her Brooklyn home taken by fashion photographers, and in freelance photographs taken by news outlets featuring the author's latest literary achievements.

No longer content to recycle the authorized publicity photos—however heavily stylized—news outlets bearing the most visible corporate imprimaturs began to produce their own images of the star's fragile beauty and allure. For example, the online publication of the *San Francisco Chronicle*, sfgate.com, shot a photo of Lahiri seated on the ground in the corner of a stark, white room, dressed in a pink dress, arms wrapped around her knees, staring into the camera. A *Time* magazine feature, meanwhile, depicts the writer dressed similarly in pink but standing up with arms folded demurely in front of her (see fig. 2.4). The slightly altered mise-en-scène, lighting, and pose allow the artist to appear unique and without equivalence. And yet these photos also proliferate anew the graphic inscriptions of feminized and sexualized ethnic beauty that viewers recognize as the visual substrate of the book jackets' glam shots.

FIGURE 2.4. "The Quiet Laureate." *Time*, May 8, 2008. (Photograph by Bill Wadman)

These graphic traces of Lahiri's feminine beauty became standardized across various media in part because they capitalized on preexisting cultural referents of Indian beauty, which included both the global visibility of Indian beauty queens and also the celebrated beauty of the Indian writer and literary celebrity Arundhati Roy. Roy's literary celebrity emerged during the explosion of Indian Writing in English (IWE) on the subcontinent that subsequently took the global literary marketplace by storm. Bishnupriya Ghosh has described the way that Roy's publicity photo, which appeared on the book jacket of her Booker Prize–winning novel *The God of Small Things* (1997), motivated both visual and verbal expressivity in Indian media around Roy's "curls" and "collarbones." These physical features became graphic traces of "an appropriately delicate femininity...that could be quickly mobilized for commercial or political promotion" across various global media (B. Ghosh, *Global* 153).[19]

Roy's public image as a "Booker Prize glamour girl" was culturally situated within a preexisting symbolic domain of Indian women in beauty pageants who were exploding into global markets (B. Ghosh, *Global* 141). As Lahiri secured the Pulitzer just two years after Roy's Booker Prize win, Lahiri's public image was easily harnessed to the "Roy phenomenon."[20] It is this symbolic domain of Indian beauty, in fact, that allows Lahiri's literary predecessor Bharati Mukherjee to claim Lahiri as "the renowned novelist and Bengali beauty" in Mukherjee's latest novel on Indian female call-center workers, *Miss New India* (2011), a title that itself riffs off the global purchase of the Indian beauty queen.[21]

Several fan sites devoted to Lahiri's star image abstract Lahiri's beauty and sex appeal from her larger social value as a literary star. But the vast majority of visual and verbal expressions of Lahiri's beauty circulate as a kind of surplus value to her literary value, which is calibrated in terms of literary talent and appeal. These discussions often emphasize ethnic difference in Lahiri's stories as secondary or incidental to her presumably more universal themes of intergenerational or romantic conflict. Yet Lahiri's value-added beauty in these discussions actually allows the author's Indian ethnicity to shore up her globality (where globality is rooted in claims about the universality of Lahiri's fiction) and to obscure what I have been calling Lahiri's literary feminist cosmopolitics. For example, one literary blogger, after expressing some disappointment that Lahiri has not yet moved "outside the sphere of the Indian American experience, which clearly constitutes her comfort zone," at the same time admits, "On the other hand, it won't bother me if she doesn't. She has made that world so real, so vivid—and so universal." The blogger concludes her post with *The Namesake* glam shot of Lahiri, ostensibly in a gesture of the author's visual signature. Yet the glam shot proves to be more than this. Before signing off, the blogger writes, "My husband just walked by the computer and exclaimed, 'What a jaw-dropper!' I figure if she gets worn out from all that writing, she can make movies instead!" ("Unaccustomed"). Such seemingly supplementary and non sequitur exclamations about Lahiri's disarming beauty are commonplace within the popular form of the literary blog.[22]

What is perhaps more striking than references to Lahiri's beauty within the public content of literary blogs is the way that such expressions circulate across more authorized media content as well. In a review of *Unaccustomed Earth*, for example, the *San Francisco Chronicle* writer Adair Lara's opening words make explicit reference to Lahiri's beauty and echo the sentiments of the blogger just quoted: "Expensively and chicly dressed, Pulitzer Prize–winning writer Jhumpa (pronounced Joompa) Lahiri is at 36 as beautiful as any movie star." A particularly guiling (and galling) instance of the surplus value of Lahiri's beauty can be found in the visual image that accompanies Boris Kachka's review of *Unaccustomed Earth* in *New York* magazine. In the article, titled "The Confidence Artist," Kachka declares that there is "no hook" in Lahiri's writing, "just couples and families joining, coming apart, dealing with immigration, death, and estrangement." Kachka sees such universal themes as somehow a part of and yet fundamentally distinct from an ethnic identity that he calls the "Bengali-American experience" and that he sees as resonating across Lahiri's fiction. Yet the title "the confidence artist" points not just to the mere transposition of ethnicity onto universal themes of family, love, death, and immigration in Lahiri's fiction. More specifically, the term points to a suspicion around this transposition, one laced with racist undertones. The label "confidence artist" is, of course, longhand for "con artist," a term that is applied to those who are adept at earning the false trust of others in order to swindle or cheat them and that resonates with the historical characterization of Asian Americans as duplicitous "double agents" (T. Chen).

Kachka suggests that Lahiri's literary value has to do with the way that ethnicity operates as a ruse for the global appeal of her fiction. Yet the photograph of Lahiri that accompanies the article, presumably serving as visual authorial signature, performs the act of conjoining ethnicity to global appeal that Kachka finds so suspicious in Lahiri's fictional worlds. The highly stylized black-and-white headshot of Lahiri (see fig. 2.5) maintains many of the graphic traces of the previous publicity photos of the writer's beauty, with the exception of Lahiri's eyes, which are averted down. The downward gaze, along with the use of black-and-white film stock and severe (though aesthetically appealing) lighting, remediates Lahiri's ethnic beauty through the "universal" aesthetic of old Hollywood female glamour. As such, the image works semantically to ameliorate deep-seated racist (and sexist) fears of the ethnic con artist.

Such visual and verbal expressivities have become standard fare within public images of Lahiri's literary celebrity. Even more recently, however, the mass-mediated beauty of Lahiri's literary star image has become the raw material for Lahiri's transformation into the more highly abstracted commodity form of a global fashion icon. In these images, it is Lahiri's beauty that is the primary text, while her literary celebrity provides surplus value. Two images in particular capture this transformation. The first is a watercolor illustration of Lahiri against

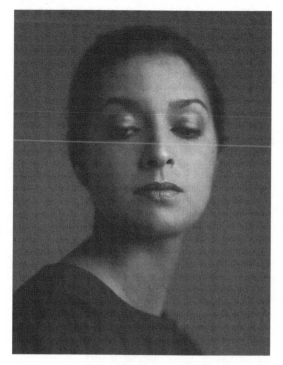

FIGURE 2.5. "The Confidence Artist." *New York,*
March 31, 2008. (Photograph by Peter Hapak /
Trunk Archive)

a sepia background, featured in an October 2009 *Vogue India* fashion
spread called "You're the Inspiration" (see fig. 2.6). The spread features
global female celebrities whom various Indian fashion designers claim
as the "muses" for their fashion designs and all of whom are painted
in the clothes of a different designer. In the painting of Lahiri by the
Vogue freelance fashion illustrator Cecelia Carlstedt, Lahiri is dressed in
a merino-wool quilted jacket with kimono collar and a yoked silk skirt,
Lycra leggings, and sandals, designed by the Indian fashion moguls
David Abraham and Rakesh Thakore, whose painted faces peer out at
us from behind Lahiri's full-body image.[23] In Carlstedt's painting, Lahiri
appears as a fashion model on a runway: her hip thrust to one side, hands
in pockets, gazing, so it seems, into an imaginary audience of fashion
enthusiasts. The caption reads, "Jhumpa Lahiri has brains, beauty, and
writes compassionately about belonging and displacement." The *Vogue*

Muse: JHUMPA LAHIRI
"Jhumpa Lahiri has brains and beauty, and writes compassionately about belonging and displacement"
—DAVID ABRAHAM, ABRAHAM & THAKORE

FIGURE 2.6. "You're the Inspiration." *Vogue India*, October 2009. (Illustration by Cecelia Carlstedt)

caption echoes the visual and verbal expressions around Lahiri's beauty in literary mass-media outlets, building her social value as a literary star.

Yet the relation of Lahiri's social value to her literary stardom becomes more attenuated when placed within the larger context of the *Vogue* fashion layout. The layout features such female fashion muses as the Hollywood actress and model Uma Thurman, the Bollywood actresses Dimple Kapadia and Kareena Kapoor, the former model and Miss World Priyanka Chopra, the American music icon and fashion maven Madonna, Chanel's French spokesmodel Vanessa Paradis, the Italian supermodel Linda Evangelista,

FIGURE 2.7. Louis Vuitton Diwaali party, November 2010.
(Photograph by Billy Farrell / BFAnyc.com)

and the Indian fashion models Sheetal Mallar and Lakshmi Menon, among others. The *Vogue* spread allows Lahiri's star image to accrue social value through her equivalence with these other highly recognizable fashion and beauty icons, remediating her global literary celebrity into that of an iconic fashionability. Lahiri's photographed appearance with the Indian American jewelry designer Waris Ahluwalia, at a Louis Vuitton Diwali Party in November 2010 (see fig. 2.7) secures the increasing abstraction of Lahiri's fashion iconicity from her literary value. In this image, Lahiri is not just fashion savvy or simply a muse for the Indian fashion industry but, through her association with Ahluwalia (who later became the victim of a fashion scandal, which I discuss briefly in the epilogue), an active fashion industrialist.

The processes of repetition and standardization that inform the mass-media circulation of Lahiri's beauty and fashionability illustrate how the proliferation of such public images, despite circulating within emerging and established global markets for Indian beauty, must also be disaggregated from the fictional gaze that Lahiri maintains on Indian beauty's affects at the dawn of the twenty-first century. As these public images of Lahiri clearly reveal, this is a gaze that is very much directed toward Lahiri as well. Yet the political stakes of Lahiri's cosmopolitical feminist gaze lie not in the way that such a gaze challenges proliferation of such images—the fictional diasporic women that I have discussed in this chapter are still singularly beautiful, charming, and alluring, after all. But Lahiri's fictional gaze does begin to loosen the ties that bind mass-mediated representations of Indian beauty to its neoliberal attachments, in ways that open onto the nonhegemonic affects of its transnational itineraries.

3 / Fashioning Diasporic Citizens in Literary Youth Cultures of Beauty and Fashion

In the previous two chapters, I examined how Indian beauty's materiality and affectivities generate desires for, but fail to secure, national and transnational mobility and belonging for a range of South Asian, non–South Asian, and diasporic subjects in what are by now canonical South Asian American literary texts. In this chapter, I examine a lesser-known archive of South Asian American fiction written about and for young Indian women, in which diasporic cultures of South Asian beauty and fashion animate the limitations and possibilities of diasporic citizenship, or "full belonging within the diaspora" (Siu 106). In distinction to the modes of belonging that I mapped in chapters 1 and 2, in which belonging is articulated primarily in relation to dominant national culture and nation-based understandings of transnational affiliation, diasporic citizenship has to do with the way that "diasporic communities contest, forge and reaffirm their identities" (Siu 106) through their global connections to other South Asians on the basis of shared ancestry and cultural practices. This chapter also marks a shift in the way that *Fashioning Diaspora* conceives of beauty as an assemblage of materialities and affectivities. In the previous two chapters, Indian beauty is primarily a physical attribute of the diasporic woman's body. In this part of the book, I locate Indian beauty as taking on a multiplicity of social forms within diasporic girlhood, including beauty pageantry, colonial histories of dress, and the global fashion industry.

In this chapter, I examine beauty as a public event organized around the judgment of young Indian women's femininity (a short story about the Miss India USA pageant). I then turn to an examination of fashion as a gendered discourse about Indian colonial modernity (a young-adult novel about an Indian anticolonial girl fashion doll) and then as a young Indian American girl's place within the US fashion media complex (a young-adult "chick lit" novel about fashion journalism). Since beauty-as-assemblage allows us to apprehend texts as a "collection of multiplicities" rather than as linked through analogy or equivalence, the diasporic Indian beauty queen, the Indian American Girl doll, and the aspiring young, Indian American, female fashion reporter that are the subjects of this chapter circulate as heterogeneous but connected narratives about young women's understandings of diasporic citizenship. Across these texts, beauty and fashion produce temporary and fleeting diasporic affiliations across class and citizenship divides; a politically conscious diasporic consumer nationalism; ethnic affiliations; and racial consciousness about the economic links between skilled and unskilled South Asian workers in the global fashion industry.

In locating fashion and beauty's socializing capacities within literary youth cultures of diasporic girlhood, this chapter expands on and intervenes into existing feminist scholarship on racialized girlhoods. US feminist childhood studies scholars have shown how childhood is a "potent force in the cultural and economic structures of the nation" (Sanchez-Eppler xxii). These scholars have attended to the role of the child in the formation of class identities, norms of domesticity, social reforms, and the emergence of the United States as an overseas empire.[1] Yet the role of the child—and of racialized girlhood in particular—in the making of diasporic public cultures has remained virtually unexplored within childhood studies. This chapter, then, like the few other works on racialized girlhood that currently exist, places young women of color and diasporic girls at the center of citizenship practices (Jiwani et al.). When I talk about beauty and fashion as socializing forces in youth literature, I mean not only that youth cultures of beauty and fashion are central to the formation of diasporic community. I mean also that beauty and fashion do the work *of* socialization: they are, whether implicitly or explicitly, pedagogical tools through which young women learn about the social value of an ideal diasporic subjectivity. This pedagogical role, particularly in the two young-adult novels that I examine, is to some degree inherent to the genre of children's literature, a literary industry that often colludes with the childrearing agenda of schools, parents, and other childhood "experts" to educate children into being responsible, civil subjects. At the same time, I argue that literary youth cultures of beauty and fashion also reveal young women and girls to be "forces of socialization" (Sanchez-Eppler xv) in that they showcase how girls and young women can be agential in scripting social relations and in defining diasporic community through their engagements with fashion and beauty.

Girl cultures present a particularly rich site for examining beauty and fashion's production of diasporic citizenship because like beauty and fashion, racialized girlhood and young womanhood are seldom recognized as central to the making of national and diasporic public cultures. This has to do with the way that both beauty and girlhood are most often associated with political passivity and mass consumerism, those realms of culture that Lauren Berlant, as I discussed in the introduction, has called the "juxtapolitical." It also has to do with the way that dominant critiques of "girl power," a discourse of consumer feminism that circulates in the marketing of toys, games, and books for girls, typically cast girls as helpless victims of consumer culture and therefore in need of adult protection and supervision.[2] Beauty and fashion are often at the heart of these critiques. Girls must "stay pretty and accessorized" as consumer subjects, even when they are represented as socially empowered (Lamb and Brown 168). These critics thus lament the puerile feminism of a "girl power" that does little to challenge a "pink-n-pretty" model of girlhood (Lamb and Brown 168). By claiming to take pressure off girls to conform to consumerist beauty ideals of girlhood and to cede control over the well-being of girls to parents, studies of girlhood almost always reproduce the figure of the girl-child as in need of adult (usually parental) rescue. Such critiques of consumer feminism rarely if ever focus on racialized girlhoods, and those that do most often reproduce a multiculturalist account of racial difference that leaves intact the figure of the girl (of color) as inhabiting a universal state of innocence and vulnerability. In examining young South Asian American women's and girls' positioning within beauty and fashion literary cultures, this chapter shows that neither diasporic young womanhood/girlhood nor the public domains of beauty/fashion can be marked off as socially, economically, or racially "innocent."[3] Rather, these young women's participation in beauty and fashion cultures do a lot of work to upend upwardly mobile definitions of diasporic community and culture, to promote a vision of politicized diasporic girlhood that challenges the requisite liberal multiculturalism of girl consumer cultures, and to construct girls as racially conscious workers, and not just consumers, in a new global economy.

Affective Economies of Pageantry in Pallavi Dixit's "Pageant"

In the opening scenes of Pallavi Dixit's "Pageant" (2009), a short story about a Miss India USA beauty pageant, the story's protagonist, Miss India Kentucky, sabotages a fellow pageant contestant, Miss India New Jersey, by ripping apart her sequined evening gown during the pageant's intermission. After Miss India Kentucky completes her transgression, she walks out the back door of the pageant hall and upon exiting finds herself in the parking lot, where two of the pageant's South Asian male waitstaff are taking a cigarette break. In an unlikely and unexpected encounter between the middle-class pageant contestant and the South Asian service-sector workers, a discussion ensues about the Miss India USA pageant and its judgments of Indian beauty and femininity. This discussion as well as the scene of improvised pageantry that it produces draws into affective proximity Indian coethnics who are otherwise stratified by differences of gender, class, and citizenship. Whereas in Lahiri's "Interpreter" diasporic beauty and femininity promise but fail to realize affiliations between Indian coethnics with differing class and national affiliations, in "Pageant" diasporic beauty and femininity deliver, however ephemerally, on this promise.

Dixit, an emerging South Asian American New Jersey–based writer,[4] wrote "Pageant" on the basis of her experiences reading about Miss India USA pageants in *India Abroad*, a widely read, US-based, and Indian-owned news publication about culture and politics in India and the diaspora, and after befriending South Asians whose friends and relatives had competed in the pageant. Realizing that pageants are popular public events in the diasporic community, Dixit wanted to explore "what it would mean to be considered 'perfect' or prize-worthy" within them (Dixit, interview). The popularity of Miss India USA is tied to a much longer history of ethnic beauty pageantry within Asian immigrant and diasporic communities. Since the turn of the twentieth century, beauty pageants have been central to defining citizenship and belonging within these communities (see, e.g., Wu). Though dubbed "beauty pageants," diasporic community pageants such as Miss India USA are organized around a range of performances of diasporic femininity that travel under the sign of "beauty." Miss India USA contestants participate in an evening gown, Indian dress, and interview and talent competition, with evening gown and Indian dress counting for 40 percent each, and talent/interview counting for 20 percent.[5] The judgment of beauty at Miss India USA, like at most beauty pageants, is part of a larger project of mediating differences among pageant contestants in order to produce a "structure of common difference" in the judging of diasporic femininity (Wilk 117). In the context of diasporic pageants, the structure of common difference in turn determines "the criteria for an idealized diasporic subjectivity, the criteria against which belonging in the diaspora is measured" (Siu 106). The Asian woman's body at these contests is thus charged with the task of representing what counts as official belonging within the diaspora.

Latent within Miss India Kentucky's hostility toward Miss India New Jersey in the opening scene of "Pageant" is the way that diasporic regionality operates as an unmarked structure of difference in the judging of Indian femininity at Miss India USA and, concomitantly, the way it betrays Miss Kentucky's feelings of regional inferiority within the pageant scene. The unmarked nature of regional difference in this opening scene is otherwise belied by the way that regionality is a rather explicit part of the format of national-level beauty pageants, in that contestants are identified first and foremost by their regional affiliations. "Pageant" follows this convention within pageant culture, in which pageant contestants—Miss Kentucky, Miss Florida, Miss New Jersey, and so on— become "nameless representatives of entire regions" (Dixit, interview). (Replicating this convention of depersonalization in the pageant's organizational structure, the waitstaff, too, remains nameless, known only by their assigned roles as hired labor for the pageant.) Yet at the same time, Miss Kentucky's act of sabotage against Miss New Jersey reveals that state-based regionality is far from a neutral mode of contestants' representation. As part of the larger organizational structure of Miss India USA, regionality structures Miss India Kentucky's feelings of hostility toward Miss India New Jersey and toward the larger diasporic community who has gathered to watch the pageant.

Defined alternately as a cultural backwater, a nonmetropolitan space, or a rural area that is often cast as tangential or marginal to dominant national culture, the geographic designation "region" critically challenges dominant cultural geographies such as the nation and/or the global. An emerging body of work in feminist, queer, and ethnic studies has begun to explore how regions, in their positioning as ex-centric to urban, metropolitan national spaces, can allow for—rather than prohibit—the emergence of alternative genders, sexualities, and racial formations and intimacies than those that remain within metropolitan-centered national and global frameworks.[6] This scholarship highlights how regions, which often stand as spaces of national neglect and political, cultural, and economic divestment, can operate subnationally, as spaces that remain below the threshold of dominant definitions of national citizenship and as spaces that enable new global connections based on nonmetropolitan affiliations.

Expanding on this growing body of work situated at the intersections of regionality, queer, and feminist studies, I argue that regionality can also challenge dominant *diasporic* narratives of gender and sexuality, insofar as diasporas—regardless of whether they are constructed as complicit with or oppositional to nationalist narratives of gender and sexuality—are often naturalized as urban and metropolitan. As a pageant contestant from Kentucky, Miss Kentucky hails from a region that has remained almost invisible in scholarship on South Asian American culture—the US South. This scholarship has tended to focus on East Coast and West Coast cities such as New York, San Francisco, and Toronto as the most representative spaces of diasporic culture, despite the large number of diasporic populations that reside outside these metropolitan centers, including especially regional southern cities.[7] Despite the fact that the US South is home to the third-largest population of Asian Americans, Jigna Desai and Khyati Joshi argue in their introduction to a recent collection of essays on Asian Americans in the US South that the South is a region often positioned as "discrepant and antithetical" to the figure of the Asian American. Asian Americans, they observe, are associated with "immigration and borders, globalization, and contemporaneity" and the US South is frequently cast as trapped in a time warp of lingering (black-white) racial divides, rather than as marked by a dynamic multiracial cultural geography (1). Within this framing, "Asian Americans in the US South become quirky exceptions to the larger story of Asian America that is configured through its bicoastal . . . paradigm" (2). The conclusion of Dixit's "Pageant" squares with this characterization of Asian American southerners, when as Miss Kentucky performs her talent of singing a *ghazal* (a classical South Asian musical form), the audience wonders if "there are a lot of Indians in Kentucky" (10). Though they find the ghazal performance "simple and sweet," they then "forgot about her" (10). The audience's understated and dismissive reception of Miss Kentucky's talent is hooked into their lack of knowledge about "Indians in Kentucky" and thus attests to the invisibility and provincialization of nonmetropolitan, diasporic southern contestants within Miss India USA.

The provincialization of Miss Kentucky vis-à-vis her southern regional affiliation accrues even greater significance when situated within the story's setting in Edison, New Jersey, a state with a long history of involvement in the organizational structure of Miss India USA. New Jersey is part of the northeastern "tri-state" region, which includes New York and Pennsylvania, where the Miss India USA pageant originated in 1980; New Jersey is also home to the India Festival Committee (IFC), the governing body that oversees selection of Miss India USA pageant candidates for state and national competitions.[8] Candidates from the tri-state area have the advantage of being selected at large by the IFC to compete at the national-level competition. By comparison, those who come from states outside the tri-state area must compete in IFC-sponsored regional state pageants in order to determine which young women will compete at the national level. At these state-level pageants, an IFC-elected representative is required to attend and, on some occasions, to judge the contest. The IFC's modes of governance thus contain a clear regional bias. This bias privileges pageant representation from tri-state South Asian populations,[9] while non-tri-state populations, such as those in the US South, are seen as carrying less referential density than they do on the East Coast. Indeed, at the end of "Pageant," the audience's guesses about who will win Miss India USA include "Miss Pennsylvania, Miss New Jersey, or Miss Washington, D.C." (10) but not, unsurprisingly, Miss Kentucky.[10] The city in which the pageant takes place, Edison, New Jersey, is widely regarded as a veritable South Asian diasporic "mecca" because of its long history as a place of South Asian migration and settlement and because of its reputation as one of the most desirable South Asian food and retail enclaves, or "little Indias," in the United States. Dixit, who grew up in Edison, describes it as having a "very strong, tight-knit Indian community" that is "different from other Indian communities" around the country in which South Asians may be too dispersed to form strong social bonds with one another (Dixit, interview). Edison's Royal Albert Palace, the banquet hall in which "Pageant" takes place, has also been the venue of choice for many Miss India USA and Miss India Worldwide competitions.

"Pageant" does not reveal the precise nature of Miss New Jersey's "sarcastic comment" (3) toward Miss Kentucky, which prompts the latter to sabotage the evening gown competition. Nor does it reveal why Miss New Jersey has been "mak[ing] fun of people" (3) during the pageant's dress rehearsal. Yet such forms of sabotage and disparagement attest to the cultural authority that Miss New Jersey, as a tri-state South Asian, commands at Miss India USA. Miss Kentucky's hostility toward Miss New Jersey during the opening scenes of the story, then, is tied to the way that Miss New Jersey's "size zero body," "fake eyelashes," and ridicule of other pageant contestants (3) is a result of her deployment of her cultural authority not only as a physically beautiful subject but as a regionally normative one. Miss New Jersey's familiarity with the Edison South Asian community allows her a measure of social capital at Miss India USA; she thereby reinforces Miss Kentucky's cultural inferiority within the pageant and in relation to Edison's South Asian diaspora more generally.[11] Much like Miranda's feelings of provincialized white femininity upon her phantasmatic encounter with Madhuri Dixit's Bollywood sexuality in Jhumpa Lahiri's "Sexy," Miss Kentucky's encounter with Miss New Jersey reinforces her own provincialized diasporic femininity. Miss Kentucky is aware, for example, that her "orange lehenga" (a long skirt that is usually embroidered and pleated) is tame in comparison to the "sparkly and revealing outfits" (5) of the other pageant contestants in the Indian dress competition. Though these observations do not directly cite Miss Kentucky's regional identity, they do point to her lack of familiarity with the normative conventions of highly sexualized diasporic femininity at Miss India USA. Bakirathi Mani notes in her ethnography of the 1999 Miss India USA pageant in San Jose, California, for example, that despite being billed as "family fun," Miss India USA includes explicitly "sexualized performances" of Bollywood femininity during the talent competition and during the wildly popular fashion shows, which include "dance and musical items performed by male and female fashion models" that resemble Bollywood performances ("Beauty" 740). Miss Kentucky compares such sexually explicit performances by other pageant contestants to her own "demure" femininity (5), which, in addition to her simple orange lehenga, is performed through her "simple and sweet," but ultimately forgettable, singing of the much less popular ghazal.

Though Miss Kentucky's provincialized femininity impels her encounter with the waiters through her feelings of exclusion from the pageant, her cultural authority as a middle-class subject is made legible within this scene of encounter. The most explicit reference to class differences between coethnics occurs when the older waiter accuses the younger one of wanting to "impress" Miss Kentucky by speaking knowledgeably about the pageant contestants. He warns him that she will never be "impressed by someone who comes to work on a bicycle" rather than a car (6). Here the older waiter alludes to the unequivocally middle-class ethos of Miss India USA. Contestants are folded into model minority aspirations of the diasporic community and are expected to become "units of skilled labor for the US State" (Mani, "Beauty" 725), despite the class heterogeneity that often exists among the pageant contestants themselves.[12] Miss India USA is funded and organized by prominent entrepreneurs in the Indian American community who groom contestants to enter professions in medicine, law, business, and engineering. The model minority ethos of the pageant, in turn, shapes relations between organizers and contestants, which take on the quality of a "fictive kinship" (Mani, "Beauty" 725). Pageant contestants refer to pageant organizers as "aunties" and "uncles," while the Indian business community refers to the contestants as "our children." Mediated through a discourse of real and fictive kin relations, the pageant's construction of diasporic community reproduces middle-class narratives of diaspora at every level, from funding to crowning.

Both Miss Kentucky's observations about the waiters and the wait-ers' observations about the pageant variously express an investment in this middle-class narrative, one that excludes working-class, noncitizen diasporic subjects like the waiters from its definitions of diasporic com-munity. Upon entering the pageant parking lot, Miss Kentucky distances herself from the waiters, observing that the younger waiter "appeared as though he had just gotten here from India" and that both men "are prob-ably not supposed to be sitting around out here" (4). Miss Kentucky here silently polices the waiters' occupation of this public space, which she understands as violating the terms of their employment. After noticing Miss Kentucky in the parking lot, the young waiter tells his compatriot that Miss Kentucky stands a good chance of winning because of her "fair skin" and that she should have received higher marks in the Indian dress part of the competition. Despite Miss Kentucky's hearing the waiters openly discuss the viability of her beauty with each other, she "pretend[s] not to hear them" and is surprised that the young waiter "didn't seem to care that they had not introduced themselves or that she was a contes-tant and he a waiter" (4). Miss Kentucky's observations about the waiters' presence in the parking lot, the waiters' discussion of the pageant contes-tants, and her avoidance of them betray Miss Kentucky's class-marked assumptions within this scene of encounter, namely, that working-class status warrants noninterference with, or at the very least deference to, middle-class subjects such as herself.

The older waiter carefully observes these class distinctions between contestants and workers as well, primarily by policing the younger waiter's judgments about Indian beauty and the pleasure he takes in the spectacle of the pageant. When, during an ongoing conversation between the two of them about the pageant contestants, the younger waiter expresses his opinion that Miss Florida is "too too dark" to win, the older waiter tells him not to "say things like that in front of her [Miss

Kentucky]" (5). The source of the older waiter's scolding lies not only in his perception that the younger waiter is speaking out of turn by judging contestants' beauty but also in the younger waiter's presumably mistaken assumption that a light-skinned beauty bias on the subcontinent is as fully entrenched in the diaspora. (We might recall that skin color was the major criterion by which Indian media judged the 2014 Miss America winner Nina Davuluri's "Indian" beauty as not Indian "enough.") Similarly, as the young waiter begins to dance to the music booming from within the pageant hall, the older waiter tells him that he has a lagging "work ethic," to which the young waiter obligingly responds, "I know. Only with working hard can I get a visa" (5). Here, the young waiter seems to parrot his older compatriot's didactic platitudes about the value of hard work (rather than, presumably, the lack of such values that he exhibits in "goofing off") as holding out the promise of permanent US residency, rather than temporary guest-worker status. The older waiter's management of the younger waiter's pleasure—his scolding of the younger waiter for his enthusiastic judgments of Indian beauty and for his dancing—reveals how the pageant's middle-class ethos of hard work regulates and disciplines not only young Indian women who "embody the values of hard work and upward mobility" into pursuing lucrative professions (Mani, "Beauty" 725). It also disciplines working-class South Asian subjects with quasi-legal status who exist on the periphery of the pageant as a diasporic cultural event. While the service labor of the waiters is vital to the successful production of the pageant, they are excluded from participating equally in the pageant's spectacle and production of pleasure.[13]

The starkest example of the tenacity of class divides between coethnics at Miss India USA occurs in the various references to Miss Kentucky as a beauty queen. As a title that proclaims the winner a diasporic cultural figurehead, the title "beauty queen" is exposed as frivolous within working-class South Asian communities. When, for example, at one point in the story the younger waiter expresses concern for his neighbor's wife—whom he suspects is the victim of domestic violence—the older waiter warns him against involving himself in issues regarding the wife's safety. He explains that if the younger waiter were to report his missing neighbor to the police, the police might falsely question the waiter instead of her husband for her disappearance, and then, he says, "No one will save you. Not you, not this beauty queen here, no one" (6–7). Despite the grandiosity of the beauty queen's title, she is here rendered ineffectual as a cultural figurehead when it comes to protecting the welfare of recently arrived, noncitizen immigrant subjects, who are the most vulnerable to criminalization and deportation. Furthermore, the older waiter's admonishments for the young waiter to concern himself only with "his own wife" in India rather than the neighbor's wife in the United States reproduces a focus on the diasporic family form over more expansive definitions of community: "In America, we worry about our own families only. There is one thing they say here. Mind your own business. Number one rule here, mind your own business" (6). The extended ethnic kin networks to which the younger waiter implicitly appeals—and with which he is undoubtedly more familiar as a cultural norm on the subcontinent—violate the prioritization of "our own families" in defining diasporic community in the United States; they are thus deemed unworthy of the young waiter's affective investments. Because they stand to exacerbate the precariousness of citizenship for working-class, quasi-legal subjects, such affective investments threaten these subjects' social mobility within the nation.

Despite these observable differences of class and citizenship, though, the encounter between Miss Kentucky and the waiters in the pageant parking lot also produces an alternative scene of pageantry than the one taking place at Miss India USA. The parking lot is an open public space that exists at a physical remove from the official judgments of beauty and femininity taking place within the closed, communal public space of the pageant. Neither fully inside nor fully outside the pageant, the parking lot is thus a liminal space in which Miss Kentucky and the two waiters are brought together as an ununified group of pageant outsiders. The judgments about diasporic beauty and the performance of diasporic femininity that take place in the parking lot produce an affective community of pageant outsiders, in which diasporic affiliations across differences of class, gender, generation, and citizenship can materialize.

Miss Kentucky's disavowal of the title of beauty queen catalyzes this alternative scene of diasporic pageantry. It first sets in motion a set of direct and even intimate exchanges about diasporic beauty and femininity between these coethnics, exchanges that were otherwise precluded by these subjects' policing of class and citizenship divides. When the older waiter tells the young waiter that even Miss Kentucky cannot save him from potential deportation, Miss Kentucky responds to him by saying, "I'm not a beauty queen. . . . No, I wouldn't call myself that at all" (7). Whereas prior interactions between Miss Kentucky and the waiters consist primarily of mutual indirection and avoidance, Miss Kentucky's disavowal of the title of "beauty queen"—a rejection that we are to assume has to do with her lack of social capital as a diasporic southerner—earns the waiters' captive attention: "The old man halted near her and the young guy turned and sat up straight. . . . The men continued to stare at her" (7). At this point in the story, the younger waiter faces Miss Kentucky directly and begins to convince her that she is, in fact, worthy of the very title that she has just disavowed: "Do you think those other girls can beat you? The other contestants are ugly next to you! Ugly. . . . I saw the Indian dress competition and really you were the best. Others were not Indian at all. But you, you were Indian. Absolutely. First class" (7). In issuing such judgments of Miss Kentucky's beauty, in which he implicitly conflates beauty and Indianness (to be "ugly" is to fall short of being a "first class" Indian), the waiter certainly makes an essentialist claim about authentic Indian beauty. But his comments are also intended to point to his cultural authority on the subject of Indian beauty, in that his status as a recently arrived immigrant marks him as more authentically Indian than the diasporic community of judges, contestants, and audience members who participate in the pageant's productions, displays, and judgments of Indian beauty. Thus, whereas his working-class status otherwise precludes him from fully participating in the pageant's official judgments of Indian beauty, his recently arrived immigrant status marks him as more intimately knowledgeable about what constitutes "first class" Indian beauty and femininity.

Moreover, the younger waiter's proclamations about Miss Kentucky's "first class" Indian beauty blatantly challenge Miss India USA's official criteria for judging diasporic femininity (evening gown, traditional dress, and talent/question-and-answer). He makes the point that Miss Kentucky's fitness for the Miss India USA title has less to do with these official criteria than with her willingness to cross precisely those class divides that the pageant is so invested in maintaining. He explains, "Some [contestants] showed their bodies more, and they were slimmer than you, but this is not the kind of girl who should win. . . . They are not nice girls. . . . They would never sit here like this. They would never talk to me" (7). For the younger waiter, Miss Kentucky's diasporic citizenship is contingent not on the sexualized performances of beauty and femininity exhibited during the talent and dress competitions but on her willingness to engage with working-class South Asians who are excluded from the pageant's official narratives of diasporic community.

Miss Kentucky's disavowal of her title as a "beauty queen" also allows for an unscripted performance of her talent—the singing of a ghazal—that produces an affective relay of loss and longing between coethnics.

After the conversation with the young waiter about the Indian dress competition, the older waiter asks Miss Kentucky to reveal what she plans to perform as her talent. Upon replying that she sings, the older man is suddenly and inexplicably reminded of his wife, who, the story implies, is either dead or has been left behind in India. Miss Kentucky and the younger waiter notice that the older waiter "seemed not to be looking at them but to be thinking of someplace else. Turning his back to the young guy and girl, he parted his lips as if about to say something" but instead "looked up at them. 'My wife sang,' he said." At the mention of his wife, Miss Kentucky "stared down at the old man. She hadn't noticed how little hair he had, or how his shoulders hunched over when he sat. It was the only thing left to do, so Miss Kentucky closed her eyes and sang a sad, slow, ghazal" (8). The ghazal here stands in for the plenitude of spoken language; it is sung in response to the older waiter's memory of and loss of his wife, as well as to Miss Kentucky's recognition of his aging body, referenced by his balding head and hunched shoulders. The older man's "fixed . . . gaze on Miss Kentucky" (8) as she sings the ghazal and Miss Kentucky's act of "star[ing] into the old man's face as if trying to read something there" (9) after she completes her singing draw the older waiter and Miss Kentucky into affective proximity with each other. Miss Kentucky's performance of the ghazal also neutralizes tension between the two waiters, whose relationship until this point is defined by differences in age and generation and who differ in their willingness to judge the pageant contestants' performances of diasporic femininity. Whereas before the older waiter admonished the younger waiter about his uncensored judgments of contestants' beauty, after hearing Miss Kentucky's ghazal, both waiters stand united in their shared judgment that her singing is so "superb" that the pageant "cannot eliminate" her (8). Their united judgment of Miss Kentucky's suitability for the title of Miss India USA in turn prompts Miss Kentucky to consider telling the waiters about "what she had done [in cutting Miss New Jersey's evening gown] and why she had done it exactly" (9). The ghazal thus also marks a shift in Miss Kentucky's own mode of relationality, from one of avoidance to one of intimacy.

In opening up what was previously a closed affective field between coethnics—one registered by dissociation, indirection, and physical distance—Miss Kentucky's singing of the ghazal produces an ephemeral "community of sound." Gayatri Gopinath uses this phrase to refer to the way that "auditory cultural forms and practices powerfully mobilize affective loyalties," connecting diasporic subjects across "time and space" (*Impossible* 43). As a musical genre constituted by a "volatile emotionality" (Qureshi 120) that is rooted in the expression of the pain of separation or loss, the ghazal is a cultural form that is particularly well suited to the creation of an affective community of sound. The ethnomusicologist Peter Manuel, for example, has shown that the mournful tonalities of the light classical ghazal appealed to both lower and elite classes in nineteenth-century India, despite its later circulation in the mid- to late twentieth century as "a reified, commodified music, a catchy tuneful song" that catered to middle-class Indian and diasporic audiences (354). Miss Kentucky's ghazal is "sad" and "slow," likening it more to these earlier classical forms and even to the ghazals sung in 1970s and 1980s Bollywood cinema, which were often used to bridge differences of generation as well as class. The ghazal is thus a musical form that, by its very definition, participates in the "transmission of affect," the process whereby "the enhancing or depressing energies" of affects or emotions in one person can "enter into another" (3). As a melancholic diasporic form, the ghazal affectively sutures coethnics to each other through its transmission of pain and loss between the older waiter's loss of his wife, the younger waiter's exclusion from participating in the middle-class pleasures of pageant spectatorship, and Miss Kentucky's provincialization within the pageant's metropolitan definitions of diasporic femininity.[14]

In connecting diasporic coethnics across time and space through shared feelings of loss, the ghazal is also an art form that challenges the dominance of Bollywood idioms in defining diasporic community at Miss India USA. Bollywood idioms are among the most popular and well-received displays of diasporic talent and are thereby "the primary modality of ideas of Indianness" at the pageant (Mani, "Beauty" 729). Mani describes the way that these talent performances consist of singing, dancing, and reenacting dramatic scenes from well-known Bollywood blockbusters. These explicitly sexualized performances are sanctioned and rationalized within the pageant in much the same way as they are within Bollywood films, not as vulgar sexualized displays of the Indian female body but as "a form of middle-class family entertainment" (740).[15] Despite claims to feminine modesty (such as the absence of a swimsuit competition from the pageant), these performances reveal the compatibility of Bollywood sexuality with middle-class definitions of diasporic community. The ghazal's melancholic form and its capacities to transmit affects of loss and mourning across differences of generation, citizenship, and class fall outside these culturally sanctioned performances of Bollywood femininity. As a cultural form that remains peripheral to dominant performances of diasporic feminine talent, the ghazal also destabilizes the pageant's reproduction of middle-class definitions of diasporic kinship and allows for alternative definitions of community. Miss Kentucky's unscripted performance of the ghazal produces a community of sound that resonates across a range of social divides such as homeland/diaspora, first generation/second generation, and working class/middle class.

Such assemblages of affect among coethnics are, of course, ephemeral. This alternative scene of pageantry takes place during the intermission, which constitutes a temporary break within the linear temporal progression of the pageant. As such, this scene operates beyond the purview of anything like recuperative affiliations. As Gilles Deleuze and Félix Guattari write of assemblages, "You may make a rupture, draw a line of flight, yet there is still a danger that you will reencounter organizations that restratify everything" (9). At the end of Miss Kentucky's ghazal, she and the waiters hear the music that signals the end of intermission and feel pressed to return to their assigned roles within the pageant: "[Miss Kentucky] smiled quickly at the two men, still sitting, and walked back inside through the door she had first come from. The two men got up too and the young guy picked up his pitcher and followed the old man inside through their own door near the garbage" (9). The two doors—one near the main entrance and one near the garbage—serve as proximal spatial reminders of the class and citizenship divides that separate working-class South Asians from the middle-class consumers of and participants in the pageant. At the same time, this contingent affective community of coethnics produces a lingering rupture within the multiply stratified space of the pageant. In the most basic way, it delays the resuming of the pageant:

> The lights above the audience were switched on and off and only the stage was illuminated. The audience looked up at the stage and awaited the first act. They thought it was strange that it was taking so long for the show to get started. What could be the delay? They imagined a girl retying her red silk sari. A girl pulling the skin beneath her eye in order to get dark eyeliner inside her bottom lid. A girl stretching her arms above her head in preparation for her Bharatanatyam [classical South Indian dance] performance. . . . No one imagined a girl cutting a dress. . . . A girl talking to waiters who filled glasses with water. (9)

The audience can imagine the cause of the delay only in terms of the pageant's scripted performances of diasporic femininity that occur backstage—the tying of a sari, the application of makeup, and the preparation for a classical dance routine. They cannot imagine, in other words, the cause of the delay in terms of unofficial judgments of beauty and unscripted performances of talent that occur offstage and outside the official space of the pageant.

This affective community also reverberates against the *failure* of the pageant to produce the idealized diasporic subjectivity that is its intended purpose. For "Pageant" does not conclude with a triumphant and exuberant crowning of a new Miss India USA as a representative figure of diaspora but tellingly stops short of this climax. It registers the audience's silently shared assessment about the inability of the pageant successfully to produce a structure of common difference in the judging of diasporic femininity: "The audience began to lose track of who was the best performer, the best looking. All the girls were talented and pretty. All had bright futures. There was no reason to believe that one stood out above the others" (10). The ending of "Pageant" thus reveals the collective difficulty in producing the pageant's requisite judgments of beauty. Such difficulty throws into crisis the very legitimacy of the pageant as a diasporic public event—to determine who is most deserving of the title Miss India USA and to produce a coherent definition of diasporic citizenship on the basis of that determination. In the face of this impossibility, "Pageant" instead makes possible an ununified and ephemeral diasporic community of affect, one that nonetheless emerges from within the very structure of Miss India USA as a diasporic public event.

"Modern Girl" Fashionability, the New Swadeshi, and the Indian American Girl Doll Neela Sen

Whereas in "Pageant" the community of beauty-pageant outsiders produces an affective economy of pageantry that disrupts the Miss India USA pageant's upwardly mobile definition of diasporic citizenship, here I examine how youth citizenship is produced through a diasporic engagement with the politics of fashion in colonial India. If beauty can be defined as a set of physical attributes, embodiments, and performances that circulate within the realm of aesthetic judgment and pleasure, fashion can be defined as the practice of dressing, styling, and adorning bodies through the use of clothing and other decorative accessories. By "fashion," then, I mean the creative input, economic processes, and production of aesthetic value that are required to translate the raw material of clothing into the symbolic meaning of style (fashionability) *and* the habits of dress that inform everyday practices of the self (sartoriality).

Here I turn to an examination of South Asian fashions in a little-known object of diasporic consumer culture—the politically conscious, anticolonial Indian, American Girl (AG) fashion doll Neela Sen. The historical-fictional young-adult novel that is sold with the doll, *Neela: Victory Song* (2002), written by the well-known South Asian American author Chitra Divakaruni, situates the Neela doll within a larger social script about the role of fashion in shaping diasporic girlhood. I examine Neela as a toy and literary object that positions diasporic girlhood at the intersections of Indian colonial girlhood, Indian consumer national-isms, and post-9/11 US multiculturalism. In doing so, I extend Robin Bernstein's claim that dolls are a "defining feature of girls' culture" that allow us to see how "girls and girlhood" are central to the historical pro-duction of US racial formations (19) into the contemporary transnational cultural arena. I pay special attention to the girl protagonist Neela's negotiations of colonial-era fashions in shaping her anticolonial feminist subjectivity; I also attend to the way that the politics of clothing in *Neela* overlap with and diverge from the overall mission of American Girl—the widely popular, Mattel-owned, multicultural girl-toy brand—of politi-cizing girlhood through consumer culture.

I approach *Neela* as a fictional text that circulates independently of the doll and as the doll's narrative "supplement." This double-sided approach parallels the way that AG novels are marketed and consumed. On the one hand, the novels are among a range of accessories that can be purchased with the dolls. They are thus part of the larger consumer apparatus by which toy dolls invite certain forms of imaginative play and that produce girls as particular kinds of consumer-citizens. On the other hand, the novels circulate independently of the dolls and thus demand consideration as commodities that are, to quote a well-known toy-ad dis-claimer, "sold separately." The books' relative affordability—the average cost of an AG doll is about $85, while the average cost of an AG novel is $7.95—not only allows them to circulate more pervasively within con-sumer markets but also makes them affordable for public educational use; indeed, many of the novels have been stocked in school libraries and have even been included as part of elementary school history curricula.[16] AG books' unique positioning as both supplemental to and independent of the doll figurines thus makes them worthy of examination as objects of material culture in their own right.

Set in 1939 in colonial-era Bengal, *Neela* is the story of twelve-year-old Neela Sen, a village girl of modest means who longs to join the Indian independence struggle. Neela's nationalist fervor is roused when a group of freedom-fighting "bandits" ride into her village, demanding donations to purchase guns and to make bombs and other weapons for the nationalist cause. Neela's father, though moved by the freedom fighters' nationalist rhetoric, firmly expresses his opposition to the use of violence and goes to Calcutta to join the Gandhian swadeshi movement, confiding only in Neela of his plans.[17] Awed by her father's love of country and eager to escape the mounting pressure from her mother and community to marry, Neela secretly hopes to join her father. Her chance to be a part of the freedom struggle comes when Samar, an injured boy freedom fighter, seeks refuge in Neela's family's barn and after Neela learns through a local minstrel that British soldiers may have captured her father. Determined to rescue her father, Neela disguises herself as a boy street urchin and secures passage on a train to Calcutta, undetected. Once in Calcutta, Neela meets Samar's cousin, Bimala, who hails from a wealthy, elite Bengali family and whose political sympathies lie with the British. After feeding and clothing Neela, Bimala agrees to help Neela find her father and reunites her with Samar. Neela and Samar then hatch a plan to hijack a British truck headed for the Andaman prison colony; their plan is successful, and they free the prisoners, among them Neela's father. British officials then storm a train that Neela has boarded with her father and Samar, at which point Neela outwits the British officials, enabling their successful and uneventful journey home.

The Neela fashion doll was part of a short-lived AG series called Girls of Many Lands. Launched in 2002 and discontinued in 2005 due to faltering sales, Girls of Many Lands "was intended to help girls ages 10–12 explore the world by expanding their knowledge and understanding of different cultures and the events that have helped shape world history" (Jevens, interview). Girls of Many Lands thus bears the imprint of a US brand of global multiculturalism in which American girls can learn about girlhood in non-US nations. This global brand of multiculturalism expands on the US-centered multiculturalism of the original AG line, which includes a few nonwhite American girls, including the ex-slave Addy, the indigenous Nez Perce girl Kaya, and the former inner-city Latina Marisol. (Some of these dolls have received a fair amount of attention in both the popular and scholarly press for their perpetuation of uncritical racial and even racist stereotypes.) Just as with the original AG line, specific authors were commissioned to write the Girls of Many Lands novels. They were chosen based on "their ability to capture the essence and voice of the people they were depicting in the stories, as well as a discernible sense of time and place," and whether the authors' own ethnic heritage matched that of their doll subjects (Jevens, interview).[18]

In contrast to the original AG line, which features eighteen-inch, six-to eight-year-old girls from different historical periods in the United States, the dolls in the Girls of Many Lands line were designed as nine-inch girls, were targeted at a slightly older tween market, and were sold with slightly longer fictional-historical novels. The dolls were priced at about fifty dollars each when they were released and are now highly collectible. In addition to India, the Girls of Many Lands collection included dolls from England, France, China, Alaska (the only US state featured in the line), Ethiopia, Turkey, and Ireland. The places of origin chosen for the line had to do with AG's ability to combine "both story potential and outfit potential for the accompanying doll" (Jevens, interview). Girls of Many Lands achieves its stated mission of cultivating global multicultural girl citizenship not only through its fictional-historical storylines but also in the way the dolls and novels teach girls about different traditions of national dress. Indeed, like other AG novels, Girls of Many Lands novels frequently describe in detail the outfits in which the doll figurines appear and even incorporate the outfit into the narrative so as to allow for a stronger synergy between doll and story.

In many ways, the Neela doll and the *Neela* novel are unexceptional within the multiculturalist imperatives that structure AG's choices in authorship, costume, and narrative. Divakaruni is, like Bharati Mukherjee and Jhumpa Lahiri, a literary celebrity of South Asian American adult fiction. Divakaruni's first collection of short stories, *Arranged Marriage* (1996), won the American Book Award, and her first novel, *Mistress of Spices* (1997), was both much maligned and much lauded for using Indian spices to "package[e] ethnicity within a palpably 'exotic-ethnic' framework" (Mannur 91). Divakaruni's choice to use spice names as chapter titles, her descriptive use of spices, and her deployment of arranged marriage as highly recognizable tropes of South Asianness have been the focus of these framings and easily fulfill the multicultural criteria of AG authorship. Neela's costume—she is wearing a silk, orange sari and accessorized with gold earrings, gold bangles, and a gold necklace—also fulfills what Jevens calls "outfit potential." Saris, as I discuss more in chapter 5, are widely recognized by South Asians, diasporic subjects, and non–South Asians as quintessential garments of Indian femininity and are thus highly visible and easily digestible markers of ethnic Indianness.[19]

Finally, Divakaruni's portrayal of Neela as an educated, fiercely self-reliant, yet family-oriented, girl is typical of a liberal feminist strain in much AG fiction. Even though AG does not announce its mission or its products as feminist, some cultural critics have described the AG brand as emphasizing a "revisionary history that offers girls new stature" as educated, socially conscious, and civic-minded subjects (Susina). The doll characters' appearance and storylines are often understood as offering girls (and their parents and guardians) a political and pedagogical alternative to a depoliticized vision of global girlhood, one most infamously represented by Mattel's best-known brand, the Barbie doll.[20] For this reason, some critics have dubbed AG dolls the "anti-Barbies" (Inness) or "Barbies with a sense of history" (Susina). The novels, in particular, encourage girls to see their dolls not just as material objects of imaginative play but also as fictional-historical subjects capable of social and political change.

Even with civic-mindedness and social consciousness written into narratives of girlhood, AG dolls still circulate as fashion dolls. As the childhood studies scholar Jan Susina notes, "simply because their costumes are historically accurate does not exempt them. . . . The natural fibers and attention to detail make the clothing for the *AG* Collection much more expensive on a per item basis than Barbie's bright colors and high heels" (134). I will return a bit later to a discussion of how Neela fits into this frequently made comparison between AG dolls and Barbie dolls when I discuss Neela in relation to the popularity of Mattel's Indian Barbie. For now, though, it is simply worth noting Susina's point that, even if AG dolls are less overtly sexist or antifeminist than Barbie dolls, their "historically accurate" and high-quality clothing makes them consumable as objects of fashion and collectible as historical fashion objects. (Indeed, as if in recognition of AG as a fashion-conscious toy brand, in 2014 the producers of the hit reality-television series *Project Runway* asked the show's fashion designer contestants to "update" for contemporary American girls the outfits of their assigned AG dolls in an episode called "American Girl Doll.")

In what follows, I examine *Neela* within AG's marketing of its dolls as multicultural, politically conscious, fashion dolls. I look specifically at how late colonial-era ideals of Indian womanhood and national identity are routed through the novel's sartorial imagination. If *Neela* combines a sense of fashion ("outfit potential") with a narrative of girl feminism ("story potential"), then it does so in ways that put considerable pressure on AG's multiculturalist pedagogy of celebrating and appreciating national-cultural difference. I argue that fashion is central to locating the novel's interlocking political projects of diasporic consumer feminism, nationalism, and British and US anti-imperialisms.

The orange sari that is the Neela signature fashion statement meshes well with the tween market toward which Girls of Many Lands was targeted, since, in addition to being a quintessential garment of Indian femininity, the sari typically marks an Indian girl's rite of passage into womanhood. In *Neela: Victory Song*, Neela receives the orange sari as a gift from her mother for her sister's wedding and revels in the way that it "transform[s] her into a princess," exclaiming, "It's gorgeous! It makes me look at least fifteen!" (24). The novel also draws attention to Neela's instruction in sari wearing, in which young readers learn what a sari looks like and how to wear it. While Neela knows that a sari is "six yards of material," she requires the help of her Cousin Rani to tuck "the pleats of the orange silk into the top of Neela's petticoat" and then arrange "the end of the sari so that it fell in neat pleats from Neela's shoulder down her back, using safety pins to secure it to Neela's silk taffeta blouse" (24). At the same time that Neela is fascinated by the skill required to tie the sari and charmed by her own womanly appearance in it, sari wearing emerges as a contradictory practice of young Indian womanhood, for Neela also finds wearing it to be extremely cumbersome. As she tries to follow Rani's instructions to "take small, gliding steps," "her feet kept getting caught in the pleats of the sari," and she wonders, "how do women manage to wear these things and still do all their housework?" (25). The gendered dilemma of walking in a sari, one that will reemerge in an altogether different guise in my examination of live performance in chapter 5, is here presented as both an embodiment of and an obstacle to the realization of a preindependence ideal of Indian womanhood, the ideal of the *bhadramahila*. A Bengali colonial prototype of the respectable Indian woman, the bhadramahila "inhabited a procreative, middle-class femininity within the terms of heterosexual marriage" (Ramamurthy 158). Neela's reference to performing housework, which follows her cousin's excitement that Neela will soon be married and have children of her own, clearly invokes this ideal. Yet Neela also remains skeptical about the practicality of the sari in achieving this ideal. In this and other moments of sari wearing, Neela lifts the sari up to her knees to allow for quicker movement when no one else is noticing (25, 78). Such small acts of bodily disobedience and sartorial impropriety accommodate AG's brand of girl empowerment in that they allow Neela to question the bhadramahila ideal without rejecting it altogether.

Beyond the novel's scripting of Indian colonial girlhood through Neela's relationship to her sari, it also presents clothing as central to her embrace of Gandhian swadeshi (a term that means "of one's own country"). An anticolonial nationalist idiom defined by economic self-sufficiency, a critique of consuming British-made goods, and self-discipline, the discourse of swadeshi merged economic independence with political freedoms by denouncing Indian dependence on British-made goods—notably, "mill-woven British cloth"—and consumerism as necessary to achieving self-rule (Mazzarella 6). Neela is introduced to the political ideals of swadeshi when a group of nationalist freedom fighters, known by the villagers as "bandits," ride into her family's village on the eve of her sister's wedding day, explaining to the villagers that the British "treat Indians no better than dogs" and that they must donate their riches in order to reclaim a "life of dignity" (30, 31). After observing that the village landowner refuses to donate his treasures to the nationalists while the poor villagers donate money and prized belongings, Neela is moved to contribute her treasured gold necklace—which her parents have set aside as part of her wedding dowry—to the swadeshis. Both Neela's selfless act and her mother's subsequent reprimand that Neela has chosen "motherland" over "family" insert Neela into yet a different nationalist ideal of Indian womanhood, that of the New Woman. The New Woman "expressed her agency" by "protesting foreign consumption, especially of cloth and foreign fashion" (Ramamurthy 159). Neela remains undeterred by her mother's chiding for choosing love of country over love of family and even judges her own family for their lack of politicization around matters of dress. She discovers, for example, that among the dowry gifts that are to be presented to her sister Usha's husband, which include "traditional Indian clothes in both silk and cotton—*dhotis*, the long pieces of cloth tied around the waist and reaching to the feet, and *kurtas*, the tunics that went over them"—are black leather shoes with the words "Made in Great Britain" embossed on the soles (43–44). In feeling that her family has "betrayed the freedom fighters" (44) by purchasing British-made shoes, Neela's aspirations to uphold the nationalist ideal of the bhadramahila gives way to the anticolonial nationalist ideal of the New Woman.

New Woman ideals of sartorial self-renunciation and the eschewal of British-made fashions come into conflict with yet a third category of colonial-era Indian womanhood in *Neela*, the Modern Girl, who "embraced and reworked fashions from elsewhere" (particularly the West) (Ramamurthy 159). In the novel, Modern Girls bear the mark of an overly Westernized modernity and punitively apolitical girl subjectivity. When Bimala takes Neela to her Drama Club dress rehearsal, Neela notices that the members of the Drama Club were, like Bimala, the daughters of rich, old Calcutta families who did not want their children getting involved in anything as messy as politics. For the most part, the children didn't want it either, as Neela could clearly see by all the imported clothing, shoes, and makeup they wore. Their manners were affected and Western—and, Neela thought, quite comical. Why, she thought in surprise as she listened to them heatedly discussing a new hairstyle they'd seen in a British magazine, "even I know more about the world than they do!" (138)

Neela's judgment of the rich Bengali girls' clothing, shoes, and makeup, as well as their conversations about British hairstyles, marks them as politically unconscious or at least as less politically conscious than the girl swadeshi, Neela. Neela's judgments about Bimala's friends' adoption of Western styles of dress and their consumption of British-made goods to enhance it echo Gandhi's judgments about Modern Girls as unfit for political participation in the nationalist movement on the basis that they were "self-fashioned through artifice" (Ramamurthy 159–60). Just as Neela's aversion to British-made clothing politicizes her, the elite girls' desire for Modern Girl fashions signals their lack of interest in the "messiness of politics."

Yet rather than dismiss the figure of the Modern Girl as inherently antithetical to the nationalist cause, Divakaruni's novel rehabilitates it by linking it to Gandhian ideals of swadeshi. This happens through one of the novel's storylines around political passing. When Bimala rescues Neela, she encourages her to abandon her boy-street-urchin disguise and dresses her in a dress of "pale pink, with lace at the neck and cuffs and pearly buttons down the front" (116). Though Neela obliges, she also feels "guilt" "because the dress was obviously foreign-made" (116). To assuage her guilt, Bimala urges Neela to think of the dress as a "disguise" that allows the aspiring freedom fighter to "fit the role" of an elite Bengali girl, which will in turn allow her to spy on the elite classes' knowledge of the British counterinsurgency. Neela's British frock is here likened to her "disguise" as a boy street urchin and appeals to Neela's revolutionary aspirations. Similarly, in a rather bizarre turn of events toward the end of the novel, Neela uses a box of makeup that Bimala has given her as a gift. Like the high fashion of elite Bengali girls, the makeup is imported and therefore marked as "foreign." She applies the makeup on her father's skin to manufacture the illusion of smallpox so that British officers will be deterred from discovering his identity as a freedom fighter.

In response to Neela's clever use of the makeup, which allows Neela's father to remain undetected as a fugitive prisoner, Neela's boy sidekick, Samar, excitedly exclaims, "Where did you learn to apply makeup like that? Maybe you could join our freedom fighters group!" (179). Rather than marking Neela as a fashionable, foreign, and Westernized modern subject, Neela's imaginative use of makeup marks her fitness for anti-colonial nationalism. It allows the politically insurgent male body to avoid surveillance through its appearance as abject, unapproachable, and terrifying.

The passing narrative, as we saw in chapter 1, is a common one in both ethnic-minority and young-adult fictional narratives because it provides culturally disempowered subjects access to forms of social power that are otherwise historically unavailable to them. Yet what is striking in *Neela* is the way that Divakaruni inverts the normative function of this narrative convention by showing how access to social power can be used to claim a less socially empowered but more politically desirable identity. In using imported makeup, Neela exploits her access to fashionable Modern Girls in order to claim a revolutionary and strikingly less fashionable ideal of Indian womanhood. Whereas Gandhi himself cast Modern Girls as incapable of political participation in the nationalist cause, claiming that their "sartorial zest" revealed an artificiality that made them incapable of nonviolent and courageous forms of protest (Ramamurthy 159), Divakaruni allows Modern Girl fashions to accommodate New Woman political ideals. In showing how Modern Girl commodities such as imported makeup can be used to facilitate brave acts of political subversion, Divakaruni reconciles the figures of the Modern Girl and New Woman instead of presenting them as two disparate ideals of colonial Indian womanhood.

Operating beyond the multiculturalist appeal of Neela's signature orange sari, *Neela's* larger sartorial imagination can be understood as constituting Divakaruni's feminist diasporic rearticulation of what William Mazzarella, in his ethnography of Indian advertising campaigns in the 1990s, calls "the new swadeshi" (5). Unlike the Gandhian discourse of swadeshi, which encouraged the sublimation of consumerism as part of the Indian national subject's self-discipline, the new swadeshi of the 1990s explicitly meshed Indian national identity with consumerist desire in Indian advertising campaigns.[21] To be sure, the Neela doll and novel do not rely on the consumer aesthetics of the Indian commodities that Mazzarella describes. Yet insofar as Divakaruni's fictional-historical narrative promotes the nationalist ideal of swadeshi as part of its girl feminist consciousness, it can be read as a diasporic rebranding of the Indian new swadeshi. The novel's narrative appendix, titled "A Girl's Life Then and Now," in which Divakaruni educates girls about homespun cotton, ethnic dyes, and the Indian boycott of British-made clothing during the late colonial period, further advances this pedagogical narrative of diasporic consumer nationalism. The novel's promotion of Indian-made cloth and its rejection and repurposing of Modern Girl fashions circulate within the consumer feminism of the AG brand even as they are rooted in the anticonsumerist ethos of swadeshi.

If, as I described earlier, AG dolls are marketed and consumed as "anti-Barbies" or "Barbies with a sense of history," then how does Neela's brand of anticolonial girl feminism challenge Barbie's depoliticized model of consumer girlhood? To answer this question, we should consider Neela's emergence on the diasporic girl-toy market in 2002 in relation to the widely popular Indian Barbie doll's entry into Indian markets in the late 1990s. Indian Barbie, as the feminist scholar Inderpal Grewal observes, became a successful commodity in India only after the transnationalization of the Indian fashion and beauty industries, when Barbie could help promote Indian girls' careers in fashion modeling, fashion design, and beauty contests (89). Barbie became such a powerful signifier of Indian and diasporic consumer girlhood in the late 1990s in part because the dolls could be marketed as "Indian" and "American" at the same time. As a white-skinned doll dressed in Indian clothes such as saris and other ethnic costumes denoting tribal and regional affiliations, Barbie was marked as ethnically Indian but also American enough to be attractive to middle-class Indian consumers who increasingly saw themselves as connected to the lives of middle-class Indians in the United States.

Though certainly part of a similar diasporic girl-toy market as Barbie, *Neela*'s fictional engagement with colonial-era fashion stands in sharp contrast to Barbie's promotion of fashion-oriented professions as normative aspirations for Indian girl consumers. Contra the fashion-conscious Indian Barbie, which was used to promote fashion design and modeling competitions in urban schools and Euro-American ideals of beauty and femininity among Indian female consumers and professionals, *Neela* deliberately politicizes fashion through the figures of the bhadramahila, New Woman, and Modern Girl. AG's Neela thus participates in what Sarah Banet-Weiser and Roopali Mukherjee have called "commodity activism," or "the participation in social activism by buying something" that they see as an inevitable part of neoliberal contemporary cultures (1). The discourse of new swadeshi in *Neela* operates as a form of transnational consumer activism in that it allows South Asian American girls to understand their racialized American identities and feminist subjectivities as irrevocably bound to the historical formation of the Indian nation and, more importantly, to politicized discourses of Indian femininity. By deploying the consumer nationalism of the new swadeshi, *Neela* demonstrates the powerful potential of fashion to shape diasporic political consciousness. Neela's boycotting of British-made fashions and her acts of sartorial self-renunciation can be read as a diasporic critique of a transnational Indian "vanity industry" that Indian Barbie helped to inaugurate seventy or more years later (Grewal 108). Situated over against the successful marketing and sales of Indian Barbie, *Neela*'s anticolonial politics of fashion precedes—and even prefigures—the formation of this very industry. Moreover, whereas Mattel steered clear of "a dark-skinned or brown 'Indian' Barbie" (Grewal 96) in order to ensure that Indian Barbie was attractive to Indian consumers who wanted to identify with dominant American standards of beauty and femininity, Neela's dark skin rejects the reproduction of whiteness and white ideals of femininity in the making of diasporic girl consumer-citizens. As a fashion doll whose sari, brown skin, and rejection of Modern Girl fashions mark her anticolonial subjectivity, Neela promotes a diasporic branding of the new swadeshi as its form of commodity activism within diasporic consumer cultures.

Unlike Indian Barbie, there is nothing definitively "American" about Neela as an American Girl. Yet the novel's politics of fashion and Neela's dark skin *do* produce a narrative about the US nation, one that is difficult to reconcile with the corporate multiculturalism of the AG brand. The girlhood studies scholar Robin Bernstein's claim that dolls, like children, are "effigies that substitute uncannily for other, presumably adult, bodies and thus produce a surplus of meaning" (23) is instructive in locating the absent presence of the US nation in *Neela*. If we consider Neela as an "uncanny substitute" for Divakaruni's adult body and for politicized discourses of diasporic womanhood more broadly, then Neela's anticolonial fashion choices—her unwillingness to embrace fashions made in the imperial metropole and her politically subversive use of Modern Girl fashionability—produce a "surplus of meaning" that links racial hegemonies in postcolonial India to those of the post-9/11 US nation. Divakaruni claims that in writing children's literature, she wanted to challenge the Anglophilia of much British children's literature written in the postcolonial period, such as Enid Blyton's adventure stories about English children. Blyton's stories, which made Divakaruni wish that

she had "light skin and golden hair and a name like Felicity and Gwen-
doline" ("Chitra" 217), became the impetus for her own foray into writing children's novels. Though she did not let her children "grow up with
that sense of [racial] inferiority," it was not until the events of September 11, 2001—an event that made her "rethink the whole enterprise of
writing"—that Divakaruni made the decision to begin writing literature
for children (217). She recounts a day in the weeks following 9/11 when
she and her young son were verbally harassed by a truck driver while
leaving a grocery store in her hometown of Oakland, California: "The
driver leaned out and shouted expletives at us. He ended by shouting at
us to 'get out of America, and go back home'" (218). After that incident,
she became aware that "the climate in America seemed different, that
on the streets . . . strangers eyed [her] askance" (218). That racist verbal
attack and the violence against South Asians that followed in the weeks
and months following 9/11 prompted Divakaruni to write for children of
both South Asian and non–South Asian descent in order to contest the
US state's decision to "close down the borders" in an effort to "redefine
what it means to be a good American" (217). Divakaruni's account of her
decision to write children's literature thus connects two historically and
geographically distinct narratives of South Asian belonging—postcolonial India and the post-9/11 United States.

Neela's dark skin, her orange sari, and her anticolonial sartorial politics challenge the Anglophilia that Divakaruni recalls reading in much
postcolonial children's literature. Divakaruni's choice to educate girls
about colonial-era Indian fashion can also be understood as a diasporic
reclaiming of South Asian fashions during a time in which clothing and
dress has become an increasingly politicized marker of US racial minority identity and has operated both to reinforce nonwhite populations as
ineluctably foreign, dangerous, or simply unassimilated, and to claim a
racialized identity as a political response to sartorial surveillance. Such
a reclaiming of fashion as racialized identity has occurred, for example,
as Muslim American girls and women who did not previously practice
veiling regularly began to wear the hijab as a way of asserting a legibly
Muslim identity after 9/11. Divakaruni's politicized narrative of fashion
gestures to new forms of girl consumer citizenship that parallel the way
that immigrants, African Americans, and other racialized constituen-
cies have historically used the US market "to mitigate and challenge
racist practices and cultural exclusions" (Banet-Weiser and Mukherjee
7). I return more explicitly and at greater length to these intersections
between South Asian fashions, anti–South Asian racisms, and diasporic

racial formation in chapters 4 and 5. Here, however, I turn to an examination of diasporic girl subjectivity within the global fashion industry, in order to attend to the ways that diasporic girlhood takes shape not only through practices of consumption but also through the representation of girls as workers in the new global economy.

Economic Citizenship, Racial Consciousness, and the Global Fashion Industry in Kavita Daswani's *Indie Girl*

Whereas *Neela* in one sense prefigures and critiques the transnationalization of the Indian fashion industry in its diasporic rearticulation of the new swadeshi, in the fashion journalist-turned-novelist Kavita Daswani's young-adult "chick lit" novel *Indie Girl* (2007), it is this very industry that contributes to the development of a diasporic racial consciousness as part of its narrative of girlhood. In *Indie Girl*, the sixteen-year-old Indian American girl protagonist, Indie Konkipuddi, aspires to become a fashion reporter for the fictionalized US fashion magazine *Celebrity Style* (likely modeled after the real-life fashion magazine *InStyle*). I examine Indie's struggles to become a fashion reporter as a set of struggles around her economic citizenship. Though Indie understands herself as possessing the skills and style sense to work in the US fashion industry, her future as a fashion professional is circumscribed by her assigned role as exploited racialized labor within this industry. At the same time, through an extended ethnic kin network, Indie develops a racial consciousness about the global fashion industry that produces her emergent identifications with Indian female garment workers and prominent Indian fashion designers on the subcontinent.

Written for a popular, female, teen literary market and clearly informed by Daswani's own career as a fashion journalist, *Indie Girl* is part of an emerging subgenre of South Asian American young-adult literature called "chick lit." In the United States, chick lit is a genre of popular literature written by and about middle-class women, in which typically white heroines achieve both personal and professional fulfillment through the pursuit of romance, fashion commodities, and marriage. Though liberal feminist critiques of white adult chick lit tend to emphasize these novels as "postfeminist" because of their emphasis on consumer culture and compulsory heterosexuality, the feminist scholars Pamela Butler and Jigna Desai have recently provided a much-needed corrective to such postfeminist readings of chick lit as "tawdry" and "apolitical" (4). Focusing their analysis on ethnic chick lit and South

Asian American chick lit in particular, Butler and Desai argue for reading chick lit by women of color through a transnational feminist framework. Such a framework, they argue, pushes against postfeminist dismissals of the genre, highlighting the struggles of women of color for ethnic and national belonging through their participation in global consumer culture (16).

My examination of *Indie Girl* expands on this emerging feminist scholarship on South Asian American chick lit by shifting attention away from the intersections of South Asian womanhood and consumption and toward the intersections of South Asian girlhood and labor. Indie's aspirations to join the global fashion industry as a fashion writer expose a set of structural constraints on her economic citizenship, or her right to work in the global capitalist economy.[22] Several scholars have argued that, whether through a metonymic identification with money or through conspicuous consumption, Asian Americans' involvement in circuits of economic exchange has historically defined the way that they seek out national belonging, transnational mobility, and even racial healing.[23] *Fashioning Diaspora* is certainly sympathetic to these claims about representations of Asianness, insofar as diasporic beauty and fashion are always imbricated in the transnational circuits of economic exchange that define diasporic consumer cultures. Yet claims about Asian American economic citizenship all too often leave unexamined the particular *types* of labor and exchange that secure economic citizenship for Asian Americans in the first place. Such an examination can help to unsettle either the assumption or the conclusion that Asian Americans have unfettered access to the capitalist market. *Indie Girl* complicates the construction of Asian American subjects—and South Asian American subjects in particular—as quintessential economic citizens by demonstrating how Indie's lack of social capital and aesthetic capital (having the right "look" for the job of fashion reporter) precludes her unimpeded entry into the industry of fashion. The global fashion industry in *Indie Girl* belies a neoliberal market logic in which the idea of racism is contradictory to the idea of a "free" market.

As an aspiring fashion reporter, Indie is part of a group of fashion industrialists that includes not only fashion models and fashion designers but also fashion media industrialists. If, as I suggested earlier, one way to define fashion is as the creative input and economic processes that are required to translate the raw material of clothing into the symbolic meaning of style, then fashion reporting can be defined as the professionalized labor of thinking and writing about the symbolic meanings of clothing as style. As someone charged with the task of disseminating news about the latest style trends, designers, and runway models, fashion reporters play integral roles in the fashion media complex. The fashion media complex includes blogs, magazines, newspapers, books, and television shows devoted to reporting on the aesthetic dimensions of fashion as well as the fashion celebrities, icons, models, designers, and fashion houses that they feature wearing, purchasing, and producing fashion. The fashion media complex is thus integral to what Roland Barthes, in one of the earliest book-length scholarly works on fashion, calls "the fashion system." In his book by the same name, Barthes studies not the "real garment" of fashion but the representation of women's clothing in fashion magazines (9). These visual and written representations of fashion are for Barthes just as much a part of the fashion system as are the garments that they represent. It is after all the fashion media—and not designers or other industry experts—that most powerfully shape consumers' desires for fashion and their understandings of what is fashionable and what is not.

At the same time, fashion reporting is, like fashion design, a form of creative labor, in that an appreciation of the aesthetic dimensions of fashion are often just as much a prerequisite for writing about fashion as is formal or informal training in fashion design as a field of study. In this latter sense, fashion reporting bears some similarity to the art and labor of fashion blogging. In a study of Asian American fashion bloggers, Minh-Ha Pham describes the way that "fashion and style bloggers, no matter their sartorial sensibilities, share in the activity and enjoyment of producing, consuming, and exchanging the material and immaterial goods of fashion and beauty" ("Blog" 9). Though fashion bloggers are most often known as "citizen-journalists" of fashion, a term that distinguishes them from the (paid) professionalized labor of fashion reporting (13), some fashion bloggers do go on to become credentialed fashion reporters for high-profile fashion magazines or for other major magazines and newspapers, because of their ability to forecast fashion trends and their roles as arbiters of taste in the fashion media complex. Fashion journalism, then, requires not only the professionalized skill of writing about fashion but also a keen aesthetic sensibility that allows fashion writers to be style trendsetters in their own right.

The editorial internship at *Celebrity Style* to which Indie applies requires both forms of formal and informal fashion knowledge. The job calls for someone who is "interested in fashion and journalism," so that she can learn to write compellingly and knowledgably about fashion. It also requires someone with enough style expertise to "manage the fashion closet" for celebrities who are featured in the magazine and to "accompany senior fashion staff to interviews and photo shoots" of celebrities wearing the latest fashions. Finally, the intern must also attend "product launches" so that she can learn about fashion designers' latest creations (16). Informally, Indie studies fashion by spending her time outside school perusing the latest fashion magazines, trolling shopping malls, or surfing online fashion websites. Indie also sees herself as possessing a highly attuned sense of ethnic style, which she gauges by her ability to combine Indian and Western fashions and by her use of Indian clothing as style accessories. While dressing for her school's Career Day, for example, Indie combines "bootleg corduroys" with "Nepalese beads around [her] neck, and pointy-toed Payless shoes on [her] feet." She then takes a "slim chartreuse-colored dupatta and [weaves] it through [her] belt loops" and then adds "four mirrored bangles, their slim wooden bases knocking against each other," to the Timex watch she wears on her left wrist (13). Indie's aesthetic sensibility distinguishes her from the more mainstream stylishness of her predominantly white, wealthy, Los Angeles schoolmates and friends and allows her to earn a degree of cultural distinction among them: "In the right things, like I was wearing today, I could shine. I could stand out and be distinctive. Fashion, in that sense, was really the only thing that helped me make any kind of mark" (14). Yet such performances of ethnic style always involve the constant negotiation of not appearing too ethnic (which risks mere sartoriality) and looking ethnic enough (which signals stylish innovation). Indie is all too aware, for example, that her peers' perception of her "innate fashion sense" (13) could easily slip into their assessment of her "ultra Indianness" (14). She must therefore take care to "wear the right things" (14)—to wear Indian fashions in a way that ensures their legibility as style rather than sartoriality. The line between the two, as will become clearer in chapter 4, often marks the boundary between maintaining the symbolic ethnicity of Indianness and bearing the social costs of a racialized South Asian identity.

Beyond the development of Indie's highly cultivated, individual sense of ethnic style, fashion is for her "a serious academic exercise." Her approach to fashion as an academic field of inquiry allows her to differentiate herself from "girls [her] age [who] loved to troll through the mall, checking out the cool clothes in store windows" (9). Indie describes her discovery at age eleven, for example, of the American fashion photographer Melvin Sokolsky's black-and-white photography collection *Seeing*

Fashion (2000), which featured female fashion models floating in bubbles and which Sokolsky shot from 1959 to 1971 while working for *Harper's Bazaar* and *Vogue*. Indie notes, "I studied all of them, memorizing not just the setting but the clothes, staring at [the models'] hair and makeup, taking note of the designers whose clothes the models were wearing" (9). She also studies the *St. James Fashion Encyclopedia: A Survey of Style from 1945 to the Present* and writes "pretend reports from the catwalks" and "perceptive analyses of recent runway events that [she] had seen on the Internet" (2) to acquire the skills necessary to become a knowledgeable fashion writer.

In approaching fashion as a profession that requires serious study, skill, and hard work, Indie frames fashion reporting as more like, rather than unlike, the professional managerial labor of model minority South Asians. Indie's framing of fashion as a skilled profession in fact helps to challenge her family's perception that her "fascination with clothes and shoes and supermodels" (5) is at best a frivolous hobby, and to force them to see fashion as requiring the skill and prestige of careers in "medicine or engineering or government" (4) into which her father encourages her to enter. Relatedly, Indie herself invokes the model minority ethos of hard work to supplement her fashion skills and expertise. In addition to "wow[ing]" the editors at *Celebrity Style* "with [her] enormous knowledge of and passion for the subject [of fashion]," Indie also hopes to impress them with her "reliability, efficiency, and punctuality" (17). Like the pageant waitstaff who are disciplined by the Miss India USA's entrepreneurial ethos of hard work as the path to middle-class national belonging in Pallavi Dixit's "Pageant," Indie here mobilizes this ethos as the way to guarantee her an economically secure career in fashion.

Indie's innovative fashion sense, her pursuit of fashion as an academic subject, and her hard work ethic should, by all accounts, qualify her for the internship at *Celebrity Style*. But these attributes cannot compensate for her lack of social capital, the social and institutionalized networks that operate as valuable resources necessary to help her secure a career in the fashion industry.[24] Indie's lack of social capital forces her to see herself as a racial minority in the fashion industry (instead of merely as a stylishly ethnic subject among her peers) and to grapple with the structural limits that this minoritized status imposes on her economic citizenship. Though Indie is economically privileged as the daughter of a neurosurgeon dad and a stay-at-home mom, her parents have no ties to the fashion industry—"their combined fashion knowledge amounted to which fabrics would shrink in the clothes dryer" (29). She also lives in the suburbs of

Agoura, California, forty miles outside Los Angeles, where "fashion really happened" (29). Indie's father reinforces Indie's lack of social capital by discouraging her from pursuing a career in fashion because South Asians have had relatively little success in creative industries:

> "What kind of high-profile success have we, as a community, had in this country in the arts or media? Ismail Merchant made beautiful movies, but it's not like he was ever as well known as Steven Spielberg. And that girl, that wonderful actress from *Bend It Like Beckham*, that Parminder Nagra—how many Americans even know her name? But her English sidekick on the movie goes on to Oscar nominations and all that. . . . Look at Aishwarya Rai, the most famous person in all of India, the most beautiful," my father continued. "She appears on 60 Minutes, even hires a Hollywood agent. There is talk of her being a Bond girl. Ha! It didn't happen. It could never happen!" (93–94)

Indie's father attributes the invisibility of diasporic South Asians in the arts to a pervasive racial glass ceiling, rather than to a lack of social capital per se. But his citations of the few South Asians who have managed to gain mainstream visibility in US and British fashion, media, and film nonetheless reinforce Indie's understanding of her lack of social capital as an Indian American daughter of professionally skilled but creatively unskilled and fashion-unconscious immigrant parents.

Indie's lack of social connections in fashion is seemingly at odds with the kin networks that have allowed other Asian Americans to achieve a measure of success and visibility in the US fashion industry. It is therefore worth pausing briefly to consider the history of these connections in order to better understand why Indie struggles to gain even a small foothold in the fashion media complex. Thuy Linh Nguyen Tu describes in her study of Asian American fashion designers how intimacies between a younger generation of designers and an older generation of parents, aunts, and uncles who worked as sewers, sample makers, factory owners, and garment workers for clothing retailers helped to launch designers' careers. By drawing on the older generation's knowledge of traditional Asian designs, their sewing skills, and their manufacturing connections, younger designers had access to the material and creative resources that allowed them to successfully execute and market their designs, despite their lack of formal training in fashion design.

Though there are certainly differences between fashion reporting and fashion design, Tu's tracing of the "dense connections" (6) between Asian immigrant sewers and Asian American designers is instructive for understanding Indie's lack of social capital as an aspiring fashion industrialist. Whereas Chinese, Korean, and increasingly Vietnamese Americans could cultivate social capital within the fashion industry because of their direct ties to an older generation of Asian immigrant workers in the apparel industry, South Asians have been inserted into professional managerial labor (doctors, engineers, businesspersons, professors), low-skilled service-sector labor (motel owners, convenience-store clerks, taxi drivers), and even high-skilled technological labor (the IT industry) but not garment work.[25] Though there are now highly successful South Asian American fashion designers, unlike other Asian American groups, most of them do not possess familial or ethnic ties to the US and global garment industries.

In the absence of sufficient social capital, Indie develops a racial consciousness about the fashion industry: she learns that she can "enter" it only by performing feminized service labor. After denying Indie the internship at *Celebrity Style*, the editor in chief of the magazine, Aaralyn Taylor, instead offers to hire Indie as a nanny for her son, so that she can spend more time expanding *Celebrity Style* into global markets. Aaralyn tells Indie, "I hear that people from your part of the world [India] are good with domestic duties" (36). Like the South Asian immigrant heroine Jasmine, whom I discussed in chapter 1, Indie's brownness marks her legibility only as racialized labor to white, wealthy Americans such as Aaralyn. Despite having nothing to do with her interest in the art and labor of fashion reporting, Indie's care work is nonetheless crucial to Aaralyn's professional goal of developing *Celebrity Style* into a global brand. Though clearly aware of Aaralyn's trafficking in racist stereotypes of a feminized global care industry, Indie hopes that she can convert her domestic labor into enough social capital to earn her an internship as a fashion journalist.

Yet Indie realizes that her job as a nanny ultimately makes this kind of conversion structurally impossible. When Indie's father asks Indie what she hopes to gain professionally from working as a nanny for Aaralyn, Indie replies, "'I've always been interested in fashion journalism. . . . So when she [Aaralyn] asked me to help look after her child on weekends, I figured it would, you know, get me closer to her.' . . . I did have a plan: to make myself so invaluable to Aaralyn and her family that she would find a place for me at her magazine" (92). Yet instead of seeing Indie as "invaluable" to the global branding of *Celebrity Style*, Aaralyn begins to exploit Indie's labor and to treat her in culturally demeaning ways. She first requires Indie's parents to drive Indie an hour each way to and from her home in Beverly Hills for her babysitting job. She then refuses to allow Indie to speak in Hindi to her toddler son. And after promising Indie the opportunity to attend Milan Fashion Week, Aaralyn demands that Indie spend all of her time, including the fourteen-hour flight from Los Angeles to Milan, caring for him rather than attending the fashion shows for which Indie had prepared.

Aaralyn's exploitation of Indie's labor also forces Indie to realize that despite having a sense of ethnic style, she does not possess what might be called aesthetic capital, or having the right "look" for a career in fashion reporting. After her first experience babysitting Aaralyn's son, Kyle, Indie says,

> I could only see myself through Aaralyn's eyes. I didn't have the kind of physical qualifications that would ever endear me to a woman like her. It didn't matter, I suddenly realized, that I had something of a unique sense of style. I didn't . . . have those pretty light-skinned looks and willowy bodies of the girls that are employed by these magazines. I didn't have the connections or the clout. (100)

Indie, like Jasmine in chapter 1, here experiences a form of double-consciousness in the Du Boisian sense: the cultural capital that Indie possesses among her white, suburban peers who envy her ethnic style is distinct from the aesthetic capital of "pretty light-skinned looks and willowy bodies" that she realizes she must also possess in order to be taken seriously as a fashion professional.[26] Whereas Indie's ethnic style allows her to capitalize on her Indianness without incurring the social costs of racialized difference among her white peers, not possessing normatively white standards of beauty forces her to incur that very cost as an aspiring fashion industrialist.

Yet even as Indie lacks conventional forms of social and aesthetic capital, her social ties to her local Indian community provide her with unexpected and indirect forms of social capital that have hitherto eluded her within the fashion world. The civic and philanthropic work that the Los Angeles Indian community performs in India and the diaspora and its upholding of cultural traditions such as weddings and festivals allow Indie to see India—rather than the United States—as a global fashion center. Indie's ethnic kin networks also provide her with the material resources necessary to break a fashion news story about Indian garment workers in the global fashion industry and to demonstrate her currency as a fashion journalist.

Initially, Indie believes that her pursuit of fashion as a career is fundamentally at odds with her ethnic community's investments in maintaining overly traditional and model minority narratives of Indianness. Her impression of her local Los Angeles Indian community is best illustrated by a group of young Indian women whom she calls the "Inky sisters." Praised by the community for "their straight A's, their skill at Bharatanatyam dancing, the fact that they could sing the latest crop of Hindi film songs as well as something from forty years ago," the Inkys embody precisely the kind of "ultra Indianness" that Indie tries to avoid exhibiting through her hybrid ethnic style (64). Yet when she reluctantly agrees to attend a community wedding with her parents, she is shocked to see the wedding guests wearing cutting-edge Indian fashions, against which her own carefully chosen lehenga seems outdated. While dressing for the wedding, Indie is initially pleased with the lehenga's "traditional bandini design" of "tiny, multicolored polka dots, arranged over the crushed silk fabric, with gold beads sprinkled over them" that had "recently become popular in the West" (140). Yet upon entering the wedding hall, she discovers "an array of terrifically fashionable Indian clothes" that makes her own presumably stylish outfit seem "dated and boring" in comparison (142). She takes in the "flowing palazzo pants with lace inserts paired with short embroidered tunics," "heavily embellished halter-neck blouses set off with a simple sari," and a "satin *ghagra choli* ... in the most divine shade of chocolate, studded with turquoise stones and accented with raffia," and notes that all of these styles are "fresh off a designer catwalk" (142). At the local community wedding, Indian fashions are not merely accent pieces for Western clothing, such as "clam-diggers and a draped tee," as Indie treats them in dressing for school (140). The wedding guests' outfits instead reflect Indian designers' appropriation of Western-style designs and material such as palazzo pants, halter tops, and satin; these Western styles are innovative updates to more conventional Indian fashions, such as saris, sari blouses, and *ghagra cholis* (long embellished skirts paired with sari-style blouses or bodices). In realizing that "there were plenty of girls here who obviously followed [Indian fashion] trends as much as [she] followed Western ones" (140), Indie recognizes and revises her Anglocentric definitions of fashion.

The community wedding also provides Indie with access to a breaking fashion news story that is taking place in India. The story allows her to expand her understanding of the fashion industry beyond US borders and to see how US fashion is connected to the Indian fashion and garment industries. She learns from the Inky sisters that a prominent member of an Indian civic organization, the India Association, has agreed to be a cultural liaison between a philanthropic A-list Hollywood celebrity, Trixie Van Alden, and an Indian village where "the women sit for hours a day and do all the beading and embroidery for the big fashion brands and are paid practically nothing for it" (148). The Inky sisters inform Indie that, in addition to exposing how large fashion retailers use exploited, offshore labor to execute their designs, Van Alden intends to employ the Indian village women to make her a wedding dress and to pay them a fair wage for doing so. Van Alden's plan is that the village Indian women will "get all the publicity" instead of "French couturiers and New York and Los Angeles designers" (148). When Indie learns of Van Alden's trip to India, her plan to expose French and American wedding-dress designers and brands as globally exploitative, and her desire to pay Indian women garment workers a fair wage, she realizes that she now has information "that could make [her] invaluable to people in the media" (148). Yet when Indie breaks the story of the garment workers to Aaralyn in an effort to be hired as a fashion intern for *Celebrity Style*, Aaralyn not only refuses to hire Indie but also fails to cite Indie as a source in breaking the fashion story, effectively expending Indie's social capital and further exploiting her labor.

Indie's social connections to the local Indian community fail to secure her a place in the fashion media complex. Yet, when read through Indie's eyes, the visual-textual composition of *Celebrity Style*'s published story about Indian garment workers and European and American couturiers also produces Indie's diasporic racial consciousness about the globalization of the Indian fashion industry. It exposes the garment workers' exploited Indian labor within global fashion as paralleling Indie's exploited labor within the fashion media complex. At the same time, the story introduces Indie to an alternative career in the Indian fashion industry. The story about wedding-dress garment workers is accompanied by a fashion spread on the popularity among US and British celebrities of Indian-inspired fashion designs, or Indo-chic, a topic toward which I turn in chapter 4, as well as the emergence of Indian designers onto the global fashion scene. The *Celebrity Style* spread includes a picture of "Cate Blanchett in rich gold Indian jewelry at the Oscars," and a "shot of Madonna in her mehndi and bindis" alongside photographs of well-known Indian fashion designers such as Ritu Beri[27] and the "fashion design duo Abu-Sandeep" (168). The appearance of Indian designers—and not just Indian and Indian-inspired designs—in the fashion spread makes Indie's "heart [swell] with pride" (168); it contributes to her understanding that India is now a "bonafide fashion capital" (140). The article in *Celebrity Style* thus captures India's *and* Indie's place within the global fashion industry, as emerging at the intersection of sweatshop and catwalk, of exploitative Indian garment manufacturing and Indian aesthetic innovation. Indie's various roles within the fashion industry— exploited care worker, style innovator, and aspiring fashion writer— reveal diasporic girlhood as taking shape at the intersections of cultural globalization, labor, and economic citizenship. Indie's desire to enter the fashion media complex thus challenges a model of girlhood as contingent on "racial innocence," as adult protectionist and racially hegemonic discourses of girlhood might have us believe. It instead constructs the relationship between diasporic girlhood and the fashion industry as inextricable from the acquisition of a diasporic racial consciousness.

Moreover, rather than affirming that Indie does not "have the right look for the job" of a fashion reporter, the *Celebrity Style* fashion spread on Indo-chic and Indian designers affirms Indie's prospects as a style trendsetter and fashion expert as contingent on the globalization of the Indian fashion industry. In chapters 4 and 5, I examine the role of Indo-chic and Indian fashions more broadly in defining diasporic belonging, in ways that exceed the pursuit of economic citizenship. For Indie, combining Indian and Western fashions and using Indian fashions as style accessories always involves the terse negotiation of the line between clothing as garb and clothing as fashion. The feminist media artists that I discuss in chapter 4 visually experiment with precisely this line. For them, Indian fashion emerges as the site of dense connections to practices of labor, migration, and embodiment that, as we will see, remain virtually untold within the story of Indian-inspired fashions, or Indo-chic.

4 / Oppositional Economies of Fashion in Experimental Feminist Visual Media

Whereas the diasporic literature that I examined in chapters 1–3 illustrates the capacities of Indian beauty and fashion to produce emergent affiliations across class and generational divides and between diaspora and nation, what remains to be more fully explored is the *visual* field within which fashion and beauty exert their material and affective force. In this chapter and chapter 5, I turn to an examination of South Asian clothing and fashion within diasporic feminist and queer visual and performance cultures. These artists' engagements with South Asian fashions might be understood as furnishing a form of what the Asian American art historian Margo Machida calls "expressive capital," a "repertoire of collective responses to [society's] moment and place in the world" (6–7). The popularity of Indian-inspired clothing, accessories, and designs—known as Indo-chic—is central to the "moment and place" of the artists I discuss in this part of the book. During the 1990s through the middle of the first decade of the twenty-first century, bindis, *mehndi* (henna), saris, sari borders, as well as Indian-inspired textiles and home décor, could be found on high-end fashion runways and designer boutiques, as well as in more affordable retailers and arts-and-crafts stores.

I approach South Asian diasporic visual and performance artists' engagements with South Asian fashions and rituals of adornment as existing in productive tension with the cultural economy of Indo-chic. In the simplest terms, Indo-chic is the story of fashion industrialists using South Asian fashions to cultivate economic and cultural capital in an increasingly competitive global economy, usually in ways that "[presuppose] a cultural remove and enact a cultural distancing" from the South Asian cultures that inspire them and from which they "purportedly emerged" (Tu 23). By contrast, the use of South Asian fashions in the art that I examine here can be situated within and against this narrative, as telling a rather different story about globalization and South Asian fashion. This is a story in which South Asian fashions are the "raw material" not for aesthetically innovative and culturally distant use within the dominant fashion system. Rather, they are the raw material for forging connections to histories of labor, migration, and diasporic belonging that remain virtually untold within the story of Indo-chic. While Indo-chic does not necessarily comprise the primary visual and performance-based subject matter that I examine here, it nonetheless provides the cultural occasion for these artists' to visualize these connections in ways that allow them to accrue expressive capital, to issue an aesthetic response to the racial and gender politics of fashion in culturally relevant and expedient ways.

For Swati Khurana and Prema Murthy, the visual artists whose artworks I discuss in this chapter, the bindi's appearance as an everyday practice of dress and a popular fashion trend serves as the basis for their parodic resignifications of it. The bindi is a dot fashioned out of powder or adhesive felt and plastic designs and placed between the eyebrows. Historically, the bindi, particularly in its form as a red powdered or felt dot, has denoted Hindu women's marital status (though some Muslim women in South Asia also wear bindis), female wisdom within Hindu spiritual traditions, and a woman's age and/or class status. In more recent history, South Asian women and girls wear the bindi, particularly in its form as an embellished, variously shaped, multicolored adhesive sticker, as a fashion accessory sometimes with and sometimes without Indian clothes. Khurana's and Murthy's "bindi art" conceives of the bindi as a fashion accessory that counters the orientalizing aesthetics that structure the bindi's circulation as Indo-chic style by exploring where the bindi-wearing South Asian woman "fits" within the cultural economy of Indo-chic. In a one-woman show by the performance artist Shailja Patel, which I discuss in chapter 5, Patel's narrating, wearing, and handling of a quintessential garment of Indian femininity—the sari—is set against the historical backdrop of and acquires greater political traction within the cultural economy of Indo-chic. I thus approach Indo-chic, South Asian dress, and visual/performance art not so much as distinct cultural domains but as constituting fashion-as-assemblage. These assemblages of fashion animate what fashion can *do*—the forms of embodiment and affect that fashion generates across various diasporic registers.

Visual Parody in Swati Khurana's and Prema Murthy's "Bindi Art"

This chapter focuses on two experimental artworks in which the bindi features prominently, Khurana's video *Dothead* (2001) and Murthy's fake pornographic website *Bindigirl* (1999). Though widely divergent in form and content, these feminist media deploy parody as a shared visual aesthetic that produces what I call oppositional visual economies of fashion. Khurana and Murthy visualize the bindi's parodic appearance on the body of the South Asian woman in ways that both challenge and exploit Indo-chic's orientalizing aesthetics. But they also refuse to capitulate to the orientalizing demands of cultural authenticity, in which South Asian women who choose to wear the bindi are positioned outside culturally dominant definitions of fashionability and/or are deemed the rightful inheritors and transmitters of authentic culture.

Parody's postmodern associations with culturally degraded versions of high culture are central to Khurana's and Murthy's respective parodies of the bindi as both fashionable accessory *and* everyday fashion. Most theories of parody locate its origins in "low culture" such as mass media, photography, film, and pop art, which have been used to discredit it as a postmodern form of derisive critique that is more playful than political.[1] In contrast, I argue that parody is a diasporic feminist art practice that can serve to "politicize representation" through a pointed refusal of aesthetic gravitas and a self-conscious embrace of aesthetic play (Hutcheon 95). For Khurana and Murthy, parody enables a feminist materialist critique of fashion that complicates conventional understandings of parody as an overly ludic and depoliticized art practice and fashion as a depoliticized symbolic good. In *Dothead*, parody functions as a form of derisive humor that calls into question the commodification of bindichic. Khurana's video reassesses the bindi's status as a fashion accessory by framing it as a visual marker of difference that triggered racial violence against South Asian immigrant communities in the 1980s and 1990s. Rather than deflecting attention away from such acts of violence, Khurana's parodic visual engagement with the bindi draws into productive tension the materiality of violence and the largely symbolic value of fashion. By foregrounding acts of violence as part of the bindi's diasporic cultural history, *Dothead* forces viewers to question the very distinction between the sartorial and the fashionable on which the dominant fashion system relies in order to create aesthetic and symbolic value. Murthy's

Bindigirl, on the other hand, experiments with the creative practices of adaptation and reinterpretation through which Indo-chic accrues symbolic value within the dominant fashion system. Murthy experiments with the bindi's accessorization by rejecting its associations with chaste heterosexual womanhood and by explicitly sexualizing it. She refashions the bindi into an accessory of a feminine body that is itself an object of mass consumption—the body of the South Asian female porn artist.

Parody is particularly well suited to these artists' aesthetic engagements with the politics of fashion, since some forms of parody share with Indo-chic the aesthetic signature of imitation with a difference. Even though a design must appear original and without equivalence in order to be considered new in fashion, "fashion is by nature notoriously unoriginal" (Tu 117). The production of difference thus becomes vital to "turn[ing] the raw material of Eastern sartorial traditions into the stuff of style" (Tu 116). Sometimes the creative labor of producing this difference involves an aesthetic remaking of existing South Asian designs or garments, such as when saris are cut and their borders restitched so they can be worn as shawls or used as "vintage textiles" for curtains, pillow cushions, or other home accessories. Other times this distance involves simply altering how or where a fashion object is worn, such as when embellished bindis designed to be worn on the forehead are marketed as "body jewelry" to adorn the belly, arm, or shoulder.

But even as parody and Indo-chic share the aesthetic signature of imitation with a difference, these forms of difference ultimately are, of course, quite distinct and circulate within disparate regimes of social value. Indo-chic's imitations and adaptations of existing South Asian fashions produce the designer's "value-adding function" (Tu 116) to the existing garment or design, shoring up the designer's creativity and cultural authority. Imitation and adaptation are thus forms of creative labor that are understood as value-added innovation in the global fashion system. By contrast, parody both "legitimizes and subverts that which it parodies" (Hutcheon 101), calling into question the very notion of aesthetic originality and undermining the idea of artistic cultural authority in deploying imitation as an aesthetic. In this respect, parody in Khurana's and Murthy's visual art inverts Indo-chic's visual economy, wherein "the copy [is] always more valued than the original, the aura not lost but enhanced by its reproduction" (Tu 117). Parody, by contrast, destroys "the Benjaminian 'aura' of an original work through its reproduction" (Hutcheon xv).

The playful and ridiculing structure of parody allows Khurana and Murthy to dismantle the orientalisms that shore up the commodification of Indo-chic. It also allows them to expand the gender, sexual, and racial politics of diasporic fashion beyond popular accusations that Indo-chic is a form of cultural appropriation. Charges of cultural appropriation (as well as those who claim that charges of appropriation are "really" misrecognitions of cultural appreciation)[2] abound among South Asian, diasporic, and other racially conscious fashion consumers in the blogosphere, especially around the bindi's more recent resurgence as a popular feminine style commodity.[3] Several of these blogs specifically targeted the pop singer Selena Gomez, who wore the bindi in her Bollywood-inspired dance routine at the 2013 MTV awards, and the actress Vanessa Hudgens, who sported it as part of her everyday attire among the Hollywood-hipster crowd that attended the independent arts festival Coachella in 2012.

The discourse of appropriation among diasporic subjects is itself a highly variegated one. For some people, appropriation is a form of cultural theft that denies the cultural origins and cultural significance of South Asian fashions. Ishra Aran, who blogs for the edgy online women's lifestyle blog *Jezebel*, lambasts the bindi's fashionability at Coachella, arguing that the sporting of the bindi "doesn't take from Hindu culture on Hindu culture's terms. It takes from Hindu culture on American terms and negates the Hindu aspect. . . . Bindi trend-sporters aren't celebrating a cultural symbol. They're celebrating themselves." For other bloggers, the problem with the bindi's fashionability has little to do with the failure among its wearers to acknowledge its cultural significance. For them, concerns about "cultural dilution" are smokescreens for more pressing issues that are at stake in the bindi's trendiness, which have to do with the forms of racial privilege that are at work in determining under what conditions—and on what bodies—the bindi can be read as fashionable in the first place. In a blog post titled "Beyond Bindis: Why Cultural Appropriation Matters" for the South Asian American lifestyle magazine *Aerogram*, twenty-four-year-old Jaya Sundaresh argues that what makes "the non–South Asian person's use of the bindi problematic is the fact that a pop star like Selena Gomez wearing one is guaranteed to be better received than I would if I were to step out of the house rocking a dot on my forehead. On her, it's a bold new look; on me, it's a symbol of my failure to assimilate." For bloggers like Sundaresh, appropriation is problematic not because it effaces intimate knowledge of South Asian culture. It is problematic because it requires that fashion maintain an inherently uneven cultural and racial playing field, in which Indo-chic marks non–South Asians as fashionable and South Asians as merely embodying their ethnic heritage.[4] While recognizing these differences within cultural appropriation discourse, I also contend that even when those who express their discomfort with Indo-chic do not explicitly cite cultural theft, the appeal to cultural restoration subtends the various strands of this discomfort. Because it is highly unlikely that South Asian women wearing bindis as part of their everyday or even occasional dress will suddenly be seen as fashionable subjects within the dominant fashion system, the recourse to cultural restoration becomes a kind of default political position, perhaps the only viable political response in the face of racial hegemony and the structures of privilege that dictate the meanings of fashionability.

We can see the overlaps of these two strands of cultural appropriation discourse—those who appeal to South Asian cultural theft and those who appeal to the racial politics of South Asian fashionability—in debates about the emergence of Indo-chic during the 1990s and beginning of the twenty-first century. In a study of *desi* (second-generation South Asian American), college women who used the popularity of Indo-chic as an opportunity to stage fashion-themed culture shows and events such as "Mehndi Night" at their universities in the first few years of the new millennium, Sunaina Maira observes that these young women were "active participants in [Indo-chic's] commodification process" ("Indo-chic" 230). These young South Asian American women appealed to their peers' desires to be decorated with "henna tattoos" as a way to educate them about this particular facet of South Asian culture. Such events allowed these South Asian women to position themselves as, at least nominally, arbiters of fashion. Yet these women also shared "an underlying fear that the popular appetite for Indo-chic might muddy the category of 'real' South Asian culture" (Maira, "Indo-chic" 232–33). They expressed anxieties about the unfair appropriation of South Asian designs and styles by fashion industrialists, even as many of them admitted to having little or no knowledge of the multiple geographical origins of mehndi (which include South Asia, North Africa, and the Middle East) or its cultural significance within South Asia and beyond.

Cultural appropriation arguments are useful to the extent that they raise "questions about who controls and benefits from cultural resources" such as fashion (Fung, qtd. in Pham, "Fashion's"). Yet the danger of these arguments is that they can also produce fictions of authentic culture in the process of safeguarding those very resources. Parody allows Khurana and Murthy to point to the political limits of appropriation discourse, which can all too easily, even if unwittingly, devolve into pious, anxious, or uncertain defenses of pure culture.[5] Specifically, parody in these artists' early experimental media makes visible the way that Indo-chic's orientalizing gestures *and* counterdiscourses of cultural appropriation rely on highly gendered assumptions and norms about South Asian fashion. In particular, appeals to Indo-chic as a form of cultural theft invoke the normatively feminine South Asian body as the authentically adorned/fashioned body from whom "culture" is stolen. This body vaguely inspires and yet is virtually invisible within the marketing and consumption of South Asian style commodities. Both South Asian American lifestyle bloggers now and South Asian American women in the 1990s explicitly or implicitly reproduce(d) the authentic South Asian woman as the subject who can restore fashion to its "proper" and rightful mode of embodiment, reinforcing how, as a number of feminist scholars have argued, contests over cultural authenticity are most often waged on the body of the diasporic or immigrant woman.[6] Insofar as parody typically challenges cultural authority, and insofar as feminist art forms challenge the heteronormative and heteropatriarchal structures of that authority, parody lends itself to a distinctly feminist visual aesthetics.

By parodying the bindi's status as both Indo-chic commodity *and* authentic sartorial accessory, Khurana's and Murthy's bindi art makes visible politically resistant forms of feminine embodiment that remain unseen within the fashion genre of Indo-chic and the politicized counterdiscourse of appropriation, or "exploitation chic."[7] Such forms of embodiment also avoid succumbing to what Machida has called a "politics of victimization" (32). Machida uses this phrase to capture the multiculturalist pitfalls of overidentification with the racial injuries of state exclusion in Asian American visual art; but her definition can be expanded to include the multiculturalist pitfalls of claiming racial injury from exclusion from cultural economies such as fashion as well. Khurana's and Murthy's different uses of parody reject the idea that South Asian subjects are somehow fashion's "victims"—subjects whose South Asianness inspires the dominant fashion system and yet who are all too often systematically excluded from its definitions of style and from its economic gains (as we saw in my examination of a South Asian girl's aspirations to enter the fashion industry in chapter 3). These artists steer clear of this narrative of cultural victimization, even when, as my discussion of Khurana's *Dothead* will show, South Asians are targeted subjects of racial surveillance and anti-immigrant violence.

Yet Khurana's and Murthy's refusal of a politics of victimization is by no means tantamount to a jettisoning of the political potential of parody.

On the contrary, through parody, they reveal how fashion-as-style and fashion-as-authentic-culture are negotiated on the bodies of South Asian women. In Khurana's *Dothead*, the bindi-wearing South Asian woman is, I argue, a parodic figure whose appearance generates a set of racialized feminist fantasies about fashion and sartoriality; these fantasies, in turn, allow her to function as an agent of racialized countersurveillance. Murthy's fake porn site *Bindigirl*, by contrast, parodies the orientalist appropriations of the bindi by deploying appropriation as a visual aesthetic that results in the bindi's vanishing point as a material object of fashion. I show that the bindi's proliferation and heterogeneous forms generate a confusion in the digital visual field in which the bindi is neither merely ethnic style nor authentic accessory but a digitally interactive icon that both adorns and provides users access to the culturally inauthentic and eroticized South Asian female body.

Finally, it is worth noting that, despite these two artists' differing visual engagements with the gendered and racialized politics of the bindi, both use looping and sped-up video footage, as well as video and digital self-portraiture, as highly experimental, low-budget modes of media production. Such low-end technologies were and continue to be popular among female media artists and among feminist-of-color women media artists in particular, because it allows artists with "'low social power' [to] modify existing technologies" for their own political ends (Nakamura 13). As examples of early do-it-yourself (DIY) media technologies in the 1990s, these forms of media production attest to the political urgency of Khurana's and Murthy's feminist responses to the cultural politics of Indo-chic. These techniques facilitated quick and inexpensive production,[8] which could allow for the relatively immediate consumption of these artworks within an ongoing present of racial violence and commodification.[9]

Racial Violence and Sartorial Countersurveillance in Swati Khurana's *Dothead*

Khurana's three-minute installation video *Dothead* (2001) made its public art debut at the South Asian community arts activist festival Diasporadics in 2000.[10] It was later shown in its final edited version as part of a South Asian Visual Arts Collective (SAVAC) curatorial project at the Hamilton Artists arts center in Hamilton, Canada, in 2001. Though *Dothead* is Khurana's first publicly displayed artwork, in many ways it prefigures her larger aesthetic concerns with "the seductive promise of rituals" (Khurana, interview), namely, the Hindu wedding ritual. *Dothead* includes images of Khurana's bindi-clad face, which I analyze in more detail shortly, taken from Khurana's own three-day Hindu-Punjabi wedding. These images, as well as others from her wedding video and from photographs of her wedding, appear across several of her artworks, including her reshot wedding video *Bridal Guide*, her mixed-media installation *Ten Years Later*, and her video trilogy *Love, Life Support, and the Pursuit of Marriage*.

As an early artwork in Khurana's oeuvre, *Dothead* does not focus on the wedding ritual per se. It therefore sits at a slightly oblique angle from much of her later work, in which the feminine rituals associated with weddings constitute a "wedding aesthetic." Nonetheless, the appearance of the bindi in *Dothead* is part of Khurana's political project of "examining personal agency or lack of agency in . . . rituals" that pervades her larger body of work (Khurana, interview). I argue that the repeated appearance of Khurana's bindi-clad forehead in *Dothead* enacts the repetitious nature of the daily ritual of wearing the bindi that some married immigrant and diasporic women practice. This mode of representation counters both the orientalisms of Indo-chic and the orientalist assumptions that South Asian women who wear the bindi are simply "passive" or "perpetuating a traditional mode" of femininity (Khurana, interview). Instead, Khurana's repetitious visual representation of the bindi insists that the ritual wearing of it is agential within both orientalist modes of thought.

Khurana describes *Dothead* as an exploration of how "racism impacts South Asians in the US by looking specifically at the bindi" and by questioning whether the "popularity of the bindi is just fashion" ("Dothead"). The title *Dothead* refers to the racist slur ascribed to the red round circle that some Hindu women place in the center of the forehead to designate marital status. Though "dothead" nominally designates women as the primary targets of anti–South Asian racism, the term circulated widely in the 1980s and 1990s as a broader racist characterization of South Asians, especially those who immigrated to the East Coast during this time as part of a largely working-class labor diaspora.

Dothead's form follows in large part from the metonymic function of its namesake: the reference to the bindi as a "dot" that is placed in the center of the forehead stands in for a larger repertoire of visual representations of South Asians. Khurana's video installation consists of two highly sped-up and repeated loops of played-back media footage of South Asians. One television monitor, placed in the center of the installation, displays both of these loops simultaneously across a split screen. Two additional television monitors, flanking the split-screen monitor on both sides, play each loop of footage independently. The installation is set up so that all three monitors play their respective loops simultaneously.

One loop—which plays on the left side of the split-screen monitor and independently on the monitor positioned to the left of the split-screen—includes footage of South Asian American public culture and public life in and around Jackson Heights, a South Asian commercial and residential center in New York City. On this loop, we see South Asians shopping at local grocery stores, outdoor markets, and clothing retailers; protesting unfair labor practices toward South Asian taxi drivers; or dancing and singing at public events like outdoor festivals and weddings. The second loop—which streams on the right side of the split-screen monitor and independently on the monitor positioned to the right of the split-screen—plays back clips from orientalist media about South Asians. Such clips include the figure of the "savage sabu" in the Hollywood film *Gunga Din* (1939), directed by George Stevens, which was loosely based on the British author Rudyard Kipling's poem by the same name and which rationalized the need for British colonial rule and civilizational rescue in India; and the "royal," turban-wearing Indian male savages whose Kali goddess worship, practices of human sacrifice, and unsavory eating habits threaten the everyday life of village Indians in Steven Spielberg's film *Indiana Jones and the Temple of Doom* (1984). (Many viewers remember the almost comically offensive scenes of Indian village royalty eating chilled monkey brains, eyeball soup, and baby snakes.) This channel also splices together scenes from the animated television show *The Simpsons*, featuring the Indian immigrant character Apu and his recently arrived immigrant wife, Manjula, who wears a bindi and to whom Bart and his kid sister Lisa direct questions about the bindi's cultural significance. All three screens are overlaid with written text, which include racial slurs against South Asians (such as "dotheads," "cow worshipers," "cab drivers," "cyber coolie," "white man's burden," "sand nigger," "wog," "towel head," "model minority," and "Paki"); quotes from news-media coverage about verbal and physical attacks against South Asians; and Khurana's own written commentary on the bindi as an object of ethnic style and of racial violence. As even this brief description suggests, Khurana's video is organized primarily by an aesthetics of contrast, in which the images portrayed in orientalist media bear little to no resemblance to images of everyday South Asian American public life.

The three-monitor format gives viewers the option of watching all three monitors at once or of watching each monitor individually.[11] The visual dissonance generated by Khurana's aesthetics of contrast provokes an explicitly antiracist mode of visual consumption, as the footage of the everyday lives, politics, and cultural practices of South Asians on the first loop undercuts the representational truth of the orientalist footage that plays beside it on the second loop. These two competing strategies of South Asian representation—those of everyday South Asian American culture and those of orientalist media—renders ironic Khurana's use of the term "dothead" in the video's title.

Dothead emerged onto the diasporic arts scene just at the pinnacle of the millennial Indo-chic craze and a decade after the bindi accrued meaning as a racially charged marker of South Asian identity within diasporic communities. Indian-inspired style commodities such as the bindi, henna "tattoos" (a dark plant-based paste applied in elaborate designs on various parts of the body), and saris/sari borders took the Western fashion world by storm at the end of the last millennium. Indian-inspired clothing and motifs could be found adorning the models on the catwalks of such haute couture fashion designers as John Galliano, Jean Paul Gaultier, and Yves Saint Laurent. Though the popularity of Indian-inspired styles, clothing, and fabrics waned during the first decade of the new millennium, these style commodities—and the bindi in particular—have made a popular resurgence and can be found adorning the bodies of such pop icons as Gomez, Hudgens, Katy Perry, and Miley Cyrus, to name only a few female celebrity fashion trendsetters of bindi-chic.

Dothead's emergence early in the first decade of the new millennium marked a feminist response not only to the racial politics of Indo-chic but also to the racial politics of violence against South Asians. Khurana also created Dothead in the political aftermath of acts of anti–South Asian violence, in which the bindi came to saturate South Asian bodies with disgust, inassimilability, and violability. While the term "dothead" is generally derogatory, Khurana's usage references specific vicious physical and verbal attacks against South Asians in New York and New Jersey in the 1980s and 1990s. A multiethnic (white and Latino) gang of middle-class youth called the "Dotbusters" claimed that the rise in South Asian immigration to and settlement in the area—precipitated by structural adjustment programs on the subcontinent that led to an influx of working-class labor migrants made up mostly of taxi drivers, newsstand owners, and domestic workers—threatened the city's largely white,

European-immigrant entrepreneurial and residential community. The name "Dotbusters" cloaks the gang's acts of racial violence in a kind of vigilante heroism reminiscent of the 1980s film *Ghostbusters*, in which the four male heroes save their beloved New York City from an invasion of ghosts. Vowing to "'go to any extreme' to drive Asian Indians from Jersey City," the Dotbusters imbued the bindi with the markings of an inassimilable South Asian immigrant identity in perpetrating racist hate crimes (Hanley). The gang brutally attacked Rishi Maharaj, an American-born, nineteen-year-old, Indo-Trinidadian man living and working in Queens, New York. Maharaj was walking home with his two female cousins after dinner at his uncle's house in Queens' South Ozone Park neighborhood when three gang members attacked him with baseball bats, resulting in multiple skull fractures. A Pakistani gas-station attendant was beaten to death with a baseball bat two days later in Long Island. These attacks reinvigorated a string of racist hate crimes against South Asians living and working in northern New Jersey in the late 1980s, which culminated in the brutal murder of a thirty-year-old New Jersey bank manager, Navrose Mody, as he left a Hoboken café (Texeira).

The image-texts of *Dothead* force viewers to consider how the bindi's popularity as fashion depends on the erasure of such histories of racist violence. In this respect, Khurana's video elaborates on the tensions between beauty and violence that play out in Mukherjee's *Jasmine*, discussed in chapter 1. Whereas Jasmine's Indian beauty mitigates the threat of anti-immigrant violence, Khurana's aesthetics of contrast in *Dothead* insists that the bindi's fashionability instead must be made accountable to histories of racial violence. Viewers encounter these histories through excerpted text taken from mainstream and community news accounts of anti–South Asian gang violence that is overlaid onto the two loops of played-back media footage. Such text includes proclamations by a fourteen-year-old, white, male youth who claims "it's us against the Hindus" as well as interviews with white residents claiming that South Asians should not "have the smell they have, dress the way they do, dress in curtains, and walk around in tribes."

Some of the text detailing anti–South Asian sentiment is superimposed onto highly recognizable clips of 1990s Indo-chic, such as pop-music mavens Madonna and Gwen Stefani sporting the bindi and henna in their music videos. The clips of Madonna are taken from her music video "Frozen" from her album *Ray of Light* (1998), which most clearly displayed the pop diva's infatuation with Indo-chic during the late 1990s. In these clips, the material girl's henna-adorned hands and arms move in a style that simulates the South Indian classical dance style of bharatanatyam (in which women dancers also typically wear mehndi on their hands, arms, and feet). The footage of Stefani sporting the bindi is from the music video "Just a Girl" from the album *Tragic Kingdom* (1996) by the band No Doubt, of which Stefani is the lead singer. The bindi—which she was encouraged to wear by her Indian band mate and boyfriend Tony Kanal—became a signature of Stefani's more everyday punk-feminist style.

By creating a montage of news accounts of Dotbusters' violence and Madonna's and Stefani's highly recognizable performances of 1990s Indo-chic, Khurana frames the racial politics of South Asian fashion squarely outside the logic of cultural appropriation. The splicing together of these image-texts makes visible what the dominant fashion system *cannot* appropriate—lived realities of racial surveillance and anti-immigrant violence that follow from the bindi as an everyday—rather than fashionable—South Asian accessory.[12] Yet what is worth noting in Khurana's aesthetics of contrast is the way that the bindi-wearing South Asian woman is most often absent or at best marginalized in both sets of image-texts. The news and community accounts of Dotbusters' violence that viewers encounter in *Dothead* cite South Asian *men* as the explicit target of physical attacks. In some accounts, South Asian men were attacked while accompanying or in close proximity to South Asian women in public, as in the aforementioned incident involving Maharaj. There is no evidence that the male victims of such hate crimes were wearing bindis (though some South Asian men do wear the bindi to signal their Hindu religious affiliations) or that the South Asian women with whom they were in close proximity were wearing bindis (though this is likely given the large concentration of South Asians in and around Jersey City and Jackson Heights). Either South Asian men are conflated with South Asian women in these attacks and thereby emasculated, or attackers retain a gendered social norm of not hitting a woman when a male body is available nearby to absorb the attack. If such acts of violence cannot be appropriated as part of the bindi's fashionability and if that violence is directed primarily toward South Asian men, then what representational space does this allow the bindi-wearing South Asian woman? In what ways does her everyday practice of wearing a bindi remain representable when the bindi is either racializing within the context of male-directed violence or ethnicizing in the context of fashionable femininity?

Here, I turn to an examination of the bindi's appearance on Khurana's forehead, which flashes periodically across the two-channel split screen of *Dothead*. The inclusion of these images counters two forms of abstraction taking place within the commodification of Indo-chic and within acts of anti–South Asian violence at the end of the twentieth century. The first is the tenuous visibility of South Asian women's bodies in the appropriation of the bindi as ethnic style; the second is the tenuous visibility of the bindi in acts of racial violence, since, despite the name, "Dotbusters" renders the bindi an abstract racial signifier even as it claims to target it. The appearance of the bindi-wearing South Asian woman in Khurana's video makes visible a femininity that vaguely inspires and that is yet rendered invisible within the marketing of Indo-chic and that literalizes the racial threat contained in the racial slur "dothead."

Khurana's bindi-clad face represents an everyday diasporic feminine ritual of dress; it is thus thematically aligned with the scenes of everyday South Asian public life that play on the first loop of the video. Yet the aesthetics of these facial shots actually marks them as quite visually distinct. The scenes of South Asians in Jackson Heights consist of panned-out camera shots of crowd mobility and collectivity, such as dancing, walking, marching, and shopping. The thirteen shots of Khurana's face, by contrast, isolate her forehead and eyes, so that each of these shots remains aesthetically differentiated from the second channel's scenes of collectivity. The close-up shots of Khurana's bindi also occupy (with one exception that I discuss shortly) *both* split screens on the two-channel display. As it territorializes both screens of the video, the bindi temporarily and episodically displaces the video's dominant aesthetics of contrast. As part of the facial adornment of Khurana's forehead and, most importantly, her eyes, the bindi is an accessory that, rather than reproducing "the orientalist image of . . . a woman who chooses to wear the bindi" (Khurana, interview), instead authorizes the bindi-wearing South Asian woman's gaze as she stares directly into the camera (see fig. 4.1).

The redoubled images of Khurana's bindi reference Bart Simpson's impertinently racist question about the bindi at the beginning of *Dothead*, in which he asks Apu's wife, Manjula, "Can you see out of it?" This question, however unintentionally, alludes to the Hindu spiritual belief that the bindi is a "third eye." The bindi in these shots does evoke a sense of "seeing," but it is a seeing in which the bindi returns the gaze confronting it in the first place. If Khurana's bindi-clad forehead indulges the fantasy of the bindi as a sacred third eye, then the bindi also sees (us). The appearance of a pink bindi placed slightly above the circular one shot in black-and-white silently references Bart's follow-up racist question to Apu's wife: "Does it change colors when you're ticked off?" These shots of Khurana's bindi—as a material object that

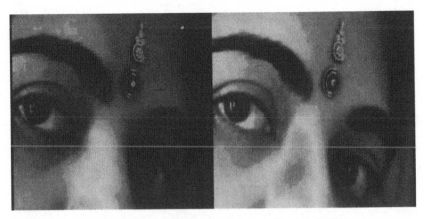

FIGURE 4.1. The redoubled bindi. Swati Khurana, *Dothead*, 2001.

"sees" and "changes colors"—playfully and defiantly indulge both of Bart's racial fantasies, answering his questions in an ironic affirmative.[13]

Khurana represents the bindi as agential (and unpredictable in its execution of this agency, since we cannot anticipate in advance when it will flash across the split screen). These shots operate as flashpoints of feminist cultural authority by making visible the bindi-wearing diasporic woman as a subject who authorizes a racialized fantasy of countersurveillance. The facial close-ups can be viewed as a feminist-of-color response to what Deleuze and Guattari have called "facialization," a method of surveillance that involves the deliberate "overcoding" of the face such that the rest of the body becomes subservient to the (over)signification of the face (181). As part of a Western capitalist, imperialist signifying system, facialization provides "a mechanism for judging faces" (177), in which some faces signify within/as modernity and others do not. Khurana upends this process of facialization in the doubled image of her bindi across the split screen. The signifiers that historically have occupied a temporality outside modernity—the bindi, the woman, the racialized subject—here emerge as surveillant. Especially when doubled, the many-eyed image turns into something of a monstrous panopticon.

The appearance of Khurana's bindi also reframes Stefani's iconic performances of bindi-chic, inserting them into a much more personal(ized) feminist fantasy of sartorial countersurveillance. This fantasy is intelligible only fleetingly, in a split-screen shot of Khurana's and Stefani's bindis, in which the word "DOTHEAD" appears in the same color over each image (see fig. 4.2). This shot is notable because it is the only instance in

FIGURE 4.2. Khurana and Gwen Stefani as "dotheads." Swati Khurana, *Dothead*, 2001.

which Khurana's bindi does *not* occupy both channels of the split screen. At first glance, the split-screen shot captures Khurana's visual play with the fiction of authenticity. The two "dothead" ascriptions underscore the stark differences between Khurana and Stefani as bindi-wearing subjects, in which Khurana is "naturally" a dothead and Stefani is not (and could never be one). Indeed, Khurana appears as though she is rolling her eyes at Stefani, who, within the context of this visual juxtaposition, is a fashion poser and therefore someone whose white female celebrity allows her to wear the bindi with impunity.

Yet I want to draw attention to another reading that makes room for this image as expressing a racialized feminist fantasy about Stefani and her bindi, one that complicates the representation of Stefani as merely a poser. The split-screen image also invites the cliché "it takes one to know one." Khurana, whose gaze is directed upward and toward Stefani, here interpellates Stefani not as a cultural appropriator but, like herself, as an inassimilable dothead.[14] This image allows Khurana to redirect a "fantasy of ridicule" that she admits to having had as a child when she heard the slur "dothead" while going to the grocery store with her mother, who regularly wore the bindi while frequenting public spaces. The contradictory meanings of the bindi, at first as "a symbol of derision, shame, instigating violence" and then as "chic (it was all over the East Village)" by the late 1990s were difficult for Khurana to reconcile: "I was physically repulsed by seeing (non–South Asian) people wear it [as a fashion accessory] because I connected it to the fear of Dotbusters and it was loaded culturally" (Khurana, interview). The shot of Khurana and Stefani as "dotheads" mediates Khurana's memory of the bindi's culturally "loaded" signification not in terms of a visual contest between authentic performances of fashion (Khurana) and appropriative ones (Stefani), though it might certainly capture this tension for some viewers. Rather, the inclusion of the word "dothead" over Stefani's face rearticulates a highly recognizable performance of 1990s Indo-chic into a racial fantasy in which Khurana and Stefani are *both* subject to racialized surveillance. By portraying both Khurana and Stefani as bindi-wearing "dotheads," Khurana brings to a visual crisis the bindi's fashionability.

This shot thus transforms the fashionable (white) feminine body into a body that is made vulnerable to violence, disrupting the context of white femininity within which the bindi accrues value as style. The feminist-of-color humor of this shot lies in its trafficking in a deliberate visual misrecognition, in which Khurana mistakes Stefani's attempts at bindi-chic for Stefani's everyday clothing. (Or, for Stefani, the bindi can never *be* "just fashion," only her everyday habit of dress.) Its humor and absurdity gains even greater political traction within the context of Stefani's puerile feminism, which will be familiar to viewers aware of Stefani's musical oeuvre. Recall that this shot, like all the shots of Stefani in *Dothead*, is taken from Stefani's music video "Just a Girl." The lyrics of the song cast girlhood as a universal experience of social constraints based solely on gender, in which being a girl is tantamount to being "some kind of freak," "so burdensome," and "living in captivity." Sung with reproach and vituperation, Stefani's lyrics express a punk-girl feminist subjectivity constrained by social expectations of feminine delicacy and propriety. Stefani's donning of the bindi in "Just a Girl" allows her to access a rebellious style of feminist self-expression in the face of these social constraints. But the phantasmatic split-screen shot of Stefani as a "dothead" in Khurana's video precludes such access. The shot frames Stefani not just as "freakish," "burdened," and "captive" as a girl but, like the bindi-wearing South Asian woman, as vulnerable to racialized regimes of surveillance and violence.

By making white feminine performances of Indo-chic just as vulnerable to racialized surveillance as are the everyday clothing practices of diasporic women, this shot of Khurana and Stefani as dotheads works to dispel the very myth of sartorial authenticity that it also ironically and humorously exploits. In this shot, authenticity becomes, retroactively, a prerequisite for violability—if Khurana and Stefani are both "dotheads," then they must both wear the bindi in ways that are perceived as authentic.

The performance of authenticity thus becomes unrecognizable as such in this visual scenario—does this performance belong to Khurana, Stefani, or both?[15] Through the unpredictable, episodic appearance of the bindi-wearing diasporic woman as an agent of sartorial countersurveillance, Khurana generates a humorously ridiculing critique of the bindi's status as both fashionable commodity and authentic sartorial object. Her parodic engagements with the bindi make mainstream fashion trends such as bindi-chic answerable to histories of racial violence, whereas violence remains otherwise inappropriable within such trends. Rather than capitulating to performances of cultural authenticity and victimization or to the late-capitalist orientalisms of Indo-chic, the act of bindi wearing in *Dothead* is refashioned into a feminist, antiracist practice of diasporic feminine embodiment.

Bindi Porn and the Crisis in Visuality in Prema Murthy's *Bindigirl*

Dothead's oppositional economy of fashion emerges most powerfully in Khurana's visual engagement with what remains *invisible* within the bindi's commodification—histories of racial violence and racialized forms of feminist agency. The digital conceptual and performance artist Prema Murthy's fake amateur pornography site *Bindigirl*, by contrast, humorously exploits the *hypervisual* terrain of online porn to counter the dominant frameworks of authenticity and commodification within which the cultural politics of Indo-chic are most often situated. Murthy's porn site produces a crisis in the digital visual field by challenging the bindi's more established connections to a sacred, conjugal, and heteronormative femininity. The bindi instead appears as a digitized dot that users must navigate in order to gain access to the illicitly eroticized, pornographic South Asian body. In what follows, I examine the cyberfeminism of Murthy's "bindi porn" through her visual experimentation with the bindi as a desacralized accessory to a pornographic femininity, as a digitally interactive dot, and in its aesthetic continuity with the appearance of the dot in avant-garde art forms.

Mimicking an amateur South Asian porn website, *Bindigirl* debuted in 1999 on Thing.net, one of the first independent online art networks that allowed an internationally diverse group of artists, activists, curators, and art critics to exchange ideas about emerging aesthetic practices in conceptual and performance art.[16] *Bindigirl* features highly sped-up and looped-together images of Murthy's avatar, a woman named "Bindi," in various sexual poses, sharing her online biography, and conducting a simulated online sex chat. Users who log on to the site can pay three dollars to sign up for regular access to more "hot pixx," "sexy sound," "live action," "erotic chat," and "exotic souvenirs."[17] Bindis appear in the form of screen icons for navigating the site, some of which cover the vaginas, foreheads, and nipples of Murthy's avatar Bindi and other unnamed, South Asian female porn artists who are featured on the site.[18] These bindis are pixelated and mimic the censorship dots that consumers of online porn typically encounter upon entry to a porn site or that are used to blot out sexually explicit body parts in any number of visual media. In addition to viewing Bindi as a porn artist, users can also buy souvenirs of their sexual adventures with Bindi. These include actual bindis (shown both adorning Bindi and in the form of packets that Bindi advertises); T-shirts, panties, and socks "worn, signed, and numbered by Bindigirl"; and goddess prints that feature digitized bindis placed over the vaginas of Hindu goddesses (see figs. 4.3 and 4.4).

In creating *Bindigirl* as a simulation of a South Asian porn site and in using video self-portraiture as the source material for the avatar Bindi, Murthy explains that she wanted to explore "going to the extreme of positioning [her]self as a sexual object" (Hickman). Implicit within Murthy's description of her site is Murthy's "passionate attachment to hypersexuality and its particular ability to critique fetishism" that characterizes a genre of twentieth-century Asian American feminist pornography (Shimizu 29). In a study of early- to late-twentieth-century Asian immigrant and Asian American female porn artists and filmmakers, Celine Parreñas Shimizu observes that the eroticization of Asian women in American porn as both docile and hypersexual is historically connected to nineteenth-century laws prohibiting Asian women who were seen as morally corrupt from entering the United States, to twentieth-century US military/colonial occupations in East and Southeast Asia, and to the burgeoning Asian sex tourism industry. These historical confluences have created the conditions of possibility for the emergence of such historical figures as the Chinese female prostitute and Japanese, Korean, and Filipina war, picture, and mail-order brides, which cater to white male orientalist fantasies about Asian women's sexuality.[19] Locating continuity across US and British colonial histories, Murthy appropriates the heightened visibility of the bindi as an Indo-chic style commodity in *Bindigirl* as a way to show how a "passionate attachment" to *South Asian* women's hypersexuality can challenge such orientalist fantasies not only about the Asian woman's body but also about fashion commodities such

FIGURE 4.3. "Souvenirs." Bindis. Prema Murthy, *Bindigirl*, 1999.

as the bindi. For Murthy, then, hypersexuality becomes the basis for her simultaneous critique of commodified South Asian fashion and commodified South Asian female sexualities.

Because the name "bindigirl" is not sexually explicit, the site may attract as many visitors who are more or at least as interested in Indochic as they are in online Asian porn. As the art critic Jennifer Hickman observes in an interview with Murthy for *New York Foundation for the Arts* magazine, "Someone can come to your Web site [*Bindigirl*] having watched Madonna and wanting to wear bindis and be thinking of an entirely different Bindigirl." Hickman suggests that the name of Murthy's site operates in part like a bait-and-switch, drawing in online consumers of Indo-chic and producing online consumers of South Asian porn. Certainly, users who encounter the site as part of shopping online for bindis might be startled by the site's home page. The page features an image of a large red bindi with a "warning" sign placed over it that indicates their imminent entry into a porn website. At the same time, as even my brief description of the site makes clear, *Bindigirl*'s reference to the bindi is not merely nominal. Upon entering the site, users encounter not just Bindi (online avatar) but also actual bindis (fashion accessories) in a number of ways. The bindi appears as a marker of Hindu married identity when placed in the middle of Bindi's forehead, as an eroticized

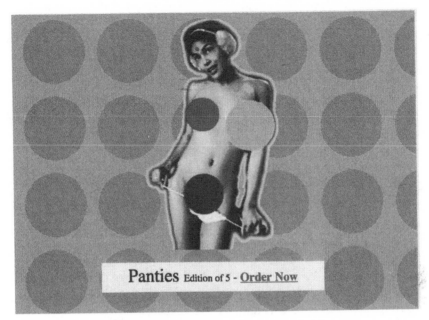

FIGURE 4.4. "Souvenirs." Panties. Prema Murthy, *Bindigirl*, 1999.

fashion accessory when superimposed onto images of nipples and vaginas of Bindi and the other South Asian female porn artists, and as a souvenir that viewers can purchase.

I examine some of these appearances of the bindi in *Bindigirl* in more detail shortly, but it is worth pausing here to consider the way Murthy's aesthetic experimentation with the bindi throughout the digital visual field exploits the bindi's inherent hybridity as an everyday fashion accessory. As Murthy explains of the bindi,

> The idea of the bindi originated to symbolize the sacred third eye. It also came to signify women's marital status in India. But even now the idea of the bindi for Indian girls has become totally decorative. Back in the day it was made with red powder. Now they're made from disposable stickers you can stick on. So, even in India the meaning has been distorted. There's been another layer of distortion added through its co-opting by pop media and pop culture. (Hickman)

In this brief and incisive rendering of the bindi's polysemy in India and in the diaspora, Murthy points out that the bindi's millennial fashionability cannot be explained solely by the orientalist appropriations of Indo-chic.

It is also tied to historical and ongoing shifts in the ways the bindi is produced, worn, and marketed on the subcontinent. For Murthy, bindi-chic is thus simply "another layer of distortion" that builds on a preexisting distortion around the bindi that originates in India itself (where it has become "totally decorative" for Indian girls). Her transnational analysis of the bindi's commodification expresses a lack of concern—and perhaps even impatience—with the politics of authenticity and appropriation that structures colloquial debates surrounding Indo-chic and the racial politics of fashion more broadly. This lack of concern may have to do, at least in part, with Murthy's identity as a biracial South Asian. As the daughter of a Filipina mother and an Indian father, Murthy grew up with a sense of being scrutinized by other South Asians, despite sometimes claiming political identities as South Asian and Southeast Asian American (Murthy, interview). As a biracial woman, Murthy's relationship to South Asianness can never be "pure" or "authentic." Positioned as always already inauthentic within the framework of identity politics, Murthy navigates the politics of the bindi's fashionability from within a diasporic framework of hybridity.[20]

If the bindi is already a "distorted" fashion object within South Asian subcontinental modernities, as Murthy explains, then its proliferation and multiplication across the digital visual field of online porn serves to further advance this distortion. One commodified form of South Asian femininity (the bindi) is layered on another commodified form of South Asian femininity (South Asian porn), a layering that repeats throughout the navigation of the site. Rather than challenge the bindi's appropriation as fashion, whether on the subcontinent or in the diaspora, Murthy humorously exploits these forms of appropriation. In layering the bindi-as-fashion onto the body of Bindi-as-porn-artist, *Bindigirl* presents users not just with "Bindi porn" but also with "bindi porn."

The bindi, after all, serves as a way of digitally enhancing the obscenity of the unclothed and sexually excessive body. Upon entering the *Bindigirl* site and scrolling over an icon of a pink lotus flower, users can click on the word "Goddess" or "Whore." Both versions of Bindi's avatar allow them to interact with and consume the bindi in a variety of contexts. Though the site nominally distinguishes between sacred and profane images of South Asian femininity, the image-texts that are included as parts of each link actually reveal very little difference between them. The word "Whore" hyperlinks to animated images (gifs) of Bindi in different sexual poses and simulating various sex acts. Bindi wears a large, eye-catching red bindi in the center of her forehead and smaller red bindis cover her nipples and vagina. Like the media footage in *Dothead*, in which both channels of images of South Asians repeat on loops, the "Whore" gifs in *Bindigirl* are hyperkinetic—sped up, spliced, and repeated on loops—so that users can make out only bits and pieces of a given sex act or sexual pose. The gifs of Bindi also feature overlaid text taken from English translations of the *Kama Sutra* by the British ethnologist and translator Sir Richard Burton. In line with the forms of heterosexual sex work and misogyny that the term "whore" connotes, these excerpts reference women's sexual subservience to men—"not acting too freely," "adapting her tastes to his liking," and "remaining silent."

Once users have completed their viewing of the "Whore" gifs, they can then scroll over the word "Goddess," which opens up a pop-up screen of vertical pink bindis in the form of television remote-control buttons (see fig. 4.5). Clicking on each bindi provides users with a simulated encounter with or information about Bindi, such as a personalized "live chat" and biographical details. The bindi features most prominently as a fashion accessory when users click on the link "harem," which takes them to a page featuring nine South Asian women's faces wearing an array of colored bindis on their foreheads. Users can click on any of the faces, which hyperlinks to a full frontal shot of the given actress in a still pornographic pose and adorned with differently colored bindis on her nipples and vagina (see fig. 4.6).

Clicking anywhere on the body of the designated artist takes the user back to the main "Harem" page, and the cycle repeats with all nine artists. The user thus confronts an endless proliferation of colored bindis as part of the experience of consuming online porn, rather than the more explicit material—genitalia, the meat shot, the money shot—for which they are presumably navigating the site. The bindi titillates even as it conceals, or titillates through its materialization of eroticized concealment. Moreover, each full-frontal image of a porn artist includes excerpts from "tantric texts on *yoni* [female genital] worship." These excerpts reference female sexuality as divine and worthy of spiritual devotion: "women are divinity, women are life, women are truly jewels," and "when she is naked men must kneel and worship her as the goddess" (Murthy, *Bindigirl*).[21] Unlike the textual excerpts taken from Burton's translation of the *Kama Sutra*, in which women are expected to act as sexual servants "silently" obliging men's sexual demands, these excerpts from uncited tantric texts purport to honor and revere Indian female sexuality as part of the act of consuming porn. Despite the name "Harem," which signals the way that women are called on to fulfill men's voracious sexual appetites, the page

FIGURE 4.5. "Remote." Prema Murthy, *Bindigirl*, 1999.

draws on these texts to represent not the subjugation but the liberation of South Asian female sexuality through its associations with sacredness, mystery, and spiritual eroticism. These excerpts thus operate ironically, as revealing how an "ancient" discourse of female sexual worship can produce a "modern" liberal feminist sensibility in which South Asian women's sexuality is something not to be denigrated but to be celebrated in the act of consuming porn. The tantric texts on Indian female sexuality in "Harem" may thus appear as examples of and appeal to something like a feminist consciousness, allowing consumers of porn to rationalize such consumption as, at least in part, a sex-positive feminist act.

If "Goddess" and "Whore" reveal little difference between the commodification of sacred and profane South Asian female sexualities, then Murthy's commodification of the bindi is central to this conflation of the sacred and the profane. Across the "Goddess" and "Whore" image-texts, Murthy reappropriates the packaging of bindis as "body art" or "body jewelry." Within the cultural economy of Indo-chic, bindis are marketed

FIGURE 4.6. "Harem." Prema Murthy, *Bindigirl*, 1999.

as ethnic style commodities that adorn not only or even primarily the forehead but also the shoulder and the belly button of its wearers. By using the bindi as adornment for nipples and vaginas, Murthy refashions it to decorate South Asian porn artists' erogenous zones. (However parodic, this form of erotic enhancement prefigures the now popular practice of "vagajazzling," in which women decorate their shaved pubic area with adhesive crystals or other jewel-like accessories in order to enhance its appearance.) Murthy also explicitly desacralizes the bindi as a marker of authentic culture when she depicts Bindi wearing decorative pink bindis on her nipples and the red Hindu "marriage" bindi on her forehead. In this unlikely and visually dissonant pairing of bindis, the red marriage bindi is made just as available for pornographic consumption as are the more decorative pink bindis, blurring the line between "what is sacred and what can be bought" within the visual field of online porn (Murthy, interview).

Even the excerpts from South Asian erotic texts that accompany the images of the bindi as an accessory of the porno body in "Whore" and

"Goddess" are more alike than different, despite differing in terms of their denigration of and reverence for female sexuality. Both sets of texts traffic in the reproduction of what Foucault calls the "ars erotica," or the erotic arts, of the "Orient." The ars erotic is a discursive formation in which travel and colonialism make possible the sexual modernity of the Occident by imbuing the Orient with sexual excess. The orientalist discourse of the ars erotica promises those who practice it a release from the sexual norms that regulate modern sexuality; or it signals a transgressive sexuality that must be disciplined and punished, even if desired. The gifs of Bindi wearing the bindi, the appearance of the bindi in "Harem," and the textual overlay from the *Kama Sutra* and tantric texts reveal the convergences of orientalist epistemologies with sex-positive feminist discourse. Routed through the orientalisms that shape both repressive and liberal discourses of Indian female sexuality, the distinction between "goddess" and "whore" becomes merely nominal.

Murthy's playful desacralization of the bindi—particularly the Hindu marriage bindi as pornographic accessory—prefigures (and arguably even anticipates, given the resurgence of Indo-chic in the early 2010s) more recent debates that have erupted within both the mainstream and diasporic blogosphere about the bindi's attachments to the reproduction of heteronormative Hindu femininity. Political and lifestyle bloggers who expressed both criticism of and excitement around the bindi's renewed fashionability, such as its appearance on pop stars Selena Gomez and Vanessa Hudgens, regularly cited Hindu leaders' objections to bindi-chic on the grounds that the bindi is a symbol of religious identity. Several blogs quoted the Hindu statesman Rajan Zed as saying, "[The bindi] is an auspicious religious and spiritual symbol. . . . It is not meant to be thrown around loosely for seductive effects or as a fashion accessory" (Joshi). Overlooking the glitzy embellishments of modern-day bindis and the mass production of the bindi as a decorative fashion accessory in South Asia, Zed's critique of bindi-chic's resurgence relies on a heteropatriarchal, Hindu-nationalist imperative to restore the bindi to its "proper" place on the foreheads of married Hindu women. In Murthy's desacralization of the bindi across the user interface of *Bindigirl*, the distinction that Zed draws between religious identity and fashionability simply ceases to exist. Indeed, the bindi as "religious and spiritual symbol" becomes exactly what Zed fears—a pornographic "fashion accessory" imbued with "seductive effects."

The feminist porn scholar Linda Williams has argued that one of pornography's central imperatives is to bring "on/scene" or into the public arena "the organs, acts, bodies, and pleasures that have heretofore been designated ob/scene and kept literally off-scene" (3). *Bindigirl* certainly simulates this form of on/scenity. But because it is a feminist *parody* of Asian porn, the pornographic images of bindi-wearing South Asian women never quite fulfill porn's promise of ob/scenity, or "unspeakable sex" (L. Williams 4). Either through highly sped-up images that refuse the user the pleasures of lingering on the porn artists' sexually explicit poses or through repeated denials of the money and meat shots or through the conflation of sacred and obscene South Asian femininities, the bindi constantly conceals the bare sex it promises to reveal.

Across the digital interface of *Bindigirl*, users encounter not only the bindi's capacity to eroticize South Asian femininity but also Murthy's eroticization of the bindi itself. I contend that more explicitly scandalous than the pornographic bodies of South Asian women is the scandalous appearance of the bindi on these bodies. For the bindi's visual enhancement of the pornographic body calls into question the very status of the bindi *as* a fashion accessory, since accessorizing typically demands the clothed body as a prerequisite. If the bindi is resolutely "on/scene"—or on display in the public arena—in its fashionability within Indo-chic markets, then Murthy brings "on/scene" the bindi's "ob/scenity" as an object that not only adorns but mediates the virtual encounter with the pornographic body. The hybridity of the bindi's material form—its "becoming dot" or its "dotness" across the noncorporeal and corporeal thresholds of the user interface—reinforces its capacities for eroticization. Given that the bindi doubles as a digital icon that users click on in order to navigate the porn site, it is often difficult to tell how and if the multicolored round objects, even when appearing on South Asian women's bodies, are "exotic" bindis, ordinary bindis, or more simply and unremarkably, just digitally interactive dots. While only a few of the bindis actually function as clickable icons, their similarity in form, color, and placement entices the user to at least attempt clicking on them. All the dots thus hold out the promise of interactivity—and often refuse it.

The bindi/dot's promise of erotic interactivity constitutes Murthy's cyberfeminist political aesthetic, an aesthetic that draws from Donna Haraway's notion of cyborg feminism. Cyborg feminism challenges the body's status as sacred and autonomous and embraces the body's intimate comingling with new forms of technological interface.[22] Digital porn on its own certainly produces this intimate comingling of body and technology since it promises the user sexual arousal while he or she navigates the digital visual field. Indeed, the mere possibility that the bindi/

dot—including its appearance on vaginas and nipples—is a clickable digital icon that will produce a more explicit sexual encounter between user and pornographic image suggests that part of what is being eroticized in Murthy's bindi porn is *interactivity* itself. As an icon of interactivity, the digitized dot parodies the pleasures of delay and deferral that distinguish online porn from other forms of pornography, such as videos and live peep shows. Zabet Patterson has argued that online porn exists not only to guarantee a corporeal encounter with the pornographic body but also to "rationalize the pleasure of surfing" for porn (109). Users not only must spend time finding the "right" site to suit their sexual desires but also must often take the time to sign on, register, and pay for access, making the eventual encounter with the pornographic image that much more satisfying because of the user's heightened sense of anticipation. The dot in *Bindigirl* extends the pleasures of delay and deferral that users experience while surfing for porn to the pleasures of delay that users experience once they have already entered the porn site—clicking on the bindi/dot produces only more encounters with infinitely deferred forms of sexual gratification.

What is notable about the blasphemous hybridity of the bindi-as-dot is the way that Murthy wrenches the bindi's dotness away from its racist attachments (as in the racial slur "dothead" and the gang name "Dotbusters") and channels it toward a feminist-of-color politics of fashion and porn. I argue that she does so by experimenting with the aesthetic continuities between the bindi-as-dot and the appearance of the dot in some late-twentieth-century avant-garde visual art forms. Murthy's cyber-feminist appropriations of these art forms becomes a way of dislodging the bindi from its status as a style commodity while also drawing attention to the South Asian woman's body as a "performing and laboring body" within the digital media genre of online porn (L. Williams 5). The dot—particularly in its form as a round, colorful polka dot—appears in the pop art photographs of John Baldessari, one of Murthy's stated artistic influences, and across various visual media by the Japanese American conceptual artist Yayoi Kusama. Baldessari, a conceptual artist who followed in the tradition of Andy Warhol's conceptual and pop art of the 1960s, famously began pasting multicolored dots over the faces of people featured in newspaper photographs starting in the mid-1980s.[23] In Baldessari's photographs, the dots flatten out subjectivity. Because viewers cannot look to faces or to facial expressions to reveal subjective uniqueness, they must look to "minor details," such as dress, stance, and ambience, in order to differentiate between the photographed subjects ("John Baldessari"). Baldessari's use of the polka dot was widely regarded by art critics as a democratizing aesthetic insofar as it located subjectivity beyond the prioritization of the face.

Murthy's use of the dot aesthetic in the pornographic visual field turns out to be the obverse of Baldessari's use of polka dots in the photographic visual field. Whereas Baldessari blots out the faces that consumers of news media most want to see, Murthy humorously blots out the erogenous zones that consumers of online porn presumably most want to see. But when users look beyond the dot blots, the pornographic visual field yields nothing by way of subjective uniqueness. Rather, the unclothed bodies, sexual poses, and icons of interactivity that the user is able to access visually only reinforce highly clichéd images of online porn. In addition, even though Murthy's audience, unlike Baldessari's, is able to see the faces of the porn artists, these faces reveal nothing unique by way of subjectivity. There certainly are differences in facial appearance and expressions of sexual pleasure and seduction, but as consumers of online porn will recognize, these differences are highly interchangeable and exchangeable within the pornographic visual field. Murthy's dot aesthetic therefore exposes as untenable Baldessari's assumption that faces hold the secret to subjective uniqueness. If the bindi's "dotness" is democratizing in *Bindigirl*, it is a democratization that is tied to the mass production and consumption of pornographic South Asian femininity. Murthy's dot aesthetic reveals how, for women of color, gender and race are categories of embodiment that remain recalcitrant within the digital visual field but in ways that are anything but democratizing. The bindi's dotness thus makes visible not so much the so-called consumerist freedoms of the digital marketplace but the body of the South Asian sex worker whose exchangeability is required to produce those freedoms.[24]

Murthy's multilayered, proliferative deployment of pink dots in *Bindigirl* is a visual aesthetic that is instead more closely aligned with the Japanese American feminist visual artist Yayoi Kusama's use of polka dots across her avant-garde oeuvre.[25] Polka dots have been a signature of Kusama's materialist art practice from the 1960s to the present and appear most often in painted form or as objects stuck onto the naked bodies of men and women, including Kusama herself. The polka-dotted self-portraitures became an aesthetic signature that earned Kusama the nicknames "Princess of Polka Dots" and "Dotty."[26] Photographs featuring a polka-dotted Kusama were often part of Kusama's publicity packages, artist statements, and press releases. The polka-dot aesthetic is part of what Bree Richards calls Kusama's "elaborate parody" of mass-media-driven images of orientalist femininity during the height of US military involvement in Vietnam. In one of Kusama's best-known photographic self-portraits, Kusama is draped provocatively across one of her three-dimensional artworks, "Accumulation #2," a couch bristling with erect phalli. Kusama appears naked, except for a pair of high heels and sprayed-on polka dots, and stares seductively into the camera.

In this and other similar self-portraits that share a "soft porn" aesthetic, Kusama links the photographic visual field to the performativity of gender. As indicated by the title of the artwork on which the 1966 photograph is based, the photograph features an accumulation of dots across Kusama's hair, buttocks, legs, back, arms, and high-heeled shoes (the most Freudian of fetishes). Much like the ludic theatricality of a polka-dotted clown, the dots across Kusama's body constitute her theatricalized production of eroticized Asian femininity. Such theatricality deliberately indulges the orientalist fantasy of the Asian woman's body as fetish object. In thus flaunting the Asian woman's fetishized femininity, Kusama holds her femininity "at a distance" (Doane 81–82). At the same time, the polka dots (and surrounding phalli) also fail to fully guarantee the total abstraction that is at work in the act of fetishization. Even as they draw the viewer's eye toward Kusama's naked body (parts), the polka dots and phalli also clutter and overtake the visual field, producing the Asian female body as a "mere surface for a swathe of pattern and repetition" (Richards).[27] In this sense, Kusama's body resists mere abstraction as it is broken up by or even blended into the proliferation of dots—it is the dots (and phalli) rather than Kusama's body that dominate the visual field.

Situating Kusama's self-portraiture alongside Murthy's souvenir self-portraitures in *Bindigirl* reveals considerable overlap in the two artists' dot aesthetic. As markings on the bodies of both Kusama and Murthy, the dots in both sets of self-portraitures enhance and obscure the sexualized Asian female body, thus humorously critiquing the mass consumption of Asian women as "little brown fucking machines" (Shimizu 211) within the orientalist and neoorientalist imagination. Murthy also refashions Kusama's dot aesthetic, in which the Asian woman's body becomes a "mere surface" for the proliferation of dots. In images of Bindi in "Souvenirs" (as shown in figures 4.3 and 4.4), large, pink polka dots decorate not Bindi herself but the background of the digital visual field. If the polka dots and phalli that overtake the visual field in Kusama's self-portraitures fail to guarantee the total abstraction of Kusama's body-as-fetish, then the pink polka dots do something similar for Murthy's pornographic body. Even as the pink dots occupy the background of the screen, their size, framing, and multiplication compel viewers to divert their gaze away from Bindi and the bindis she is selling, even if only temporarily. The proliferation of dots in the visual background thus detracts, at least momentarily, from the fetishization of the (South) Asian woman's pornographic body. In doing so, they also divert our gaze away from the bindis that Bindi is selling and thus away from the bindi's commodification.[28]

Murthy's bindi porn humorously proliferates the bindi's capacity for aesthetic "distortion," producing a crisis in its visuality. At any given time, users are uncertain of exactly what material form they are encountering—the bindi as an accessory of pornographic femininity, as an eroticized icon of digital interactivity, or as a dot that theatricalizes pornographic performance while also overtaking the visual field. To the extent that authenticity and appropriation have become virtually intractable as frameworks for understanding and debating the politics of fashion trends such as Indo-chic that possess a distinct racial dimension, we can read this crisis in visuality as a political end in itself. The bindi's endless capacity for aesthetic transformation—its commodified attachments to ob/scene South Asian femininities and to eroticized modes of digital interactivity, as well as its detachments from the cultural economy of fashion altogether—playfully disregard concerns about cultural authenticity by drawing attention to the heteronormativities that shore it up; heteronormativity is here calibrated through the bindi's attachments to noncommodified, nominally Hindu, hetero-conjugal, nonpornographic femininities. At the same time, Murthy's parodic appropriations of bindi-chic fashionability are incommensurate with the forms of appropriation that shore up the creative innovation, cultural authority, and orientalizing aesthetics of Indo-chic designs and the fashion wearer's on-trend sense of style. The bindi's blasphemous hybridity in *Bindigirl* instead operates within a South Asian diasporic feminist framework that connects the late-capitalist orientalisms of bindi-chic to the digital orientalisms of online porn. In this sense, bindi porn remains critical of orientalist practices of appropriation even as it revalues appropriation as an aesthetic practice.

The crisis in visuality generated around the bindi in *Bindigirl* also expands the scope of existing feminist materialist frameworks for the study of fashion. This scholarship has tended to focus on Indo-chic's labor economies. Feminist scholars such as Sunaina Maira, Anita Mannur, and Pia Sahni have drawn much-needed attention to the transnational circuits of racialized labor that are required for Indo-chic's successful production, marketing, and consumption. These scholars call attention to the relationship between economic restructuring and neo-liberalization policies on the subcontinent that produce India as part of a "global sweatshop where American multinationals browse for cheap labor, cheap goods, and profitable market trend ideas" and South Asian diasporic entrepreneurs who make and sell Indo-chic products in urban centers and who must compete with large multinationals in order to make a living (Maira, "Indo-chic" 235). Rather than understand Murthy's bindi porn as radically differentiated from these feminist materialist critiques of fashion's labor economies, we would do better to understand her visual aesthetics as attending to a different kind of materiality. This is not a materiality that inheres in the labors of making fashion but the materiality of "doing" fashion, the instrumentalization of fashion to advance an oppositional feminist politics of the body. In the case of *Bindigirl*, this is a politics rooted not only in a critique of commodified Indianness for the global fashion market but in humorously deploying a feminist practice of appropriation in order to disorganize the fiction of authenticity. Not only does Murthy refuse an appeal to sartorial authenticity by explicitly blurring the line between bindi and dot and by explicitly eroticizing the bindi. She also reappropriates the bindi's commodification as style in order to produce and simultaneously deny virtual access to an altogether different South Asian commodity: the body of the South Asian porn artist.[29] The blasphemous hybridity of the bindi's material form shores up the blasphemous body of the South Asian female porn artist, and vice versa. Murthy's cyber-feminist politics of porn lies in the way that her visual deployment of the bindi-as-dot makes intelligible the pornographic body as a commodified form that is inappropriable within the normatively appropriative logic of Indo-chic. It also lies in the way that it brings into view a sexually "perverse" mode of feminine embodiment that exceeds the representational limits of the bindi-wearing Indian woman as a marker of valorized and sacrosanct authentic South Asian culture.

Fashioning the Flat Affects of Bridal Adornment

In the bindi artworks *Dothead* and *Bindigirl*, Khurana and Murthy deploy the bindi as a highly experimental aesthetic form. Across these media, the bindi facilitates feminist modes of embodiment that strain against Indo-chic's orientalist appropriations and against the fictions of authenticity that are at work in many diasporic critiques of orientalism:

the bindi authorizes a feminist racial fantasy of countersurveillance in a period of anti–South Asian immigrant violence and Indo-chic fashionability; it is a style commodity that adorns the body of the South Asian female porn artist; and it is an icon of eroticized interactivity across a digital user interface that ultimately refuses access to the very orientalist fantasy of South Asian femininity that it promises. If these bindi artworks expose the fictions of authentic embodiment and even forward culturally inappropriable embodiments, as in Murthy's *Bindigirl*, then what kinds of embodiments emerge when South Asian fashions *are* linked to the production of authenticity? How do diasporic feminist visual media represent practices of South Asian dress and adornment through the lens of authenticity rather than parody, of verisimilitude rather than irony?

By way of conclusion and by way of introducing some of the relationships between gendered embodiment and sartoriality that I take up in chapter 5, I briefly consider in this final section how the feminine rituals associated with bridal adornment and the spectacle of the South Asian wedding in Khurana's "wedding aesthetic" make visible the embodied affects of bridal adornment. If cultural authenticity is consolidated through the heteronormative femininity of the South Asian woman, then the South Asian bride is in some ways the quintessential embodiment of that femininity. The bridal body is, after all, a body on which traditional rituals of feminine adornment that have come before it are reproduced in the name of consolidating and reproducing authentic culture. Across the multimedia artworks that make up Khurana's "wedding aesthetic," Khurana explores the bride's various roles in the South Asian wedding ceremony and, in particular, the rituals of fashion and beauty involved in the production of the bridal body. Though these rituals of adornment vary widely across regional and religious affiliations, the bride's performance of these rituals is perhaps one of the most visible, common, and yet spectacular ways in which South Asian cultural identity is consolidated in diaspora.

Khurana's wedding aesthetic emerged and continues to emerge from her ruminations on her own failed first marriage in 1998, which she began to consider in relation to the wedding ceremony that inaugurated it. While researching performance artists for her art degree, Khurana realized that her multiday Hindu-Punjabi "wedding was the biggest performance of [her] life" (Khurana, interview), and she began to use footage from her wedding video as source material for much of her visual art. Of particular interest to Khurana is the way that the figure of the South Asian bride allows the diasporic community of spectators who are in attendance at the wedding to "look at how adorned [the bride is] and then assess her value" (Khurana, interview). Khurana's characterization of the wedding ritual as a performance suggests first that the bride participates in the creation of aesthetic and social value for a diasporic community of onlookers who are eager to affirm her performance of authenticity. It also suggests that the feminine rituals of bridal adornment are part of creating that value and generating aesthetic pleasure.

Khurana's wedding aesthetic also draws from the exportability of the South Asian bride's aesthetic value beyond the boundaries of diasporic community, namely, the place of fascination that she occupies in the Western sartorial imagination. This fascination is due in large part not only to the popularity of Indian-inspired fashions in the global fashion industry, which the bridal body inspires, but also to the global popularity of Bollywood film, in which the wedding scene is an endlessly reproducible site of romance, allure, fashion, style, and glamour. Thus, the South Asian bride becomes "the lens, the site for projection of desire, a symbol of objectification" "in a contemporary, urban, globalized world" (Rizvi). It is within the context of the South Asian wedding ceremony that many of the fashions that inspire the style trend of Indo-chic—bindis, saris, and mehndi—take on their most ornamental and spectacular form. In consolidating authentic Indianness for diasporic communities, the fashioning and adornment of the South Asian bride can thus also double as the "projection" of an orientalist "desire" for commodified difference. This doubling occurred for Khurana when she was asked by a friend to contribute photographs of her wedding for a US bridal magazine called *Bridal Guide*, which provides would-be brides with creative inspiration for and practical advice on how to plan their weddings. Lacking anything "so colorful" as an "Indian wedding" (Khurana, interview), the magazine was eager to publish Khurana's wedding photographs, which showcased the spectacle of an "ethnic" wedding that featured in "authentic" form the saris, mehndi, and bindis as well as other Indian fabrics and designs that fashion-conscious readers would recognize as the raw material for Indo-chic or that they would misrecognize as Indo-chic commodities themselves. Because of *Bridal Guide*'s focus on wedding planning, the photographs of Khurana's wedding presumably offered the magazine's readers not only aesthetic pleasure in the viewing of these photographs but also aesthetic inspiration, an exotic visual template from which they could borrow in designing their own wedding ceremonies.

Because the bride is most often the focus of the wedding ceremony's production of aesthetic pleasure, "desire," and "objectification,"

Khurana's feminist examination of the feminine rituals of bridal adornment often involves dissociating the bride from the spectacle of the wedding, an aesthetic very much in line with the parodic and playful quality of her other artworks, like *Dothead*. In *Malabar Bride* (2005), for example, a collage series that meditates on the figure of the South Asian bride, images of bridal adornment—mehndi-adorned hands and bejeweled hands and face—taken from Khurana's wedding photographs are reproduced in the form of highly animated, black-and-white line drawings. Reduced to schematic lines and desaturated of color, such images lack the "splendor and ornamentation" normally ascribed to the figure of the bride (Khurana, interview). Instead, it is the interior walls and ceilings that make up the background of these paintings that bear the imprint of ornamentation and splendor. Whereas for readers of the bridal magazine *Bridal Guide* Khurana's wedding generates an aesthetic pleasure rooted in an orientalist desire for displays of authentic Indianness through the consumption of bridal fashion, *Malabar Bride* explicitly refuses such a desire. Viewers are forced to look not to the bride but to the background for the aesthetic pleasures of consuming Indianness.

In other visual media, though, Khurana trains her focus squarely on the subjectivity of the bride as she undergoes the rituals of bridal adornment. These artworks—*Bridal Guide* (2001), a shot and reshot four-minute video of Khurana's wedding in 1998, and *Raveling* (2008), a seven-minute video that was shown as part of the installation series *Ten Years Later* (2008) and that features prewedding love letters suspended in bird cages—stand out among the artworks in Khurana's wedding aesthetic for the way that they aspire not to aesthetic experimentation but to verisimilitude. These artworks visualize what I call the *flat affects* of bridal adornment—boredom, exhaustion, and endurance—affects that are connected to the protracted sense of time that the bride feels as she is being decorated for the wedding ceremony.

My use of the term *flat affects* expands on what the Asian American visual-culture scholar Sarita See has described as the "flat aesthetic" of Khurana's larger body of work. This is an aesthetic defined not only by the inclusion of "flattened objects" (such as bindis) as prominent subjects of her artworks but also as a "technique of superimposition [that] undoes rather than achieves a layered effect" and that "lacks depth and erases perspective," such as the clean lines and desaturated images of the bride in *Malabar Bride* (See, "How"). Yet whereas See is concerned with the visual *effect* of flatness that inheres in flattened objects, such as "pancakes, ham slices, and platters of sandwiches" (See, "How") that are peppered across Khurana's various collages, I am interested in the moments in Khurana's wedding aesthetic that visualize the flat *affects* of bridal adornment. By "flat affects," I mean the muted and even discomfited affects of the bridal self-in-process, rather than the exuberant and euphoric sensations that accompany the perception of the fully adorned bridal body (what in reality-television parlance would be called the moment of "the reveal"). If, as Khurana claims, the South Asian bride is complicit in the creation of her own aesthetic value, then *Bridal Guide* and *Raveling* visualize boredom, exhaustion, and endurance as the embodied affects of producing that value.

Bridal Guide takes its name, of course, from the magazine that requested photographs of Khurana's wedding for its feature on South Asian weddings. In addition to featuring close-up shots of various Hindu rituals that are performed during the wedding ceremony, *Bridal Guide* features close-up shots of Khurana undergoing elaborate bodily rituals in preparation for her wedding. These include the *haldi* ceremony, in which female relatives and friends of the bride rub a paste made of turmeric on her limbs and face in order to create a more luminous complexion, and the mehndi ceremony, in which Khurana's arms, feet, and legs are adorned in elaborate designs with henna, a dark-red, plant-based paste (see fig. 4.7).

As Khurana is being decorated, *Bridal Guide* cuts back and forth to Khurana's facial expressions. She appears variously bored, tired, and withdrawn. The superimposed text that appears periodically throughout the video informs us that Khurana had to remain immobile for five hours the day before her wedding as she endured the tedious process of the haldi, mehndi, and other bridal rituals. Interspersed with shots of haldi and mehndi are shots of Khurana's stationary body and withdrawn face and of friends and relatives dancing around her. The text reads, "as people danced, sang, drank, ate and gossiped I grew more and more aware of my lack of mobility." At the appearance of the word "mobility," *Bridal Guide* cuts to Khurana's exhausted eyes gazing into the camera (see fig. 4.8).

Such shots of bodily stillness and tedium sharply contrast not only with the frenetic movement of dancing and singing bodies surrounding Khurana but also with other shots in *Bridal Guide* in which Khurana is featured in full bridal attire at her wedding, smiling, waving, and at one point even flashing a thumbs-up to the videographer. When juxtaposed with the shots of Khurana's stillness and immobility, the animatedness of Khurana's fully adorned bridal self makes visible how the process of producing the bride's aesthetic value demands of the bride protracted periods of endurance and immobility. These highly gendered bodily

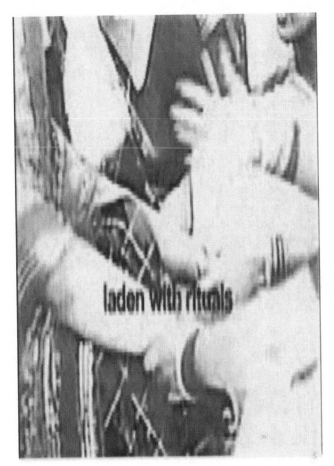

FIGURE 4.7. *Haldi*, or turmeric paste, is applied to Khurana's skin in preparation for her wedding day. Swati Khurana, *Bridal Guide*, 2001.

sensations operate as social, psychic, and somatic forms of bodily discipline. By directing focus away from the spectacle of the South Asian wedding and toward the prewedding adornment of the bride, *Bridal Guide* reveals how the South Asian wedding as a performance of diasporic authenticity demands of its star performer, the South Asian bride, the persistent management of her affect.

Raveling, which was shown as part of the mixed-media installation "Ten Years Later," requires the viewer, like the bride in *Bridal Guide*, to experience the protracted sense of time that inheres in bridal adornment

FIGURE 4.8. Khurana lacks mobility as she endures the rituals of bridal adornment. Swati Khurana, *Bridal Guide*, 2001.

rituals. *Raveling* is straightforward in its aesthetic: it is a seven-minute sped-up video of mehndi being applied on two hands and then, through a sped-up reversal of the application, being erased. Though *Raveling* truncates a process that normally takes hours to just three and half minutes, it still asks viewers to endure, like the bride herself, the process of mehndi paste being painstakingly applied to the hand. But even the expedited version of the application turns out to be a deeply dissatisfying spectacle, for the video does not conclude with the end product of this ritual, the mehndi-adorned hand. Instead of "watching in anticipation for the completion of the [mehndi] pattern" (Rizvi) or for the depth of color that will emerge once the mehndi has fully set into the skin, we watch as the mehndi pattern unravels. The process of unraveling thus empties out the aesthetic value of this ritual application. We are left to gaze not on the adorned hand of the bride but only on the blank, unadorned hand of a bride-to-be.

Bridal Guide visualizes and *Raveling* produces the flat affects—endurance, exhaustion, and the sensation of protracted time—that constitute the feminized embodiments of bridal authenticity. Whereas the artworks in Khurana's wedding aesthetic foreground the flat affects of the bridal body, in chapter 5 I examine how performed engagements with a quintessential garment of South Asian feminine fashion—the sari—produce queer forms of diasporic feminine embodiment, feminist-of-color affects, and cross-racial affiliations between South Asian and black African populations. These embodiments and affiliations challenge definitions of diasporic belonging that are rooted in the reproduction of heteronormative femininity and in a politically unified diasporic cultural identity.

5 / Histories of the Cloth and Sartorial Sentiment in Shailja Patel's *Migritude*

In 2006, the queer, feminist, spoken-word performance artist Shailja Patel launched her one-woman show *Migritude* in Oakland, California, with the tagline "come for the saris, stay for the politics, come for the mehndi (henna) and stay for the migritude." This tagline, which was posted on her blog leading up to *Migritude*'s debut, spoke to the sheer pervasiveness of Indo-chic style commodities within global fashion markets at this time.[1] While fashion magazines and designers displayed Indo-chic on white, Western women in the 1990s, by the early years of the new millennium South Asian Bollywood actresses, models, and television personalities were wearing Indo-chic designs created by South Asian and South Asian American fashion designers such as Ritu Kumar, Ritu Beri, Abu Sandeep, Prabal Gurung, Naeem Khan, and Rachel Roy. The blog's tongue-in-cheek tone capitalizes on the familiarity of Patel's audience with the global production and consumption of Indo-chic. The tagline was accompanied by an enlarged photograph of *ambi* (commonly known in the Western world as "paisley") rendered in mehndi with "MIGRITUDE" scrolled inside its curve. Ambi, a classic tear-drop-shaped pattern, has long been a popular sari design and is now a highly recognizable pattern on Indo-chic style commodities such as brocade sari borders and henna design.

For those, including myself, who were drawn to the performance in part by the prospect of seeing a display of Indo-chic orientalia, *Migritude* in some ways did not disappoint. Throughout the performance, a dozen or so sheer, ambi-adorned saris were displayed on low-sitting trapeze

FIGURE 5.1. Patel's suitcase of saris. Photograph courtesy of
Shailja Patel, 2006.

wires, and a large lit-up ambi pattern was projected onto the screen
behind Patel in the opening scene of the performance. Displayed in part
to generate aesthetic pleasure, saris and ambi are pitched as style commodities that, to borrow from *Migritude*'s bait-and-switch tagline, entice
viewers to "come" to the performance in order to get them to "stay" for
the "migritude," or the history and politics of diasporic migration.

Migritude tells the story of "three cross-continental" South Asian migrations—the early-twentieth-century colonial migration of Indians to East
Africa, the mass expulsion and political and economic disenfranchisement

of East African Indians and their subsequent migrations to the global North in the 1970s, and Patel's own journey from Kenya to Britain to the United States in the 1990s. "Migritude," which is Patel's neologism for "migrants with attitude," is a term that, as Patel claims, reclaims the "dignity of outsider status" for "South to North migrants" and eschews the migrant compulsion to assimilate ("Migritude"). "Migritude" is also a riff on the literary-political concept of Negritude, which signaled the birth of an anticolonialist, revolutionary black internationalism in the 1930s.[2] Activating the oppositional consciousness of Negritude and of a nonas-similationist migrant identity, *Migritude* is unabashedly political theater.[3] Like the concept it expresses, *Migritude* is self-consciously hybrid in form, consisting of spoken-word poetry, video and slide projection, and chore-ography that blends elements of bharatanatyam (a classical South Indian dance style), modern dance, and yoga.[4] In addition to touring in various venues from theaters to prisons across North America, Europe, and East Africa, Patel performed *Migritude* at the 2007 World Social Forum in Nai-robi, Kenya, which earned her a standing ovation. Since its Bay Area pre-miere, *Migritude* has garnered international acclaim for its ability to weave together personal history with histories of colonialism, imperialism, and global capitalism. A narrative version of the performance was published in 2010.

As a Kenyan Asian woman who has no direct personal or familial ties to South Asia, Patel stands out from the other South Asian subjects whom I discussed in the first four chapters of *Fashioning Diaspora*, who hail from or whose parents hail from the subcontinent. At the same time, Patel's performance of *Migritude* in racially conscious and politically progressive US venues such as La Peña and at South Asian American arts activist venues such as the Los Angeles–based Artwallah[5] and her own political identification as a woman of color in the United States demand situating Patel's story of migration—from colonial India to Kenya and postcolonial Kenya to England and England to the United States—within a South Asian American diasporic cultural imaginary.

Even as *Migritude*'s performance tagline and display of saris and mehndi self-consciously traffics in the orientalist idiom of Indo-chic, Patel's playful delineation between "saris" (orientalist spectacle) and "politics" (histories of empire, expulsion, and migration) also entreats the viewer to consider, inversely, the possible *connections* of saris to poli-tics in the performance. Patel has described *Migritude* as an exploration of the complex intertwining of the personal and the political, of clothing and migration: "Part of what 'Migritude' brings out is what it means to be a woman in an empire, what happens to mothers and daughters, and then my own journey, how I came into my own body, to my relationship to femininity, to saris" (Harmanci; see also Monegato). Formally trained as a political economist and an accountant, Patel regularly incorporates a critique of political economy and the global restructuring of capital into her performances and poems about everyday life in postcolonial nation-states, and *Migritude* is certainly no exception to this larger body of work.[6]

Yet while popular and scholarly reviews of *Migritude* cited Patel's economist background, few, if any, explored the possible connections in the performance between saris, femininity, and the histories of empire that Patel claims are at the heart of her performance. Some reviewers of both the performance and the published prose poem did observe that the saris were integral to the "personal" narrative of Patel's relationship to her mother. But these reviews then bracketed off this narrative from the story of empire and transnational migration that they saw as carrying the "real" political weight of the performance (see, e.g., Helgesson). Others described Patel's saris as the "connective tissue" of *Migritude* (Harmanci), as objects that are "much more than props" ("Shailja Patel") in the performance of "the personal, historical, and global historical stories" of empire (Harmanci). Yet the question of exactly *how* saris function as more than eye-catching stage props or as metaphors that bind together the narratives of empire, migration, and generationality, remains largely unexamined among both popular and scholarly reviewers.[7] Patel's invocation of saris as style commodities in the tagline to *Migritude* and her consistent and varied use of them throughout the performance impels an inquiry into the relationship between saris, femininity, and the personal and political histories of expulsion and the migrations that they engender. In this chapter, I examine precisely these connections between saris as feminine garments/material objects and the cultural politics of diasporic performance, arguing for the multiple and overlapping ways that saris animate *Migritude*'s political register.

Patel's tagline to *Migritude* invokes saris and the ambi designs and borders that decorate saris as fashions that circulate within the racial politics of Indo-chic, and Patel offers her audience a critique of the material production and consumption of these objects and designs. Those who are familiar with Patel's economist training will certainly recognize her feminist materialist approach to fashion within such critiques. Yet, as in my examination of Swati Khurana's and Prema Murthy's bindi art in chapter 4, I locate Patel's feminist materialism as also extending beyond a critique of fashion's labor economies and into an engagement with the materiality of fashion. This is a materialism more closely aligned with Louis Althusser's understanding of materiality as an embodied practice (e.g., the practice of prayer as the material form of religion) than with Karl Marx's critique of the material production of commodities. I thus attend to the forms of embodiment and affective attachments that saris make possible—what, in short, saris *do*. Patel's varied narrativization and instrumentalization of saris dislodges the sari from a set of established social scripts about the consolidation of Indian cultural identity through the performance of heteronormative femininity and from the heteroreproductive sentiments of generational love and attachment that structure that identity.

As a garment that is displayed, worn, touched, held, folded, unfolded, and so on, the sari operates as an assemblage, imbued with both representational and affective capacities that are inassimilable to a diasporic identity politics that relies on India as a unifying homeland. The first part of this chapter examines Patel's use of the sari in representing South Asian and black African women as historical subjects of colonial and postcolonial violence; the second part examines her use of the sari in representing mother-daughter generational bonds. Though I prioritize a discussion of saris as material technologies of cross-racial representation in the first part and as technologies of generational affect in the second, these discussions are intimately connected. The nonidentitarian forms of representation that I trace in the first part of the chapter enable the representation of diasporic feminist affects that I map in the second. Specifically, I argue that Patel's use of saris in representing histories of antibrown- and antiblack-female violence allows her to calibrate her relationship to her saris in terms of both generational nostalgia and feminist rage and to consider both as politically enabling diasporic affects. I thus keep in productive tension, as I have done in previous chapters, the relationship of representation to affect.

The performance studies scholar Diana Taylor's distinction between the archive and the repertoire provides a useful framework through which to examine the appearance of and references to saris in *Migritude*, as well as Patel's performed engagements with them. The archive, according to Taylor, is a collection of "supposedly enduring materials" that sustains memory "across distance, over time and space" (19). Even though materials can be subtracted and added to the archive and even though the materials housed in it can be reevaluated for new meanings, the archive nonetheless "sustains power" by separating the process of selecting and classifying objects for inclusion in it from the knowledge that the archive produces (19). The repertoire, by contrast, is a nonarchival system of transmitting social knowledge that allows for individual agency in that act of transmission. The repertoire designates "embodied and performed acts [that] generate, record, and transmit knowledge" through "gestures, orality, movement, dance, and singing" that are not reducible to written language (20). Throughout *Migritude*, archive and repertoire work in tandem. Saris are an archive of clothing passed down from mother to daughter and housed in a beat-up red suitcase; they are also a repertoire of "scriptive things"[8] through which Patel unleashes subjugated histories, embodiments, and affects of diasporic belonging.

The saris that Patel's audience sees throughout the performance are part of an intimate archive of "family treasures"—a wedding trousseau that Patel's mother gives to her daughter after giving up on the expectation that Patel will ever marry. Within South Asia, the wedding trousseau is a collection of saris (and sometimes jewelry), usually acquired over multiple generations of women and passed down from mother to daughter at the time of marriage. The sari trousseau is thus what the cultural anthropologist Lucy Norris calls a "wardrobe in waiting" that is eventually housed in the daughter's marital bedroom (64). In the *diasporic* context, the sari trousseau connects female generations across time and space through marriage and childbearing and thus can be an especially potent archive through which to preserve and assert a culturally coherent Indian identity. Yet if, as Robin Bernstein reminds us, "agency emerges through constant engagement with the stuff of our lives," then Patel's saris can also become "evocative primary substance[s]" that exceed their socially established scripts as feminine garments that reproduce the coherence of identity (12).

If, as Patel claims, "migritude" examines empire and migration as distinctly gendered experiences, then how do saris produce an embodied experience of empire and migration? How are saris part of the larger repertoire of orality, gesture, and tone that constitute these embodiments? How, to use Patel's personified and revised Marxian rendering at one point in the performance, do "saris speak"? Whereas Marx discredits the economist who imposes use value on objects that otherwise speak to each other only in terms of exchange value,[9] implicit within Patel's claim that "saris speak" is the notion that it is politically and ethically imperative for the economist—or, in this case, the performance artist—to determine the uses to which commodities are put. Patel here invokes a definition of materiality that must account not only for the sari's various histories of material production as a textile and garment but also for the intimate relationships between the sari-as-garment and the embodiments that it produces. I show that Patel's repertoire of sari wearing, sari displaying, and sari using throughout *Migritude* "speak" back to a coherent Indian cultural identity through the performance of proximate forms of anti-brown and antiblack violence, queer femininity, and diasporic feminist rage. Just as Patel moves back and forth between sari archive and sari repertoire within the performance, my own method of examining the appearance/role of saris in this chapter moves between the archive and the repertoire. In showing how saris animate the nonidentitarian, non-assimilationist diasporic political register of "migritude," I approach the publication of *Migritude* as a prose poem as an archival object, my live viewing of the performance at La Peña in 2006 as a repertoire, and the recorded performance of *Migritude* as an archive of the repertoire.

"Come for the Saris, Stay for the Politics"

As the lights come up on the opening scene of *Migritude*, Patel stands dressed in a hoodie and sweatpants with a huge, lit-up ambi pattern projected onto the screen behind her. Flashing across the screen are images of ambi—of various sizes, shapes, and designs—that appear on an array of sari borders, as well as on the hands, arms, feet, and backs of women. Two large ambi-patterned pieces of fabric flank Patel. Situating her body within the visual economy of Indian-inspired designs and style commodities, Patel begins to narrate the transnational histories of ambi and muslin, a soft, fine, handwoven fabric from which saris are traditionally made. We learn that ambi and muslin have roots in "Babylon," or present-day Iraq, the South Indian city of Masulipatnam, and Dhaka, Bengal. Through the forces of "colonial capitalism," ambi and muslin travel to the North Indian region of Kashmir, becoming the pattern and textile for handwoven shawls. The shawls are taken "by bandits, also known as merchants of the British East India Company," to Scotland, where "weavers of paisley learned how to churn out imitation ambi on imitation Kashmiri shawls," "until Kashmiri became cashmere, musoleen became muslin, ambi became paisley, and even later in history chai became a beverage invented in California."[10] Patel's wry and sardonic rendering of the prehistory of Indo-chic serves as a structural analysis of the ambi and saris that surround her. Such an analysis remains otherwise obscured within the historical emergence of Indo-chic as global fashion, in which these designs and garments occupy only the status of ahistorical spectacle for which Patel's audience is urged to "come."

Patel's references to Indian colonial subjects who are forced to buy ambi-patterned British cloth at an "80% duty" and to the chopped-off fingers and thumbs of Indian weavers who are forbidden to produce homespun cloth draw on the anticolonial sartorial discourse of swadeshi, which I discussed in chapter 3 (S. Patel 5). Patel's transnational history of the sari and ambi as South Asian fashions stolen by "bandits—known also as 'merchants'" (6)—resonates with the anticolonialist girl Neela's political protest of British-made fashions (see chapter 3). But whereas *Neela* ultimately endorses a diasporic (consumer) nationalism as the basis of an anticolonial girl political consciousness, Patel's performed engagements with the most quintessentially Indian of garments—the sari—reveals the racialized, gendered, and sexualized limitations of diasporic nationalism as the basis of an anti-imperialist feminist consciousness. The sari repertoire in *Migritude* consistently marks the culturally and politically tenuous status of the ethnically Indian female subject within a black-majority postcolonial nation and within the British imperial metropole. The sari repertoire is also a decolonizing—rather than merely anticolonial—aesthetic practice. By "a decolonizing aesthetic," I mean not only a performance practice that performs "back" to empire but "one that ironically comes most alive when identity is under erasure" (See, *Decolonized* xxvi).[11] Rather than isolating Indian women as exceptionally aggrieved political subjects within empire and postcolonial states, Patel holds Indian identity under erasure by repurposing her saris to represent violence against both Asian and black African women under empire. I thus understand Patel's decolonizing aesthetic as working against the "divide and conquer" racial logic of empire and as recognizing overlapping and intersecting histories of imperial and postcolonial state governance and political repression.

Though Patel does not return to the prehistory of Indo-chic and the anticolonial politics of swadeshi in her performance, the global story that she tells of the sari's multiple origins and travels—from Iraq to precolonial South Asia to colonial South Asia to imperial metropole and back to South Asia—sets the stage for their use in representing subjugated histories of violence against black African and Asian African women. That is, if *Migritude* first accounts for the origins of the sari pattern as rooted in multiple histories of violence, then it next accounts for the ways that the sari can be used to represent multiple histories of violence. It is worth noting here the way that the sari's material form lends itself to Patel's varied use of this garment. The sari is a single horizontal piece of cloth, six yards in length, and is therefore a one-size-fits-all garment, a feature that allows it to be worn by and exchanged between women indefinitely or until it falls apart or goes out of style. It is also an endlessly transformable material object. The sari has been and continues to be adapted for a multitude of other uses besides covering a woman's body, such as cleaning surfaces, swaddling babies, and absorbing the blood of a woman's menstrual cycle, to name only a few. Saris differ among women on the basis of preferences in and regional variations in color, pattern, texture, material, and style of draping, even as the overall structure of the garment remains the same.[12] The inherent flexibility of the sari's material form thus lends it to nonessentializing and nonidentitarian uses and adaptations.

The sari scripts a destabilizing performance of Indian identity when, for example, Patel wears it to narrate her own experience of anti-Asian racism while growing up in postindependence Kenya. In a section of the performance called "Idi Amin," the name of the military dictator who expelled Asians from Uganda—the country that neighbors Patel's homeland of Kenya, in 1972—Patel pulls a sari out of her suitcase and begins to tie it around her body. The slow, silent, and methodical nature of this performance—unfurling the sari, wrapping the end piece around her waist, pleating it, tucking it into her waistband, and then draping the *pallu* (loose end of the sari) in front of her body—to some extent indulges the part of Patel's tagline in which she urges her prospective audience to "come for the saris." Patel's draping of the sari demystifies the process of sari wearing for those in the audience who might be curious about this everyday practice of Indian feminine embodiment. In one sense, then, Patel's sari wearing could satisfy an orientalist desire, particularly among Patel's non–South Asian audience members, to "learn" how an Indian woman wears a sari. Yet Patel's tying of the sari also exceeds a strictly orientalist mode of consumption within the larger repertoire of spoken-word performance, which recalls Patel's memories of the mass expulsion of Asians from East Africa. Amin's regime sought to dismantle a local economy dominated by Asians and to concentrate economic power back into the hands of black Africans. Following Amin's expulsion of Ugandan Asians in 1972, anti-Asian black nationalism began to rise in Kenya after a 1982 military coup that threatened to take over the independent nation.

As Patel ties her sari, she rehearses a Gujarati proverb that has been passed down to her from her parents: "The night is short and our garments change, meaning 'don't put down roots, don't get too comfortable.'" She then begins to recount her memories of "the last trains coming out of

Uganda" that were "laden with traumatized Asians stripped of all that they possessed / Asian businesses wrecked and looted / Asian women / raped." Patel's draping of the sari in the very moment that she recounts her first memories of expulsion marks Indianness not as a commodifiable cultural identity but as an undesirably foreign and sexually violable one within postcolonial Kenya. Patel's performance of sari wearing here recalls the visual artist Swati Khurana's meditation on the cultural surveillance of the bindi in South Asian immigrant communities during the 1980s and 1990s, which I discussed in chapter 4. Like the wearing of the bindi, the act of tying the sari marks Indian women's bodies as targets of anti–South Asian violence and surveillance.

Yet whereas the bindi stands as a metonymy for South Asian racialization and whereas its very appearance on the foreheads of South Asian women "attracts" male-directed violence, it is not the sari itself that is the target of (state) surveillance in postcolonial Kenya. More than simply marking the racial identity of its wearer, the sari is the target of surveillance because of what it is capable of *doing*. By virtue of the folds, drapes, and tucks that constitute the act of wearing the sari, the sari possesses the capacity to conceal objects of wealth and status that differentiate Kenyan Asians from black Kenyans. Saris are quite literally portable containers of wealth in the form of jewelry, passports, and money that Asians carried with them during the expulsion, with these items often being stored in the folds of women's saris. As Patel wraps her sari, she recalls her mother telling her that in India "they didn't have banks, so they invested in jewelry": "The women of the family carried their savings . . . in their valuable saris. It was safest, you see, Shailja, and it kept them safe. They were respected because they wore and guarded the family's wealth."

For Kenyan Asians, the practice of carrying wealth in women's saris marks Asians' class privilege in relation to indigenous black Africans. The early-twentieth-century migration of Gujarati Indians to Kenya, of which Patel's family was a part, constituted a brown minority middle class of professionals, merchants, educators, and artisans. The largely commercial interests of this class of migrants buttressed British imperial interests in a way that contributed to the economic subordination of local African populations; Amin and other black Africans often cited Asians' economic power to justify their expulsion.[13] Yet the practice of hiding money and objects of economic value in women's saris during the expulsion is revealed to be a failed one within Patel's performance. Patel recalls that Kenyan military officers often searched Indian women's saris, taking "even the wedding rings, the earrings, off the women. They searched their hair" (11). The practice of carrying wealth in women's saris keeps neither the women nor their wealth "safe." Rather, such sartorial practices betray how class privilege offers Indians a false sense of economic security during periods of state-sponsored racism and surveillance.

Thus, even as the act of wearing the sari is intended to mark Patel's racial difference vis-à-vis class stratification from her fellow black Africans, the appearance of the sari does not appeal to an essentialized Indian identity. Patel instead uses the sari in subsequent segments of the performance in remarkably nonidentitarian ways. I read such nonidentitarian performances as acts of material catachresis, or an intentional misapplication of the sari's material form. Like the visual artist Prema Murthy's deliberate visual confusion of the bindi with a digitally interactive dot across the user interface of her fake porn site (see chapter 4), Patel's catachrestic use of saris challenges culturally authentic sartorial codes of Indianness. If Murthy's experimentation with the bindi's "dotness" challenges an appeal to cultural restoration in the face of the bindi's orientalist commodification, then Patel's intentional misapplication of the sari form challenges a politics of cultural restoration in the face of Indian cultural abjection within the Kenyan nation.

Saris are part of a repertoire of gendered violence that includes oral histories and testimonies of black African women that have been withheld from the official archive of postcolonial nation making. These scenes of violence include the anticolonial Mau Mau uprising, a Kenyan peasant insurgency against British colonial rule that took place from 1952 to 1960; and the genocide of the Massai tribe during British military training in Kenya from 1965 to 2001. The Mau Mau uprising, though ultimately quelled by the British, was nonetheless instrumental in forcing an end to colonial rule. In 2009, five veterans of the Mau Mau revolt launched a bid in London to win compensation from the British government over the claims that they were tortured and unlawfully imprisoned during the uprising. The British government has argued that their claim is invalid because of the amount of time that has passed since the alleged abuses took place and that any liability for these acts of torture and imprisonment rested with Kenyan authorities, and not British ones, after independence in 1963.[14]

In narrating the colonial state's violent suppression of guerrilla peasant struggles to reclaim land from the British from 1952 to 1961, Patel ties her sari in multiple loops around her neck in the form of a noose. She is then pulled by her assistant, choreographer, and dance partner, Parijat Desai, across the stage as a way of simulating the lynching of Kikuyu tribal women who participated in the revolt. While rehearsing the oral testimonies of Kikuyu women who were held in British concentration camps and whose children died because of social neglect and improper nutrition while being held there, Patel methodically ties a sari into six intermittent knots. She then gathers the knotted sari into a single bundle and draws it to her chest, as she rehearses the testimony of a survivor: "[The dead babies] would be tied in bundles of six babies. Each of us would be ordered to take a bundle and bury it with the rest of the bodies in the graves" (18). Rather than simply representing the racially and politically liminal status of South Asians within a black-majority Kenyan nation, the bundling of saris here performs the various forms of subaltern violence that are part of an untold story of black political struggle.

Similarly, Patel uses her saris in recounting the mass raping of Massai tribeswomen during British military training in Kenya from 1965— just two years after Kenya gained independence from Britain—to 2001. The greatest number of these rapes occurred in the late 1980s and early 1990s, when Patel migrated to Britain with her sister to enroll in university. The segment, titled "The Sky Has Not Changed Color," opens with Patel lying on her back clutching a train of bright-red saris that appear as though they are spilling blood from between her legs. Scooting herself backward, the knotted red saris lengthen like a trail of blood as she narrates the individual testimonies of gang-raped women who gave birth to stillborn babies or who are deemed pariahs because of their status as "unwed mothers" in their communities. Rather than invoking the alienated body of the Indian woman within the Kenyan nation, Patel's saris here represent the black subaltern female body that is subjected to British neocolonialist sexual violence. At the conclusion of the segment, Patel lifts the train of saris off the floor and begins to wrap them tightly in loops over her forearm in the gesture of a stranglehold, as she fantasizes about physically harming British soldiers who perpetrated these rape crimes but who remain absolved of them. Saris here mark a shift in the representation of violence. They shift our attention from acts of violence that remain beyond representation and therefore beyond conventional modes of historical narration to feminist fantasies about acts of retributive violence.

Patel's catachrestic use of saris in performing these scenes of violence addresses an enduring ethical question about the reproduction of (racialized) violence in aesthetic cultural forms: how does one give expression to violence without risking the violence *of* representation? How does one represent violence without, as the black feminist scholar

Saidiya Hartman elaborates in her account of the endless visual and verbal recitations of the brutalized black body under slavery, reproducing
indifference to, overidentification with, or prurience toward the spectacularization of these scenes of terror and subjugation? Patel's response to
this question, I argue, is to archive an *unfamiliar* scene of black femicide
through a *defamiliarizing* repertoire of saris. Patel defamiliarizes the
sari as a garment of Indian womanhood by using it to narrate a history
of antiblack-female violence with which we are unfamiliar because its
oral testimonial form exceeds the archive of official history. As part of
Patel's decolonizing aesthetic practice, the South Asian woman's body
and her saris become the instruments—rather than the subjects—of representation, as saris remain nonmimetic in relation to the black African
woman's body.

It is useful to understand Patel's use of saris in representing these
scenes of violence as activating a diasporic feminist poetics of "speaking
nearby." The postcolonial feminist scholar and filmmaker Trinh Minh
Ha defines "speaking nearby" as a poetics of representation that counters
acts of speaking "for" or speaking "about." Concerns about speaking for
or about the racialized or colonized Other, rather than allowing her to
speak for herself, framed many postcolonial feminist scholars' debates
about the crisis of (subaltern) representation in the 1990s.[15] As Trinh
elaborates, speaking nearby is "not just a technique or a statement to
be made verbally"; rather, "the challenge is to materialize it . . . verbally,
musically, visually" (N. Chen 87). As an intimate material archive that
is consistently dislodged from the assertion of Indian cultural identity,
Patel's saris are part of a verbal (in the form of poetic language) and
visual repertoire of antiblack female violence. Rather than speaking
"for" or "about" intimate violence toward black female subjects, Patel's
nonidentitarian deployment of saris in *Migritude* performs a diasporic
feminist poetics of speaking nearby.

This nearbyness, I argue, also constitutes a politics of form within
Patel's performance. Throughout *Migritude*, Patel draws from her
archive of saris in alternating between performed histories of South
Asian expulsion/migration and performed histories of antiblack colonial, postcolonial, and neocolonial violence. For example, Patel draws
from the sari archive first to perform the racial traumas of expulsion in
1972 and then to archive the historically overlapping genocide of Massai women. Similarly, the sari animates state and cultural racism toward
British Asian women as historically "nearby" or proximate to this act
of state-sponsored black African femicide. This performance of distinct

but proximate histories that are themselves *proximal* within the diegesis of the performance forces Patel's audience to consider the way that state violence in the Kenyan homeland is historically synchronous with state violence against brown minority subjects in the imperial metropole.

If the appearance of Patel's saris in the performance can be viewed as materializing historically proximate violences against black and brown women, then how do we account for the sari repertoire when saris remain inert or withheld from view? Patel makes visible the saris' contained or withheld presence, for example, during her account of anti-Asian British cultural racism. At the beginning of the segment that marks Patel's migration to the United Kingdom and then to the United States from 1990 to 2004, Desai removes all of Patel's saris from the trapeze wires onstage, folds them, and carefully places them into the battered suitcase from which they were originally taken. Throughout the segment, the saris remain in the suitcase, which remains in the audience's plain view, spotlighted at stage right. The contained visibility of Patel's saris signals the acts of migrant accommodation—marked by the absence of saris—that she must perform in England. As a migrant subject facing racial violence and economic and cultural disenfranchisement in Kenya, Patel must migrate to the imperial metropole under the tenuous legal status of "Commonwealth subject." Patel is made increasingly aware of her newly acquired foreign status through such racial slurs as "dirty black bastard" and "fucking Paki bitch" (52) and by being forced to work the most poorly paying jobs.

The saris' absent presence in this part of the performance recalls and revises the haunting presence of the sari in the British Asian filmmaker Pratibha Parmar's short documentary film *Sari Red* (1988). Like Patel, Parmar was born in Kenya and immigrated to the United Kingdom, where she faced virulent state and cultural racism following the expulsion and economic disenfranchisement of East African Asians. Parmar's film details the racially motivated murder of the British Asian immigrant Kalbinder Kaur Hayre in 1985. Hayre was crushed against a brick wall by three white, male youth who drove their truck into Hayre after the youth yelled racist slurs at her and Hayre yelled back, inciting their rage. *Sari Red*, which Parmar describes as a "video poem," opens with the image of a red sari rippling in the breeze and then cuts to the image of a British flag in flames ("Pratibha"). The sari's highly visible presence in *Sari Red* haunts the film's meditations on anti-Asian British racism. Conversely, it is the contained visibility of saris in *Migritude* that haunts Patel's experience of this racism. By making visible the visual containment of saris, Patel alerts her audience to the potential violability of the brown woman in a sari, of an inassimilable migrant identity in the former seat of empire.

Saris, through both their presence and absence within the performance, script an exilic and abject South Asian subjectivity alongside synchronous histories of antiblack violence. As scriptive things, saris are also part of a repertoire of racialized affects that are generated from within these histories. Specifically, saris are harnessed to the production of diasporic feminist rage against such forms of suffering and violence. Before examining the role of saris in generating feminist rage, it is first necessary to elaborate on the place of rage within *Migritude*'s affective structure. Patel mentions the word "rage" only once in the performance, in the segment titled "The Making (Migrant Song)" that opens the second part of the performance. Yet because she claims that she "make[s] this work [*Migritude*] from rage," Patel invites her audience to register rage as an affective structure of the entire performance/prose poem.

As a political concept, "migritude" riffs on the racialized affect of revolutionary rage that structures the masculinist, pan-Africanist poetics and politics of Negritude, "migritude's" political cognate.[16] The "fact of blackness," as the Caribbean postcolonial writer Frantz Fanon describes it in his seminal work on colonial masculinity, *Black Skin, White Masks*, emerges from within the experience of black populations whose histories are tied to the transatlantic slave trade and their shared struggle within New World plantation systems (77). For Fanon, blackness is a state of "crushing objecthood," one that fills the black (male) subject "full of rage at being diminished" (109, 50). Fanon later goes on to describe Negritude in explicitly affective terms, as "a paroxysm of being and fury" (138). For Patel, "the political and cultural space" that Negritude opened up was "soil from which *Migritude* could germinate" (144). Drawing from Negritude's affective structure, rage constitutes *Migritude*'s aesthetic "tone," or its "organizing affect, its general disposition toward its audience and the world" (Ngai 23).[17]

But rage in *Migritude* also exceeds the political scope of Negritude's revolutionary rage, for Patel's account of black and brown *women's* suffering is part of a diasporic feminist aesthetic that exceeds the largely hetero-masculinist genealogy of Negritude's political imaginary. Moreover, rather than being generated from within a black Atlantic slave diaspora, migritude emerges from within the historically overlapping context of a *brown* Atlantic diaspora. The history of this diaspora is more clearly tied to colonized black Africans who are not, properly speaking, part of a slave diaspora. Furthermore, the relationship of Patel, as a South

Asian subject, to black nationalism is necessarily vexed due to her class and racial difference from most indigenous black Africans. As Kenyan nationalism is irrevocably bound to "the fact of blackness," Patel possesses a melancholic attachment to blackness in this patriotic form. As a child, Patel learns, "third-generation Kenyan Asian / will never / be Kenyan enough" and "all my patriotic fervor / will not / turn my skin / black" (11, 28). Mounting anti-Asian sentiment cannot accommodate Patel's desire as a child to identify as a citizen-patriot in postcolonial Kenya. Thus, although *Migritude* rehearses what Fanon's Negritude predecessor Aimé Césaire has called a "compass of suffering" (76), for Patel the basis of this suffering exceeds a common experience of blackness.

As a poetics of *feminist* rage, *Migritude*'s structure of feeling finds its intellectual genealogy more deeply rooted in US/third-world women-of-color feminism's engagement with women's rage. Its affective mode is one that aligns with the black, lesbian, feminist Audre Lorde's conceptualization of feminist rage.[18] Arguing for the need to embrace anger as part of antiracist feminist practice, Lorde in her famous 1981 essay "The Uses of Anger" defines anger as a "grief of distortions between peers whose object is change" (8). For Lorde, anger is a feeling of loss or alienation resulting from historical distortions around the production of difference. Feminist projects must confront, rather than elide, these historical productions in order to "alter those distortions" (9). Instead of invoking a model of "solidarity across difference" in which singularities of (racial) difference remain unaddressed, Lorde posits anger as a common ground for a feminist critique of the world through an exploration of difference.[19] Patel expands the political scope of Lorde's elaboration of anger from a predominantly black/white US context to the black/brown color line of Indian Ocean nations and diasporas. The wearing, bundling, knotting, tying, spilling, and yanking of Patel's saris activate Lorde's conceptualization of rage as they express the various scales of antiblack-female violence under empire, anti-Asian black nationalism and British racism, and neocolonial occupation. Patel thus remains attentive to the historical distortions around the production of black and brown minority difference without "immobilization or silence or guilt" (Lorde 8), feelings that function merely as other forms of racial objectification.[20]

The Sari Trousseau and Generating Generational Sentiment

If Patel's saris are part of a repertoire of feminist rage through their scripting of historically "nearby" or proximate forms of antibrown- and antiblack-female violence, then what is their role in mediating Patel's attachments to her mother, a generational narrative that is consistently interwoven among these histories in the performance?[21] How or to what extent does migritude's affective structure of rage inform these attachments? The full title of Patel's piece, *When Saris Speak (The Mother): Part I of Migritude, an Epic Journey in Four Movements*, underscores the central role of saris in the story of mother-daughter generational attachments.[22] Clothing, as Daniel Miller reminds us, is more than simply a representation or metaphor of social relations; clothing objectifies, and thus constitutes, those relations, particularly through the act of clothing exchange (introduction). In this section, I examine how saris objectify Patel's relationship to her mother in contradictory ways. On the one hand, Patel's acts of wearing the sari and Patel's mother's gifting of the sari trousseau are entrenched within a maternal pedagogy of compulsory hetero-femininity and an affective economy of heteronormative love and attachment from which Patel is alienated as a feminist lesbian subject. On the other hand, Patel recognizes in her mother's gift a maternal affirmation—and even a generational transmission—of diasporic feminist rage that falls outside these normative expressions of love and attachment.

As quintessential garments of Indian femininity, saris are part of a sartorial struggle between mother and daughter that takes place within the generational narrative strand of *Migritude*. The segment "Swore I'd Never Wear Clothes I Couldn't Run or Fight In" references Patel's teenage view of the sari as a garment that would "hobble" her legs and thus impede her ability to "run" and "fight" "if a man attacked" her (22, 21). For Patel, the sari is fundamentally at odds with her understanding of unfettered bodily mobility as a young woman developing a feminist consciousness of violence against women. In Patel's child memory, the sari itself is a weapon of gendered violence turned against its wearers: "As a child, I knew of women strangled in their saris. Women doused in paraffin and burned in their saris. Saris made you vulnerable. A walking target. Saris made you weak" (21). Though earlier in the performance such references to feminine vulnerability are linked to the violences of state expulsion, here they allude to the practice of femicide as a consequence for women whose families could not pay their dowries in India. (Dowry refers to gifts of money or property exchanged as part of marriage rites.) In Patel's child mind, the sari not only prevents women from being able to physically defend themselves against an unanticipated aggressor but is also a wearable instrument of death.

Yet whereas Patel links sari wearing with different forms of gendered vulnerability in Kenya and India, Patel's mother argues that the sari, as a sartorial practice of feminine beauty, will allow Patel to mitigate the threat of violence. Mimicking her mother's voice, Patel recalls her mother telling her, "looking pretty [in a sari] is the least you can do, Shailja, ... to make up for not being a boy; you are not safe as a girl." For Patel's mother, teaching her daughter to wear a sari is part of a moral obligation to feminine beauty that is the gendered path of least resistance as a politically scapegoated subject of the postcolonial nation. (In insisting that sari wearing can mitigate the threat of violence, Patel's mother here must suspend disbelief around the sari as a garment that, as I discussed earlier, offers Asians a false sense of economic security upon expulsion from East Africa.) Patel's mother's heterosexist logic stands in obverse relation to the gendered logic of beauty that Jasmine encounters in her migrations as an undocumented woman in the United States, which I discussed in chapter 1. Whereas for Jasmine the loss of physical beauty poses a more severe threat of racial injury than does sexual violence, for Patel's mother it is the sari's role in cultivating a sexually alluring Indian beauty that will help to mitigate the threat of that violence in the first place. As Patel begins to tie the sari around her, she mimics her mother's voice:

"Don't stride Shailja, your stride is so unfeminine, how can you ever walk in a sari if you walk like that?" [Patel strides across the stage pulling up on her sari to keep it from dragging]. The only thing I ever heard was you have to be careful in a sari because you're exposing [dramatic pause and whisper] *the body*. "Don't let the *pallu* slip under the breast, that's obscene. Don't let the petticoat show the panties, that's obscene. You have to learn to allure without being sexual, to be beautiful without being aware of it, to attract without meeting anyone's eyes, you must never act as if you own your body, because your body is draped and displayed for the edification of others. Watch the women in Bollywood movies, Shailja. Combine coy virginality with hip-swinging sex appeal." (21–22; see fig. 5.2)

In this scene, Patel humorously reveals sari wearing as a practice that requires the terse negotiation of revelation and concealment, of overt sexual display and sexual self-management, at which she fails quite disastrously.

Patel's gait, posture, and stance as she walks in a sari make intelligible the performativity of clothing. Clothing, like gender, is performative in that it actively constitutes the subject by inviting certain bodily

FIGURE 5.2. Patel struggles to walk in a sari. Shailja Patel, *Migritude*, 2006.

comportments as possible over others. Through repetition, these comportments become "socially realized conventions" imbued with ideological content (Keane 194).[23] Patel's awkward and exaggerated steps perform her inability to wear the sari with the proper combination of elegance, charm, sexual allure, and sexual modesty and thus her failure to successfully embody the sartorial codes that are part of her mother's pedagogy of feminine beauty. Patel's lifting of the sari's hem and her long strides recall the awkwardness of "sari walking" for the Indian girl and aspiring freedom fighter Neela in Chitra Divakaruni's young-adult novel by the same name. For the preadolescent Neela, the difficulty of walking in a sari is normalized within a developmental narrative of late-colonial womanhood. For Patel, by contrast, the practice of sari walking involves awkward and exaggerated movements that are at odds with an efficiency of movement that she understands as part of her burgeoning feminist consciousness.

Patel's walk in one sense performs what Ania Loomba has described as the modern Indian woman's perception of the sari's "long and saggy" quality. Loomba uses this phrase to describe how popular discourses around the sari in postliberalization India and the diaspora can, in certain contexts, connote Indian women's dullness, lack of success, obedience, and dated fashion sense and thus their complicity with unmodern, patriarchal sartorial codes.[24] Yet within the context of Patel's feminine failure, Patel's showcasing of the sari's "long and saggy" quality and her revelation of the performativity of clothing might also be understood as her queering of the sari, or her rejection of diasporic sartorial codes of heterosexual femininity. Patel's feminine failure, after all, redounds against her outing of herself as a lesbian about halfway through the performance. In a segment called "Dreaming in Gujarati," which references Patel's mother tongue, Patel's "shaved head" and "combat boots" are part of a militant feminist and lesbian identity that she develops during her university education in Britain. Her performance of British punk lesbian style constitutes an explicit rejection of her mother's sartorial pedagogy. Yet such a rejection does not, as we might expect, enable Patel's unfettered access to fashion as a form of liberal feminist and lesbian "self-expression." Rather, the shaved head and combat boots fail to protect her from ongoing forms of British cultural racism and alienate her from her own British Asian community, as she is "shamed" by the judgmental looks of Indian aunties that "singe [her] western head" (51).

Patel neither embraces the sari as a form of heterosexist feminine beauty, nor does she completely reject it in favor of a Western lesbian identity premised on a heroic refusal of "the long and saggy sari." Rather, her failure to perform requisite sexual allure and modesty in a sari produces a desire for an alternative archive of sari-wearing practices. These are practices that remain unintelligible within her mother's contemporary, middle-class pedagogy of sari wearing: "No one told me about women who went into battle—in their saris / Worked in the fields—in their saris / Why didn't anyone tell me about women who labored on construction sites in their saris?" (21). Patel here references Moghul-era Indian warrior-queens who rode horseback into battle and contemporary sari-wearing practices that facilitate rural and urban Indian women's field and construction work. Indeed, when worn with the topmost pleat tucked between the legs, the sari allows for a range of bodily mobility conducive to these forms of physical activity. In the specific case of field work, the *pallu*, or loose end of the sari, also functions as a kind of "third hand" in the gathering of harvested crops.[25]

These kinds of bodily comportments are unimaginable within Patel's mother's pedagogy of sari wearing, in which the sari is worn hanging loose around the legs and in which the pallu, worn "Gujarati style," is taken from behind, passed over the right shoulder, taken across the breasts, and tucked into the waist (instead of being thrown over the left shoulder to hang freely). The contrasting sari-wearing practices of working-class, rural, and peasant Indian women working on construction sites, going into battle, and doing field labor constitute for Patel a repressed archive of sari wearing that more clearly aligns with her burgeoning feminist consciousness. Certainly, these everyday acts of sari wearing are not necessarily coded as "feminist" on the subcontinent. Such a claim would involve imposing modern political identities and middle-class subjectivities onto premodern and rural and working-class practices. Yet they are practices that nonetheless allow Patel to reclaim saris as part of a feminist sensibility in the diasporic present.[26] Patel codes the sari as "feminist" through its attachment to everyday acts of female militancy and labor that remain beyond the gendered scope of its attachments to performances of vulnerable femininity. This repressed archive of sari wearing offers Patel a form of political relief from the obligation to Indian female beauty that inheres in her mother's pedagogy of the sari; it also offers her relief from her own liberal feminist stereotypes about the sari as essentially oppressive and excessively feminine. Riding, striding, and working in saris are for Patel modes of gendered embodiment that circulate outside a normatively feminine bodily economy of sexual modesty and allure.

Saris mediate Patel's fraught attachments to her mother not only through her performances of wearing them but also in the way that Patel repurposes them as objects of generational inheritance that fail to accommodate fully a heteronormative economy of love and attachment. If, as Miller observes, the exchange of clothing constitutes social relations, then Patel's sari trousseau is part of a gift economy, a necessarily unequal and coercive process of exchange that "nonetheless facilitates and often prioritizes efforts at social connection" (Tu 22). The gift economy of the sari trousseau is one in which the exchange between mother-as-giver and daughter-as-receiver carries with it the moral obligation of a heterosexual domestic life. In a series of letters that Patel's mother writes to Patel after she emigrates from Kenya to Britain and then to the United States from 1990 to 2004, Patel's mother periodically references the trousseau in relation to her desire for her daughter to marry. A recurring theme within these letters, which are presented in voice-over, is for Patel to marry and "settle down" so that her mother can finally pass on her saris to her daughter.[27] Indeed, a repeated sentiment within her mother's reference to the trousseau is her belief that marriage will provide Patel relief from the exhaustion of her activist work. In a letter titled "Mangal Sutra" (a Hindi word referring to the marriage necklace that is worn by Hindu women and that is part of Patel's trousseau), Patel's mother explicitly positions Patel's marriage prospects against Patel's feminist endeavors:

"Since you have stubbornly refused to get married, it seems your mangal sutra has to come from your mother instead of your husband / But this does not absolve you of your duty to settle down in life! ... In the midst of all this [tragedy] is youth, with its dreams of happiness. Why not concentrate on the beauty and miracle of life, instead of on suffering and pain? Married life has its ups and downs, but ultimately, it is also great fun. ... You have had your years of sexual experimentation and feminism. Now find a wonderful man to marry and make a home with. Life is but a prize for winning LOVE." (59–60)

In this letter, compulsory heterosexuality can offer Patel what the queer feminist scholar Sara Ahmed calls "the promise of happiness," or happiness as a social good. Happiness operates as a social good through the belief that proximity to certain norms and ideals creates happiness, which make certain forms of personhood more valuable than others. Happiness as a social good means that happiness "itself becomes a duty" (*Promise* 7). For Patel's mother, happiness-as-duty involves framing feminism as a developmental life phase, one that Patel's mother believes her daughter should leave behind for the "fun" and "prize" of married life. Heteronormative happiness, according to Patel's mother, promises relief from the "suffering and pain" of racism, both personal and collective, to which she sees Patel as overly attached in her work as a poet and activist.

The sari trousseau objectifies heteronormative happiness as part of an affective economy of generational kin relations, one that is bound up with other forms of intimacy and capital as well, since typically the trousseau contains saris gifted from the daughter-bride's newly acquired family members as well as from her natal family. The quality and quantity of saris passed down to the daughter-bride by this extended network of kin objectify the bride's economic wealth, according to the expense of the saris' fabric, design, and embellishments. It also objectifies her "wealth of kin," or her social capital. For East African Asian families such as Patel's, whose migrant histories are marked by political and economic disenfranchisement and racial expulsion, the sari trousseau is also part of an affective economy that Patel, in the published version of *Migritude*, calls "shilling love." Shilling love is a form of love and attachment that is expressed and secured through the quiet pursuit of upward mobility and capitalist accumulation as responses to racial violence and political upheaval. Each stanza of the section "Shilling Love" begins with the juxtaposition of the Kenyan shilling's loss in value to the British pound, as Patel recalls that her "parents never say they love" their children but instead "they save and count / count and save" (27). The counting of money is, in effect, an accounting of the distribution of love within the migrant family, since the family's economic situation determines "who gets to leave / and who has to stay / who breaks free / and what they pay" (26). As a political economy of love, shilling love denaturalizes love as a sentimental mode of kin relations; instead, love is mediated through the historical exigencies of political and economic upheaval.

The sari trousseau objectifies Patel's mother's shilling love, a form of generational intimacy that cannot be fully disaggregated from the political economy of expulsion: it is an economic and affective archive of love and attachment that Patel's mother passes down to her daughter as a way of alleviating the pain and suffering brought on by the hardships that Patel has had to endure as a multiply migrant subject.[28] Patel of course does not fulfill the happiness duty of marriage and domestic settlement, nor does she relinquish her feminist activist work. But neither, as we know, does she dispense with her trousseau of saris. Rather than guaranteeing that Patel will fulfill her moral obligation to a heterosexual, married, settled life, Patel's materially catachrestic use of her saris to perform proximate histories of antiblack and antibrown female violence and her wearing of them to produce a queer feminist mode of diasporic embodiment circulate outside an affective economy of heteronormative happiness.

Moreover, Patel's mother gifts her the wedding trousseau *despite* Patel's failure to marry and "settle down" and in the absence of any evidence of Patel's plans to do so. Rather than viewing the gifting of saris as her mother's "giving up" on her daughter's fulfillment of heteronormative happiness, Patel understands the generational act of gifting/giving saris as one of maternal recognition of her feminist subjectivity. Patel, in her working notes to *Migritude*, admits to having been "stunned" upon receiving her trousseau: "In this act [of giving me the trousseau] my mother showed me up as the traditionalist. Appointed herself the revolutionary. Her gift showed me that the three granthis of the mangal sutra could be a blueprint for a creative life. An activist life. My life. Intention. Declaration. Execution" (93). Patel here reflects on the possibility of generational attachments secured not through the reproduction of compulsory heterosexuality but through her mother's recognition of her daughter's feminist political engagements. Within this mode of maternal recognition, the generational conflict narrative, in which the mother embodies (heteronormative) tradition and the queer feminist daughter heroically and rebelliously refuses it, remains an insufficient one in capturing this act of generational transmission. Instead, the gifting of saris secures bonds between mother and daughter through a maternal recognition and affirmation of a filial feminism.

If saris are "relational objects" (Norris 64), then Patel's mother's recognition of her daughter's feminism in the act of sari exchange also challenges a relational structure between mother and daughter that is based in a recuperative nostalgia for the mother-as-homeland. As a material archive that forges generational bonds between women, the sari trousseau typically idealizes an Indian "homeland that is left behind and continually evoked" through the figure of the Indian woman-as-mother, where the mother becomes "the embodied signifier of the 'past' of the diaspora" (Gopinath, *Impossible* 18). The sentiment that most often structures these forms of diasporic cultural preservation and female generational connection is nostalgia. Through touch, smell, style, and drape, the saris contained within the trousseau can produce for the wearer a desire for the maternal body as the lost body of homeland culture. Conventionally, the sari trousseau is also an archive *of* nostalgia in that the saris contained within it are garments that accrue sentimental value through the space and time across which they travel and the care with which they are chosen and preserved. The saris selected for inclusion in the sari trousseau "act as souvenirs, mementoes, and mnemonics of past relationships and selves through their very materiality, their physical condition, color, smell and texture" (Norris 55).

Yet instead of working in the interests of a recuperative nostalgia in Patel's performance, saris are used to forge mother-daughter intimacies through a generational inheritance of diasporic feminist rage. Patel's recognition of maternal affirmation in the gifting of saris involves her concomitant recognition that the rage that structures *Migritude*'s feminist poetics is a feeling that she has inherited *from* her mother. If, as the cultural historian Vijay Prashad writes in the foreword to *Migritude*, the sari trousseau is an "inheritance of emotions" ("Speaking" iii), then part of that emotional inheritance is rage. Patel's mother's rage in fact surfaces as part of Patel's memories of Kenya as homeland. In the segment called "I Never Wanted Daughters," the audience hears Patel's mother's voice declaring, "My daughters make me so angry! They keep seeking out danger. After everything we've done for their security, they reject us. They choose the hardest, worst, most dangerous things" (23–24). Anger is Patel's mother's response to Patel's rejection of the "security" of hetero-domesticity and capitalist mobility that she has gifted to her daughter. In Patel's mother's view, this form of security is particularly crucial for women during the political crisis in Kenya, in which "women are never safe."

Even as Patel's mother directs her anger toward her daughters for their feminist rejection of economic and political "security," she also reveals how the very process of securing these forms of security requires a militant rage, one that further advances the rage that is migritude's structure of feeling. In "Shilling Love," Patel describes her mother as "speak[ing] battle" and as "scaling the ramparts of class distinction" (26) so that her daughters might obtain the elite education that would allow them to leave Kenya and study abroad. In "Shilling Love, Part II" Patel's mother is a "general" speaking back to immigration officers who have barred Patel's parents as "third world citizens/of African passport holders" from seeing their daughters after heightened surveillance of South Asian, Muslim, and Arab-looking people seeking to enter the United States after 9/11 (57). Patel's mother, by directing her anger toward her daughters and on behalf of her daughters, privatizes her anger. Yet at the same time, her anger is also clearly directed toward the state as she acknowledges the histories of Kenyan, British, and US state violence against women and minorities that force her to wish for her daughters' embrace of "security."

Patel's use of the sari archive to represent state violence against brown and black women can thus be viewed as a performed inheritance of her mother's rage against the imperial and postcolonial state. The potential for rage, rather than a nostalgia rooted in heteronormative economies of love and happiness, to secure generational intimacies between women operates as a diasporic form of what Lauren Berlant, in the US national context, has called "countersentiment." Whereas sentiment designates "emotions as normativizing technologies that interpellate individuals into a dominant order of feeling, virtue, and ideology," countersentimentality refuses "sublimation of subaltern struggles into conventions of emotional satisfaction and redemptive fantasy" (*Female* 55). Adapting Berlant's definition of sentiment and countersentiment for the diasporic context, we could name the generational inheritance of diasporic rage as a countersentiment in that an inheritance of rage fails to guarantee the "emotional satisfaction and redemptive fantasy" of nostalgia for the mother/homeland. Rage sublimates nostalgia as a dominant diasporic affect, insofar as nostalgia means a longing for a "pure and unsullied cultural identity" (Gopinath, *Impossible* 43). The past and ongoing racial violence that shapes the racial formation "Kenyan Asian" means that the status of Kenya-as-homeland is never "pure and unsullied." While for scholars of South Asian diasporas "homeland" usually refers to the Indian subcontinent, for Patel it is Kenya, itself a diasporic site, that is the site of home.[29] Even as the sari trousseau is an intimate archive of generational attachments, the gift economy in which it circulates does not produce a nostalgia premised on an "unmediated emotional fusion" between women (Boym 227). The violence of homeland precludes Patel from investing the homeland with an imaginary plenitude of lost origins that is then reproduced through the maternal body. Patel's use of saris throughout *Migritude* instead enacts a politics of countersentimentality by allowing us to see what we have not been allowed to see or, perhaps, to imagine within an affective economy of generational inheritance: an embodied politics of feminist rage passed down from mother to daughter.

Although it might be tempting to understand rage and nostalgia as competing modes of sentiment within the generational gifting of the sari trousseau, Patel deploys them as dialectical, even intertwined, affects. At the end of *Migritude*, Patel calls out to her mother to "look" as she "forg[es] a ship of glittering songs / to sail your jewels in / staking a masthead of verbs from which to fly your saris" (62). Patel's appeal to her mother to see how she has used the sari trousseau expresses a desire for maternal recognition. This appeal resonates with Patel's elaboration of her vexed relation to her saris as a queer migrant daughter: "I came into contact with just the real beauty of interacting with these amazing pieces of clothing and the family history they carry, and all the parts of myself, which in a lot of ways, as many migrants do, cut off parts of ourselves and censor parts of ourselves . . . in order to get along in the new societies we've moved to" (Patel, interview). Patel here links saris to places and sites from which she is "cut off"—namely, the diasporic homeland of Kenya and the diasporic maternal body that still resides there—in order to survive the economic and political hardship of multiple migrations. The lament of being cut off usually implies a desire to be rejoined and emotionally fused with, a longing that is a recognizable feature of nostalgia. Yet if the inheritance of saris is at least in part about the inheritance of rage, then Patel's appeal to her mother is nostalgic in an altogether different way—it implores her mother to see how her use of saris emerges out of a longing for her mother's diasporic rage.

Come for the Politics, Stay for the Saris

In the last segment of *Migritude*, called "Born to a Law," Patel opens her suitcase of saris and unfurls each one onto the floor in full view of her audience.[30] She takes care to show off the "borders and embroidery" (95), some of which feature the same ambi pattern that has been projected from slides at the beginning of the show. As she lays out each one, she defines the word "trousseau" as "the wealth a woman takes when she leaves the home of her parents / Etymology: Old French / From trousse / bundle—and trouser / to tie up" (61). This etymology of "trousseau" resonates against Patel's use of saris to challenge being "tied" or "bound" to the dictates of a settled, heterosexual domesticity. In *Migritude*, saris generate a different kind of historical "binding" that occurs beyond the reproductive logic of blood-based affiliation and kinship: the use of saris in "binding" African and Asian women together as historically proximate subjects of empire and in binding Patel to her mother through an inheritance of generational rage. But what is Patel's audience to make of this most unabashed moment of sari display? How is this moment of display different from the images of ambi and the saris hanging on low trapeze wires that open the performance? In her working notes to *Migritude*, Patel accounts for the final, spectacular display of her saris in this way: "The audience has finally earned the right to see the saris in all their splendor. Because they've engaged with the violence and violation beneath. Sat through the unbearable and absorbed it. They've paid for the experience of beauty and sensuality, and they understand the cost" (95). Patel here invokes the language of economic exchange, casting our public viewing of her precious saris as a collectively performed act of consumption. But her references to "violence," "violation," and the "unbearable" as the "payment" for our shared aesthetic pleasure suggest that this is an economic transaction that is quite unlike the consumption of Indo-chic commodities with which she opens the performance. The practice of consuming Indo-chic depends on abstracting these style commodities from the circuits of global labor that produce them and on a lack of intimate knowledge about the resources that inspire their production. The "cost" of the sari viewing, conversely, demands an engagement with the material histories of the sari and our own intimate engagement with the intimate archive of the sari trousseau.

We as an audience have been asked to bear witness to the assemblages of materiality and affect that saris and the sari trousseau generate within the repertoire of the performance. The act of bearing witness, as performance studies scholars have argued, is itself a performance, "a doing, an event that takes place in real time" and that makes personal and collective trauma "felt affectively and viscerally in the present" (Taylor 167). "Violation," "violence," and the "unbearable" are, to quote Patel, the affective costs we pay for the aesthetic pleasure of our sari viewing at the end of the performance. The cost of bearing witness in exchange for aesthetic pleasure effectively inverts the temporality of *Migritude*'s online exhortation for audiences to "come for the saris, stay for the politics." As Patel invites us to view her saris, we are made suddenly aware that the invitation that drew some of us to the performance has in fact been deferred and reversed in a bait-and-switch: we have "come" for the politics in order to "stay" for the saris. These politics, of course, are embedded in the sari itself, and they emerge in the sari's multiple materialities throughout the performance—the sari-as-assemblage. These include Patel's transnational material history of the sari fabrics and the ambi design; her materially catachrestic use of saris in representing antibrown and antiblack female violence; the production of queer forms of feminine embodiment in wearing the sari; and the transmission of generational rage between mother and daughter in the gifting of the sari trousseau. Such affiliations, affects, and embodiments dislodge the sari from a culturally coherent notion of diasporic Indianness structured exclusively through nostalgic longing and loss. Saris are instrumentalized to represent nonidentitarian, cross-racial affiliations, queer femininities, and generational rage as central to articulations of queer, female, diasporic subjects' belonging across multiple migrations and multiple homelands.

Epilogue: Fashioning Diasporic Futures

Patel's tagline to "come for the saris, stay for the politics" and her performed inversion of it in a sense capture my own efforts at illuminating the social domains of diasporic beauty and fashion throughout this book. That is, Patel's instrumentalization of fashion to make visible practices of belonging, embodiment, and political relationality is an articulation that I hope this book has performed as well. In the face of beauty's neoliberal attachments—to social privilege and capitalist mobility, to aesthetic judgment and pleasure, to fashionability and everyday fashion—beauty is a social domain that, even when it does not take on an explicitly politicized form, nonetheless exists in "proximity to the political" (Berlant, *Female* x). The juxtapolitical terrain of beauty lies in its various capacities to disorganize dominant ways of conceptualizing belonging in the diaspora: cultural nationalism, the liberal democratic state's promise of full inclusion, elite forms of cosmopolitanism, capitalist mobility, compulsory hetero-femininity, the reproduction of gendered forms of diasporic authenticity, and even the salience of ethnicity- or race-based definitions of affiliation and belonging.

In short, my aim has been to show how an encounter with beauty and fashion can be a profoundly socializing one and how it allows us to see femininity, where beauty most often resides, as central to the practice of diaspora. These forms of femininity cannot be disaggregated from but are also irreducible to the figure of the traditional-but-modern Indian woman that has been central to the shoring up of capitalist heteropatriarchies within a dominant national and diasporic imaginary. Because beauty, unlike the nation, is not so easily harnessed to an institutional-ized model of identity and is not so easily recognizable as a social form, it lends itself to conceptualization as an assemblage. The assemblages of Indian fashion and beauty that I have mapped throughout this book make intelligible affiliations (across racial, class, and generational lines), forms of embodiment (queer, cross-gender, and politically oppositional femininities), and multiple spatial scales of belonging (national, trans-national, and global) that may otherwise remain unintelligible within frameworks of diaspora that position the Indian nation as its authoriz-ing term. This is not to discount the material links between India and diasporic communities that structure beauty's transnational itineraries. Yet it is Indian beauty and not India per se that has been this book's privileged optic; and however unlikely an optic through which to exam-ine diasporic culture, beauty is nonetheless a crucial one. The various embodiments, desires, pleasures, practices, and performances that make up these assemblages of beauty produce a model of diaspora that is orga-nized outside preconstituted collectivities and communities, or ones that we can name in advance, and that emerges instead through beau-ty's materialities and affectivities along unpredictable lines of flight. If beauty matters to diaspora, then what are its future matterings? Where, in other words, are its future habitations and what will they tell us about race, diaspora, and the social? I conclude by considering one of these possible futures, which demands expanding the social domain of beauty and fashion to include the province of South Asian masculinities.

Turban-Chic

In July 2012, a South Asian American women's fashion and life-style magazine called *Anokhi* featured a story about the French fashion designer Jean Paul Gaultier's use of "Sikh-style" turbans in his spring 2013 menswear collection at Paris Fashion Week. The theme of Gaulti-er's show—"travel"—aimed to present "a globe-trotting fashionable man who understands the very essence of traveling that is cultivating a bigger understanding and respect for various cultures" (Jakhar). Gaultier, whose collections have consistently borne the imprint of Indian-inspired fabrics, designs, and colors since his visit to India in the 1970s, did not design the turbans but used them as accessories in his nautically themed menswear collection, which did feature other Indian-inspired textiles and designs. Neither did Gaultier use Sikhs to model his creations, though the runway show did include some non-Sikh Indian male models.

In a recent post in the Sikh American community blog *Langar Hall* titled "Turbans on the Runway: What Does It Mean for Sikhs?," a Sikh American man with the screen name Brooklynwala eloquently responds to the debut of Gaultier's turbans by citing the way that "turbans have been the target of discrimination, profiling, and violence [after 9/11 and the US-led global "war on terror"] and portrayed as aesthetic objects of high fashion" (Brooklynwala). Brooklynwala calls specific attention to the massacre of Sikh worshipers at a gurdwara in Oak Creek, Wisconsin, which left six people dead and which occurred just one month after Gaultier debuted turban-chic on the runway. While he admits that there is "something amazing about seeing these models rocking turbans like they are the hottest accessories imaginable" because Sikh men are so often portrayed in Bollywood and other global media as "buffoons" and as hopelessly unmodern, he also questions the absence of Sikh male models in Gaultier's runway show and whether the use of turbans in and of themselves will "change or even challenge the reality of racism our community faces" (Brooklynwala). The *Langar Hall* blog post and Gaultier's turban-chic runway show force a consideration of the links that have yet to be fully explored between Indo-chic as part of a global cultural economy of fashion, late-capitalist orientalism, and South Asian diasporic masculinities.

In the months following the debut of Gaultier's turbans on Paris runways, several South Asian, British, and US Sikh activists, artists, and fashion industrialists drew public attention to the turban's cultural significance in their communities. The young British Asian fashion designer Jeetinder Sandhu designed jeweled turbans as part of his autumn–winter 2013 collection for Graduate Fashion Week in London. Later that year, the British Asian writer Jay Singh-Sohal published the book *Turbanology: Guide to Sikh Identity*, which was followed by the London art exhibition *Turbanology: Sikhs Unwrapped*, which "chart[ed] the colourful history of British Sikhs and the Turban rights movement in Britain—through the visual and iconic Turban" ("Turbanology"). British Sikh Pardeep Singh Bahra founded the Sikh fashion blog *Singh Street Style*, in which Sikh men are featured donning the *dastar* (Punjabi for "turban"), even if they do not tie the turban in their day-to-day lives. And Sikh American Jagmeet Sethi soon after launched his online apparel company Turbaninc.com, which designs clothing and accessories to promote Sikh pride.

As the visibility of both turban-chic and Sikh fashion industrialists grew in the public sphere, the global clothing retailer The Gap launched its 2013 "Make Love" campaign—a multicultural series of winter holiday ads featuring racially and ethnically diverse models—with the Brooklyn-based

Sikh American jewelry designer Waris Ahluwalia (who, as I discussed in chapter 2, rubbed shoulders with the literary celebrity turned global fashion icon Jhumpa Lahiri) posing alongside a white, female fashion model. Almost as soon as the ad went up in New York City subway stations, vandals began defacing it. One tried to cut Ahluwalia out of the ad, while others visually altered it to encourage Ahluwalia's and the female model's associations with terrorist masculinities and radical Islam (and in strikingly pathologically queer terms: the white, female model was transformed into a "Muslim-looking" male body); still other vandals used the appearance of Ahluwalia's turbaned Sikh identity to vilify Sikh taxi drivers as a menacing immigrant labor force. The Gap ad campaign and its aftermath eerily bears out (and answers in the negative) one of the central questions posed in *Langar Hall*: "Now that turbans are all the rage in the fashion world, will people think I am cooler in my turban, when it also comes with a long beard and brown skin?" (Brooklynwala). The turbulent—sometimes synchronous, sometimes successive—clustering of these events surrounding turban-chic produces what Jasbir Puar has referred to as the turban-as-assemblage (*Terrorist* 192–94). The turban as material object becomes a dense transfer point for a heterogeneous set of discourses around religious identity, fashionability, terrorism, and pathologized South Asian immigrant bodies and labor.

What is striking to observe here is the diasporic community's recourse to cultural restoration as a politicized response to the turban as an object of fashion and cultural theft, on the one hand, and the turban as the target of cultural surveillance practices, on the other. In chapter 4, I examined a version of this response to the fashion trend of 1990s bindi-chic and anti–South Asian violence that framed the bindi as metonymic of South Asian American metropolitan populations. In the case of turban-chic and turban profiling, as is clear from the brief account just given, the project of cultural preservation can threaten to align, however uneasily, with the very industry of fashion that diasporic communities saw as merely aestheticizing and orientalizing Sikh identity in the first place. Diasporic investments in cultural restoration, however understandable in the face of cultural appropriation and racial violence, are reinforced through redemptive consumer markets. These consumer markets call attention to the absence of Sikh bodies in the dominant fashion system and seek to make fashion "outsiders" into fashion "insiders." Sikh fashion industrialists' cultural branding of turban-chic and "Sikh chic" more broadly allows Sikhs to enter the public sphere as fashion tastemakers and trendsetters in ways that have been historically unavailable to them. Their critical engagements with the turban also counter the orientalizing aesthetics of Sikh-inspired fashions by European couturiers such as Gaultier.

Yet diasporic investments in consumer markets of fashion can also reproduce, even if unwittingly, discourses of cultural purity and narrow ethnic nationalisms. This possibility emerges in the convergence of religious and cultural equality (turban *rights*) with the celebration of religious and cultural difference (Sikh *pride*) in the art exhibit *Turbanology*; it also emerges in Bahra's reclaiming of the turban as fashionable when paired with mainstream British men's street style such as skinny jeans and, in most images, a trimmed beard. In combatting the "vulnerability of male turbaned bodies" to violence, surveillance, and cultural appropriation, such consumer markets also "[open] up the possibility of their very restoration, their rephallicization and recentering through patriarchal nationalisms" (Puar, *Terrorist* 182). Diasporic fashion cultures can facilitate the advancement of this restoration, as, for example, when the fashion blogger, clothing designer, and model Pardeep Singh requires that the Punjabi men who model his creations on his blog wear the turban regardless of their religious affiliation, with the objective of enticing Punjabi women to "embrace turbaned Sikh men" as sexually "desirable" (qtd. in Pinto).

At stake in these debates and events surrounding turban-chic and turban profiling is the question of when and whether the turban can signify a Sikh modernity. Transnational consumer markets for turban pride, for example, invariably depend on the production of convivial relations between turbans as objects of aesthetic innovation and the assertion of nonsecular forms of modern personhood. Unlike the bindi's much more secular significations on the subcontinent and in the diaspora, the turban retains strong ties to (nonsecular) "tradition." As the Sikh studies scholar Virinder Kalra observes, because the turban is for Sikhs a material object that marks a distinctive Sikh cultural identity rooted in religious affiliations, it is difficult for Sikhs (and even non-Sikhs) to consider it as just an article of clothing, much less a fashionable accessory. Indeed, Sikh and Sikh diasporic community organizations' statements about the turban, such as those who insist that "the turban is not a hat"[1] and even those who argue that Sikh fashion industrialists' sleek uses of the turban in their designs and blogs are an example of how "fashion has followed faith" ("Turbanology: Material"), attest to the difficulty of embracing the turban as just "an accepted dress of a modern person" (Kalra 84) even when it is combined with markers of modern dress, such as skinny jeans and a trimmed beard.[2]

I here turn to the South Asian American filmmaker Harjant Gill's short documentary film *Roots of Love: On Sikh Hair and Turban* (2010), a film that

I position within these events surrounding the Sikh turban as a marker of religiosity, fashionability, and violability post-9/11. In providing an account of Sikh men's everyday relationships to their hair and turbaning practices in contemporary India, Gill's film demonstrates the way that the bodily intimacies of fashion and dress continue to be a crucial site for the assertion of Sikh cultural identities and global belonging. In the film, Indian Sikh men's everyday rituals of wrapping and donning the turban, as well as their often-conflicted decisions to cut their hair (a violation of Sikh religious doctrine), are attached to a set of complex desires: to maintain visual markers of Sikh religious affiliation, to assimilate into globally modern India, and to attain transnational mobility. By turning a post-9/11 diasporic gaze on Sikhs in India, Gill documents the turban's capacities to produce heterogeneous forms of masculine embodiment that productively complicate a tradition/modernity and secular/religious binary through which the turban as a marker of diasporic Sikh identity has most often been framed.

Roots includes interviews with Sikh authority figures such as elders, parents, and scholars, who serve as the requisite "talking heads" of the documentary film genre and who share their religious devotion to, historical knowledge of, reflections on, and beliefs about the Sikh turban. Though these figures' statements reflect various degrees of Sikh orthodoxy, they are united in their claims that for Sikhs hair and turban are considered sacred parts of the body and not merely extensions of it. Gill's film also features interviews with young Sikh men who choose to forgo tying the turban and who frame their decision to do so in terms of their desire to aspire to Bollywood standards of male fashionability or to assimilate into a globally modern image of Indian masculinity, one that is based in the historical exclusion of Sikhs and Sikh culture from dominant narratives of modern nationhood. One Sikh man describes the feeling of cutting his hair for the first time, saying that seeing his shorn head reflected back to him in the mirror made him "delightful and happy. . . . It was like a fantasy world changing the way you look"; another exclaims, "It makes me feel more liberal. . . . I can do anything now." These young men appeal to deturbaning and shorn hair as forms of bodily transcendence that promise them access to masculine embodiments of fashionability, which they see as implicitly at odds with the tying of the turban.

The film's contrasting representations of the turban—as both a desirable and an undesirable marker of Sikh masculinity—are rendered with unabashed sentimentality in a brief montage in the documentary. The montage, which includes no spoken dialogue and is therefore distinct from the more or less conventional documentary format that structures

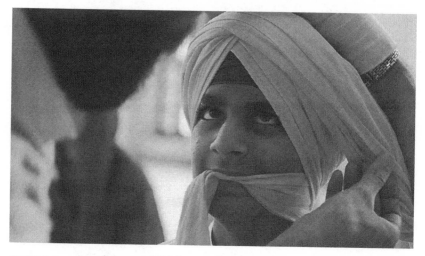

FIGURE E.1. An adolescent Sikh boy undergoes the Dastar Bandhi, or turban-tying ceremony. Harjant Gill, *Roots of Love*, 2010.

the rest of the film, is also some of the most poetically rendered footage in Gill's documentary. It begins with an adolescent boy preparing to undergo the Dastar Bandhi, a religious rite of passage in which Sikh boys tie the turban for the first time (see fig. E.1). These ceremonial shots are then interspersed with shots of a different kind of ceremonial act, that of a Sikh man undergoing the process of cutting his hitherto unshorn hair in order to pursue his dreams of entering India's Bollywood film industry (see fig. E.2). Gill cuts from close-ups of orange and pink turban cloth being folded and unfolded to close-ups of the boy's face as he undergoes the turban-tying ceremony and then from close-ups of shorn hair falling to the floor to shots of a Sikh man's face as he sets out to pursue his Bollywood aspirations. The montage signals the synchronization of modernity and tradition, the generational loss of the turban's cultural significance and the simultaneous generational continuance of its restoration.

What makes this montage so notable is the way that its visual and sonic landscape is suffused with nostalgia, a sentiment that, as I discussed in chapter 5, is a quintessentially diasporic structure of feeling. Such nostalgia accords with Gill's stated objective in making *Roots*, which is to allow audiences to see how the Sikh turban and unshorn hair are "rooted" in "love, respect, and nurturance" (Gill). As the film's dominant affective registers, love, respect, and nurturance are intended to educate viewers about how the turban is "more than a religious or

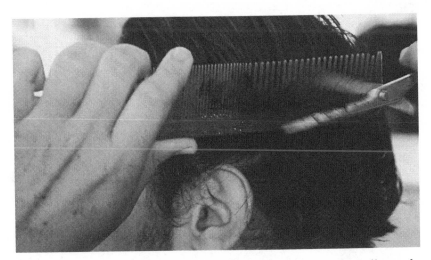

FIGURE E.2. A Sikh man cuts his hair in preparation to enter the Bollywood film industry. Harjant Gill, *Roots of Love*, 2010.

political symbol that, due to its unfamiliarity and miss-associations [*sic*] with 9/11 and terrorism, has been transformed into something threatening—to both the security of the state and the safety of the family" (Gill). Nostalgia thus functions to defuse both the perceived religious or political threat that the turban poses to the post-9/11 US state and the actual threat that it poses to turbaned Sikhs and their families who must constantly negotiate the state's perceived "miss-associations" of the turban with terrorist masculinities. Within the context of turban profiling and turban fashionability, this nostalgic rendering of turban and hair operates in the service of restoring a culturally threatened Sikh identity. Gill's use of nostalgia in this montage thus resonates with turban pride as a form of cultural restoration that is at work in British and American Sikh fashion industrialists' fashionable rehabilitation of the turban in their sartorial creations.

Yet the film's diasporic nostalgia for the turban's associations with cultural tradition is also undercut by yet a third narrative in the film, which positions the turban as a *flexible* signifier of contemporary Sikh cultural identity. This narrative is perhaps the most interesting for the way that it allows some Sikh men to claim and navigate a Sikh modernity by both wearing *and* not wearing the turban. One man in the film, who recalls "not thinking twice" about cutting his hair, responds to his parents' grief over his violation of Sikh religious doctrine by wearing the turban over his shorn hair while in their presence. He describes this choice as one that allows him to maintain "two identities," "one a cut Sardar [Sikh], one a full-fledged Sardar." Here, the turban becomes a "flexible symbol of belonging" (Gill). I draw attention to this narrative in *Roots* because it suggests that this kind of flexible embodiment is just as much a part of negotiating contemporary Sikh cultural identity as are the narratives of Sikh men who do or do not tie the turban and who do or do not cut their hair. The material heterogeneities of Sikh turbans and hair in contemporary India thus become an occasion for Gill's *diasporic* rearticulation of the turban, one that exists outside redemptive consumer markets for turban-chic, the production of fashionable Sikh masculinities, and perhaps even beyond the purview of public and consumer cultures in the diaspora (museum exhibitions, style blogs, and apparel brands).

Situated within the post-9/11 context of turban-chic and turban profiling, Gill's film negotiates the racial politics of the turban in ways that move beyond a compulsion to cultural restoration while still accounting for the way that South Asian "garb" carries with it social and political costs for immigrants and communities of color that turban-chic as fashion accessory does not. At the same time, if we situate the turban's flexible associations with Sikh modernities within the larger archive of *Fashioning Diaspora*, *Roots* also reveals some remarkable continuities with prior histories of Indo-chic and racist surveillance practices, such as those discussed in chapter 4 around the bindi. Thus, even as Gill's film is particular to a historical moment of post-9/11 vilification of turbaned Sikh masculinities and turban-chic, we might read such continuities as putting pressure on the periodization "post-9/11" as somehow radically differentiated from these prior histories and as instead what Foucault would call a discursive "truth effect." It remains to be seen how and if diasporic cultural production will engage the turban's remasculinization as a critical response to its aestheticization within global fashion markets and what creative forms diasporic engagements with South Asian male fashions and fashionability, more generally, will take.

* * *

As this book goes to press, I am struck by the sense of its timeliness, as diasporic cultures increasingly engage with beauty, fashion, and the sartorial as social domains through which to articulate diasporic belonging in a new global economy.[3] But I am also struck by a sense of its possible futures, a feeling that is itself symptomatic of this book's approach to beauty and fashion as assemblages. The temporality of assemblages is always emergent and thus unknowable because of their future orientation. My hope is that the discussion of the diasporic cultural forms of beauty and fashion elaborated throughout this book will be read as a scene of emergence, as producing an archive of the cultural political work that diasporic beauty and fashion have done and have yet to do in accounting for the material histories and diffuse affects of diasporic embodiment and belonging.

NOTES

Introduction

1. The light-skinned Indian beauty ideal is rooted in the myth that the Aryan invasion of North India in 1200 BC, which drove the "original" Indian race, the Dravidians, farther south, allowed a lighter-skinned race of Indians to emerge in the North. The Aryan-invasion explanation for skin-color differences between Indians gained traction during British colonial rule, which elevated the social status of lighter-skinned North Indians above that of darker-skinned South Indians. Though scientists have disproven the Aryan-Dravidian myth of racial difference, some Indians continue to use it as an explanation for the nation's light-skinned beauty ideal.

2. I borrow this phrase from Ann Stoler in her essay by the same name.

3. Within the field of South Asian American studies, scholars have begun to examine how the racial category "South Asian"—which emerged out of Cold War–era geopolitics and which most often includes subjects with national ties to India, Pakistan, and Bangladesh—is shaped by both North American racial formations and colonial and postcolonial histories on the subcontinent. At the same time, as scholars such as Junaid Rana have argued, post–Cold War and post-9/11 geopolitical realignments reveal how postcolonial nations such as Pakistan, despite their cultural, linguistic, and historical ties to the subcontinent, are increasingly politically, economically, and culturally aligned with the Middle East rather than with South Asia (5–17). Rana's analysis of the Pakistani diaspora in the United States speaks to an urgent need to historicize and rehistoricize "South Asian" as a racial category. Some South Asian Americans deploy the term "South Asian" to designate a politically unified diasporic identity despite maintaining various national, religious, regional, caste, and linguistic affiliations. Drawing on the constitutive heterogeneity of South Asian as a racial category, Bakirathi Mani has argued somewhat differently that this category makes sense only among middle-class South Asian immigrants in the United States, where class privilege may absorb these other forms of difference (*Aspiring* 5–11). Rana's and

Mani's arguments speak to the need to examine the historical and political contingencies of racial categories such as "South Asian." Keeping these contingencies in mind, I use the term "South Asian" in reference to cultural production that is part of a larger diasporic archive and/or when the artists under investigation use this term to describe their racial identities. I use the terms "Indian" or "Indian American" in the absence of self-conscious adoption of the term "South Asian" and/or when referring to a specific set of economic, political, and historical ties between India and the United States that shape ethnic identities.

4. Michel Foucault uses the term "governmentality" to refer both to state practices of governing populations in the name of fostering life and to forms of self-governance, or to how an individual acts upon herself. I tend toward this second meaning of governmentality, which allows us to discern how beauty and fashion operate as neoliberal "technologies of the self" that "permit individuals to effect by their own means or with the help of others a certain number of operations on their own bodies and souls, thought, conduct, and way of being, so as to transform themselves in order to attain a certain state of happiness, purity, wisdom, perfection, or immortality" (*Technologies* 88).

5. I also refer here to the scholarship on transnational feminist methodologies, particularly those that have been instrumental in reshaping feminist knowledge production on diasporas from a transnational perspective. See, for example, Grewal; Gopinath, *Impossible*; M. Jacqui Alexander; and Ong, *Flexible*.

6. See Kawamura 4–5. Kawamura's definition of fashion is clearly indebted to the thinking of the cultural theorist Pierre Bourdieu, who defines fashion as a system of belief based in "collective misrecognitions" (*Sociology* 138).

7. A person's beauty is typically understood as inhering in the physical body—facial features, limbs, figure, height, weight, skin tone, etc.—whereas fashion constitutes clothing and accessories that are put on and taken off at will and have little to do with altering the physical body per se. (This is why, for example, even people who can afford even the most fashionable clothing still at times opt to undergo plastic surgery to enhance their physical appearance.) The different bodily regimes and regimes of value in which beauty and fashion circulate is also perhaps why scholarship on beauty (colorism, plastic surgery, cosmetics) so rarely converges with scholarship on fashion (design, designers, textiles). Exceptions to this divide between beauty and fashion include scholarship on fashion modeling, such as Ashley Mears's *Pricing Beauty: The Making of a Fashion Model* (2011) and Joanne Entwistle and Elizabeth Wissinger's *Fashioning Models: Image, Text, Industry* (2012).

8. By "cultural economy," I refer to the financialization of culture, or the way that culture has become an important mode of economic production in the new global economy. To talk about beauty and fashion as cultural economies is to recognize that beauty and fashion are not merely forms of social or individual expression but cultural domains that are used to drive consumption, create labor, and generate profit.

9. If beauty sells, then it is because "images of the female body are the frequent medium of exchange for capitalism's astonishing range of material and symbolic production" (Edmonds 28).

10. More recently, the transnational dimensions of "Indian beauty" have taken an even more fascinating turn. In January 2015, the *Huffington Post* featured a news story about the Vancouver-based wedding photographer Amrit Grewal's photographs of

fashion models wearing Indian couture bridal designs inspired by Disney princesses for a newly launched diasporic bridal magazine called *South Asian Bride*. The photo spread was intended to attract Indian-brides-to-be to incorporate Disney princess themes into their weddings. In these photographs, Indian brides are represented as Disney princesses, a representation that makes ethnic Indianness desirable as part of an iconically US femininity. At the same time, the aesthetics of Indian bridal fashion operates here as a marker of global modernity that provides these iconic US figures with much-needed feminine "updates" (Weingus).

11. Food is another. See, for example, Anita Mannur's *Culinary Fictions: Food in South Asian Diasporic Culture*.

12. See Oza, esp. chaps. 2 and 4; Dewey; Parameswaran; Osuri; Grewal, esp. chap. 3; and Reddy, "Nationalization."

13. The popularity of Indo-chic—and of Asian-chic more broadly—is part of a much longer, if episodic, history of Asia's presence within a Western, and more specifically US, sartorial imagination, one that dates back to at least the seventeenth century. Yet what is new about the reemergence of Indo-chic in the United States over the past two decades are the historical, economic, and political conditions that shape it: the liberalization of India's economy in 1991 and its status as a threat to US global economic hegemony and the subsequent rise in South Asian immigration to the United States as a result of economic restructuring on the subcontinent. See Maira, "Indo-chic"; Klein; and Tu.

14. For a detailed examination of representations of Indian beauty in *Femina*, see Reddy, "Nationalization."

15. I am not implying that neoliberalism is an even or homogeneous process that operates uniformly across distinct national sites. Indeed, one of my central aims is to demonstrate the unevenness with which neoliberalism disciplines various subjects into market rationalities within the social domains of diasporic beauty and fashion. Yet as an ideology, neoliberalism operates powerfully to cohere class-based definitions of citizenship in India and in the diaspora.

16. An exception is Grewal's examination of the transnational marketing and consumption of Indian Barbie; I turn to Grewal's analysis of Indian Barbie's production of Indian and diasporic consumer citizenship in chapter 3.

17. This is a post-Enlightenment genealogy of aesthetics that begins with Immanuel Kant's *Observations on the Feeling of the Beautiful and Sublime* (1764), which has directly or indirectly impacted the most well-known and emerging feminist philosophical and cultural treatises on beauty. In addition to Kant's influence on Elaine Scarry's feminist philosophical treatment of beauty and Naomi Woolf's critique of US beauty culture, see also Brand; Etcoff; Nehamas; and Scruton.

18. The genealogies of the fetish are long and multiple, beginning with anthropological investigations into the nonsecular practices of non-Western cultures, wending their way into more conventional academic understandings of the fetish in Marxist, Freudian, and Lacanian thought, and emerging with renewed fervor within postcolonial and feminist theorizing on the colonized and feminized body. It is not my intention to rehearse the details of these intellectually rich, vibrant, and enduringly useful genealogies here. Rather, I am interested in the way that the intractability of this value-added model of racialized beauty cannot be disaggregated from post-Enlightenment philosophical discourses of beauty that carry the weight of what Mimi Nguyen,

quoting the feminist scholar Minoo Moallem, calls "civilizational thinking" (366, quoting Moallem 161). This is a mode of thinking in which colonized and racialized subjects have historically been precluded from occupying the role of judging beauty and instead relegated to the object of such judgment, thus inviting the noncoincidence of beauty and nonwhiteness/non-Westernness.

19. Feminist scholarship on Western beauty and fashion has recently reemerged onto the academic scene after a brief hiatus following Western feminist critiques of beauty in the 1990s, which castigated it as morally and ethically suspect and as arguably the most visible evidence of an oppressive patriarchal culture industry. Naomi Woolf's widely popular *The Beauty Myth* (1991) and Susan Bordo's *Unbearable Weight* (1993) are perhaps the most well known of these feminist accounts of the detrimental physical and psychological effects of hegemonic ideals of beauty—white, thin, tall, young—on Western female subjects. More recently, feminist scholarship has begun to rethink its own historically punitive stance toward beauty by recasting beauty as a site of feminist agency. The feminist historian Kathy Peiss's *Hope in a Jar* (1998) demonstrates how twentieth-century US beauty culture facilitated women's access to public life beyond the domestic sphere, while the feminist philosopher Elaine Scarry's *On Beauty and Being Just* (1999) shows how an attachment to beauty might work to forward a liberal humanist project of connecting individuals to each other and to the world.

20. This is a phrase used by Sunil Khilnani in his book by the same name. By "idea of India," Khilnani refers to the promise of diversity and democracy postindependence that has yet to be fully realized. I adapt this phrase to elaborate on Khilnani's point that "the new millennium will see many ideas of India competing to capture the imagination of Indians" (xvii).

21. See Ong and Collier; Puar, "I Would"; and Rai.

22. Here I follow the lead of new material culture studies scholars such as Daniel Miller, Webb Keane, and Susan Kuchler, who have shown that what people do with clothing—the way it is combined, worn, passed down, cared for, and exchanged— makes certain forms of personhood and relationality possible. Visual cultures exhibit strong affinities with fashion economies since fashion design, runway fashion shows, and fashion magazines rely heavily on image-based content and/or circulate within a resolutely visual field. Fashion cultures might thus be understood as visual cultures.

23. For more on the historical and economic emergence of Asian-chic, see Tu, esp. chap. 3.

24. I borrow here from Diana Taylor's understanding of "repertoire" as distinct from the archive: "The repertoire enacts embodied memory: performances, gestures, orality, movement, dance, singing—in short all those acts usually thought of as ephemeral, nonreproducible knowledge. . . . As opposed to the supposedly stable objects of the archive, the actions that are the repertoire do not remain the same" (20).

25. There exists a fairly sizeable body of article-length studies of race and beauty within US and non-US contexts. For book-length studies, see Leeds; King-O'Riain; Tu; and Edmonds.

26. Much debate has surrounded the distinction between representation and affect. Whereas a Deleuzian framework of affect understands it as what remains beyond cognition and as therefore beyond representation, other scholars point to the impossibility

of apprehending affect outside the realm of representation: "If theorizations of affect are currently being employed to supplement or counter representational analyses, then whether affect is being 'mistakenly'... hailed in the representational form of emotion or instead in the excess of emotion as it is represented (whereby the project becomes to represent the intrinsic unrepresentability of affect), it is nonetheless caught in the logic that it seeks to challenge.... All we can really enact is a representational schema of affect" (Puar, *Terrorist* 207). Following Puar's rendering, I understand affect as already caught up in the logic of representation.

27. I am grateful to Priya Shah for this useful definition of *affect*.

28. There are two discernable genealogies within the so-called affective turn in feminist cultural studies. In the first one, scholars define affects as precognitive and presubjective physiological changes in the body that cannot be codified into emotion (Massumi; Clough and Halley). In the second one, scholars argue that physiological changes and emotional responses are indistinguishable from each other (Berlant, *Female*; Ahmed, *Cultural* and *Promise*; Cvetkovich). In this book, occasionally I draw on the insights of the former genealogy but privilege the latter, which is akin to what Raymond Williams has called "structures of feeling" (132), a state prior to articulation and interpellation that is nonetheless social and material.

29. Nguyen is critiquing Elaine Scarry's recuperative treatment of beauty in *On Beauty and Being Just* (1999).

30. Scholarship on affect in beauty and fashion cultures is emerging within anthropological studies of fashion modeling. Elizabeth Wissinger's work on fashion models offers perhaps the most sophisticated reexamination of this profession through the lens of affect. Wissinger argues that the labor of modeling is best understood not as tied to the selling of a particular product (makeup, clothes, or hair products) or even as representative of a particular style that consumers want to emulate or consume but as a form of labor that is aimed at commanding attention through what she calls "affective flow": "modeling work produces value in the form of the accumulation and distribution of attention to images—a body's image and the image of bodies. Models' work is to produce content for attention-gathering and -calibrating technologies such as photography, television, and the Internet" ("Always" 235). Wissinger's interviews with fashion models reveal that these workers understand their labor as oriented less toward "creating gendered ideals of femininity, masculinity, sexiness, or beauty" and more toward " achieving a level of variability, a chameleon-like look that can be made to change at will" in order to maximize the capacity for attention (236). A model's variable look, a look that requires constant modulation of the body (hair, weight, clothes, etc.), thus works in the interest of generating attention, "[of making] an impact, however ill defined or diffuse" (250).

31. For Berlant, these are shared investments despite historical differences of class and race among female consumers.

32. Chapters 4 and 5 and the epilogue examine texts that are more overtly politicized in their engagement with objects of Indian beauty and fashion and that therefore might stand as exceptions to this claim. At the same time, these texts' self-conscious citations and engagements with the racial politics of Indo-chic style invite their consideration within consumer cultures of diasporic beauty and fashion.

33. See Eng, *Feeling*; Gopinath, *Impossible*; Ngai; and Muñoz.

34. See also V. Nguyen.

1 / Excepting Beauty and Negotiating Nationhood in Bharati Mukherjee's *Jasmine*

1. In 1991, India faced an external debt crisis resulting from a series of economic liberalization policies in the late 1970s and 1980s in which India's foreign borrowing increased while domestic output faltered. Subsequent structural adjustment programs led to the end of an era of trade protectionism and ushered in an era of foreign investment and global capital.

2. Brunetti and Leopardi's film traces the exporting of rural Indian women's hair to Europe for sorting and processing before it is sold to women in Europe and the United States and exported back to India for sale to elite urban Indian women. In Stilson's documentary, Indian women's hair is used in the production of wigs and weaves for African American women and is thus deemed "good hair."

3. See my discussion of the passage of the 1986 Immigration Reform and Control Act later in this chapter.

4. For various articulations of the historical construction of Asian Americans as model minorities, see Hattori; and Ong, *Flexible*. For the construction of South Asian Americans as a more recent articulation of the model minority stereotype, see Prashad, *Karma*; and Koshy, "Morphing."

5. As Peter McLaren argues, liberal multiculturalism is guided by a logic in which "the legitimating norms which govern the substance of citizenship are identified most strongly with Anglo-American cultural political communities" (51).

6. See Bascara; Maira, "Good"; Omi and Winant.

7. For criticism that characterizes Jasmine as a model minority, see Koshy, "Geography" and *Sexual*; and Schlund-Vials.

8. The literary critic Anne Cheng has observed the ways that racialized beauty is irrevocably linked to European Enlightenment discourses: there is a "historical complicity between the philosophical discourse of aesthetic judgment and a metaphysics of racial difference" such that racial difference (i.e., nonwhiteness) always exceeds the formulations of "aesthetic judgment" ("Wounded" 192).

9. Unlike political citizenship (the right to vote based on legal residence in a nation) and economic citizenship (the right to work), cultural citizenship designates everyday understandings of belonging and exclusion. For more detailed definitions of cultural citizenship, see T. Miller; and Maira, "Good."

10. Here I follow Chow's arguments about the relationship between ethnicity and labor. Though ethnicity is not always tied to histories of labor, "in actual practice in the contemporary world, whereby ethnicity often designates foreignness (which is, in turn, understood as social inferiority), the linkages between certain types of labor and ethnicity are ineluctable" (33).

11. The INS, or Immigration and Naturalization Service, became the United States Citizenship and Immigration Service, or USCIS, in 2003.

12. Koshy has argued somewhat differently that *Jasmine* is a novel of "postmodern passing," in which passing involves not taking on another more culturally powerful identity in order to avoid social or legal censure but consenting to "dominant scripts of exotic otherness" (*Sexual* 157, 133).

13. See Kibria; for a detailed analysis of the intermediary position of South Asian Americans in US racial formations, see Koshy, "Morphing." The events of 9/11 mark a

shift in the racially ambiguous status of some South Asian American populations, as I discuss further in chapter 3 and the epilogue.

14. Lillian herself may not possess knowledge of these histories of US racialization and passing. However, she exhibits an awareness of the difference between Jasmine's passable brownness through the African American feminine aesthetic of mélange and unpassable forms of brownness, which Lillian links to Indo-Caribbean femininity. Before Jasmine masters her "American walk," Lillian tells her that she walks "like one of those Trinidad Indian girls, all thrust and cheekiness," and then instructs her to "tone it down, girl!" (133). For Lillian, Jasmine's improvised walk signals a hyper-sexualized Indo-Caribbean femininity that is somehow legible as in excess of national norms of feminine embodiment and that therefore invites state surveillance. The "toned-down" version of Jasmine's gait is the one that Lillian deems both "jazzy" and sufficiently "American." My point here is that Lillian, whether intentionally or not, distinguishes between US-based definitions of Americanness and non-US-based ones (the Caribbean as part of the larger Americas).

15. Lillian's logic that Jasmine's brownness might somehow produce the effect of legality, while seemingly ludicrous, uncannily anticipates the racist logic of recent anti-immigrant legislation in Arizona, a state in which "looking like an illegal immigrant" was deemed a legitimate form of state surveillance.

16. It remains unclear, though doubtful, if the Hayeses here mean to reference the system of colonial Indian indentured labor that came to replace the practice of slavery in the Americas. Lillian, though, invokes precisely this history in her allusion to Jasmine's walk as evoking an Indo-Trinidadian femininity.

17. Interestingly, *Jasmine* is a rewriting of Mukherjee's short story "Jasmine," in which the eponymous heroine of Indo-Caribbean descent emigrates from Trinidad to the United States and finds work for other undocumented workers.

18. For recent scholarship on the post-9/11 "nonnational" Muslim or Sikh "terrorist," see Grewal; Puar, *Terrorist*; and Maira, "Good."

19. Jasmine in fact describes New York, the city in which she "became an American" (165), as "an archipelago of ghettos seething with aliens" "like [herself]" (140).

20. For a lucid discussion of the racialization of European immigrants as taking on symbolic ethnicities after World War II, see Waters.

21. I am here indebted to the queer feminist scholar Sara Ahmed's use of the term "stranger" to allow for a more nuanced version of the privileged figure of the "Other" in postcolonial discourses. Ahmed argues that the figure of the stranger is produced from within histories of cross-cultural, transnational encounter that are not properly colonial, a claim that is certainly germane to US racial formations. The "stranger" is a figure who is consolidated through processes of globalization, migration, and multiculturalism that (re)produce the alterity of certain bodies through different modes of proximity, or "encounter" (Ahmed, *Strange*).

22. See, for example, Chu; Carter-Sanborn; Aneja; and Warhol-Down.

23. The geographer Neil Smith defines scale jumping, in which local claims are also witnessed on a national or global level, as part of new cultural geographies that emerge within late global capitalism.

24. In foregrounding this racial logic, *Jasmine* illuminates a critically underexplored dialectic of beauty-plainness in Brontë's text: the way that the West Indian woman Bertha Mason, Rochester's "secret" wife and the "mad woman in the attic" in

Jane Eyre, is the colonized female body that shores up Jane's negotiation of plainness and beauty.

25. Gilroy is here referring to the state of postimperial British race politics, particularly following the events of 9/11. While Gilroy imagines a British "multiculture" (8) that goes beyond a consumerist model of liberal multiculturalism by issuing demands for "hospitality, conviviality, tolerance, justice, and mutual care" (99), I follow Sunaina Maira's caution that "one cannot idealize this multiculture, which is still influenced by market-driven and state-produced ideas of diversity" (*Missing* 175). There are undoubtedly important differences between the British and US national contexts, which may in fact lead to this cautionary note in Maira's reading of the limitations of Gilroy's claims to the post-9/11 US imperial culture. Jasmine's migrations repeatedly invoke and thwart the liberal notions of freedom and choice that underwrite these state-mandated and consumerist notions of diversity.

2 / Prosthetic Femininity, Flexible Citizenship, and Feminist Cosmopolitics in the Fiction of Jhumpa Lahiri

1. I draw inspiration for this section's heading from Lauren Berlant's suggestive chapter title "National Brands/National Body" in her book *The Female Complaint* (2008), which I discuss at greater length later in the chapter.

2. To take just one example from South Asian diasporic beauty cultures, a 2012 article in *Anokhi*, a South Asian American women's fashion magazine, mentioned the "immortalization" of Dixit's "million dollar smile" in reporting on the wax replica of Dixit that was created for Madam Tussauds wax museum in March 2012 ("Madhuri's").

3. Gita Rajan makes precisely this argument. Indeed, it is upon hearing Rohin's elaboration of the meaning of "sexy"—which includes a story about how his own father "sat next to someone he didn't know, someone sexy, and now he loves her" instead of Rohin's mother (108)—that Miranda chooses to abandon the tryst.

4. Berlant argues that the gazes index more than sexual desire as such, more than "half-concealing erotics" between the two mulatta women. Rather, Berlant suggests that "there may be a difference between wanting someone sexually and wanting someone's body" and wonders whether "Irene's xenophilia [her desire for the otherness of Clare's whiteness] isn't indeed a desire to occupy, to experience the privileges of Clare's body, not to love or make love to her, but rather to wear her way of wearing her body, *like a prosthesis, or a fetish*" (*Female* 109, my emphasis).

5. The mulatta woman presents a rather anomalous case for miming the prophylaxis of citizenship in Berlant's model. For the de jure white woman has the privilege of abstracting the "surplus corporeality" of black women's bodies as trademark in order to access "the artificial legitimacy of the citizen" in the public sphere of commodity capitalism. In contrast, the mulatta woman can only "trade in" the surplus corporeality of her blackness for a still disenfranchised white, bourgeois femininity. Thus, though white femininity is a "better model" than black femininity for accessing and participating in the nineteenth-century capitalist public sphere, Berlant concludes that "for light-skinned African-American women, then, the choice of public identity comes to be between two bodies of pain, not two possible modes of relief from indeterminacy" (*Female* 142).

6. Certainly, Dixit's sexual iconicity does not always challenge gendered forms of cultural nationalism and avails itself to reproducing them. Yet, given the failure of the interracial heterosexual romance and Miranda's increasing fixation on Indian women in "Sexy," I believe that it is appropriate to emphasize the feminist and nonheteronormative valences of Dixit's star image. For a detailed analysis of nationalist and nonnationalist diasporic identifications with Dixit's body, see, for example, Mehta; S. Ghosh; Mukhi; and Gopinath, *Impossible*.

7. Inderpal Grewal links up these material and ideological investments in this way: "The need to maintain relations between the South Asian diaspora and its 'home' was connected not only to colonial and neocolonial and nationalist imperatives or to diasporic needs to create an Indian identity in response to racisms and ethnocentrisms in Europe or North America, but also to the demands of the International Monetary Fund to open the country to foreign capital" (87).

8. Ong examines the way that elite transnational Chinese subjects in the 1980s and 1990s practiced flexible citizenship to "respond fluidly and opportunistically to changing political-economic conditions" within a single nation-state (*Flexible* 6). I adapt Ong's notion of flexible citizenship to the Indian context.

9. Though Lahiri does not explicitly reference Bollywood here, the genre of the "Hindi love song" conventionally refers to Bollywood film soundtracks.

10. Mary John and Janaki Nair detail how this narrative of sexual modernity follows Michel Foucault's much-cited critique of the repressive hypothesis.

11. The encounter between Mina and Mr. Kapasi, in which Mina's beauty becomes crucial in Mr. Kapasi's understanding of his own beauty and desirability, prefigures the more recent impact of Indian female beauty on definitions of Indian middle-class manhood, as evidenced by the release of the wildly popular—if controversial—fairness cream for men Fair and Handsome in 2005. Fair and Handsome is an offshoot of India's best-selling women's fairness cream Fair and Lovely, and its popularity indicates an increasing investment among middle-class men in their physical attractiveness, as light skin is now an asset for men on the marriage market. Sales of Fair and Handsome nearly tripled after Shah Rukh Khan became the spokesman for the brand in 2009.

12. This reading follows Foucault's critique of the confession as a paradigmatic mode of sexual (self-) regulation in the historical production of truth about sex in the West.

13. I adapt Dipesh Chakrabarty's call for postcolonial scholars to "provincialize Europe," or to see "the [national] modern as inevitably contested, to write over the given and privileged narratives of citizenship other narratives of human connections that draw sustenance from dreamed-up pasts and futures" (46).

14. See, for example, Bhattacharjee; Prashad, *Karma*; Gopinath, *Impossible*; and Lal.

15. Gayatri Gopinath's reading of the Indo-Caribbean writer V. S. Naipaul's *A House for Mr. Biswas* (1961) is instructive in unpacking more fully the relationship of sexual capital to diasporic domesticity in "This Blessed House." Gopinath argues that in reckoning with the traumatic histories of Indian indentured labor migration to the Caribbean, "Naipaul recognizes that within a colonial system of gender, possessing a viable masculinity is intricately tied to the ownership of property in the form of an idealized domestic space" (*Impossible* 73), as Biswas struggles to build and rebuild his home. Though Sanjeev's and Biswas's migration histories could not be more different

(Sanjeev, unlike Biswas, has not been forced to endure the traumatic histories of forced—indentured labor—migration and displacement and has come to the United States as part of a professional managerial class of South Asians), as an immigrant subject seeking successful embourgeoisement in the diaspora, he clearly shares with Biswas a concern over achieving "an idealized domestic space." Indeed, both Naipaul's novel and Lahiri's story use the house as an organizing (and titular) metaphor for the production of racialized masculinity.

16. For a detailed analysis of the way that Indian American NRIs reproduce a long-distance cultural and political nationalism, see Prashad, *Karma*; and Grewal.

17. Scholars working in the field of literary celebrity studies such as Joe Moran, James English, and Joseph Roach, among others, have examined how market forces and networks produce a system of awards and prizes that confer authorial stardom. But it is not merely Lahiri's literary celebrity that interests me here. Rather, I am interested in how Lahiri's public image is shaped by her talent and an appeal that seems increasingly harnessed to both visual and verbal expressions of her exemplary beauty.

18. I follow Bishnupriya Ghosh's description of media control as the "industrial and technological capacity to distribute, store, and recycle certain images, so that they become the most recursive images of a public figure" (*Global* 11).

19. By "political promotion," Ghosh refers to Roy's antiglobalization protests in the name of a global green politics that followed her Booker Prize win.

20. Despite the vastly different historical, political, and cultural forces that shape the two authors' fiction and media personae, popular and critical comparisons between Roy and Lahiri abound. Roy appeared in *People* magazine as one of the fifty most beautiful people in world in 1998, while Lahiri was voted one of *Esquire* magazine's "women we love" in 2001, a publication that also dubbed her a writer turned "sex symbol."

21. Mukherjee's novel details the life of an Indian village girl turned call-center worker in the high-tech city of Bangalore, India. In the novel, Indian female call-center workers are likened to Indian beauty queens because they share with these figures a glamour and sophistication that represents Indian technological prowess within a global information economy. Female call-center workers are dubbed the "Miss New Indias."

22. The blogger of a British literary blog called *The Most Cake* writes: "Lahiri, I think, is just one of those authors from whom I will read anything, and though I have favourites among her work, there is nothing that she has written that I have not wished I could read again for the first time. There is nothing particularly gladdening about her work—it's more likely to leave you in tears than with a smile—but I think the minor heartbreak I get after I finish each story is really worth it in the end. Also, I'm not going to lie, I think she's totally beautiful. Which, you know, helps" (Devil's Food Cake).

23. David Abraham and Rakesh Thakore both graduated from India's National Institute of Design in Ahmedabad before creating the Abraham and Thakore design label. The fashion designers design clothes, accessories, and home décor, and their designs are regularly featured in India during India Fashion Week in New Delhi and have also appeared as part of textile exhibitions in various global cities.

3 / Fashioning Diasporic Citizens in Literary Youth Cultures of Fashion and Beauty

1. See, for example, Karen Sanchez-Eppler's *Dependent States* (2005); Caroline Levander's *Cradle of Liberty* (2007); and Robin Bernstein's *Racial Innocence* (2011).

2. See, for example, Sharon Lamb and Lyn Michael Brown's *Packaging Girlhood: Rescuing Our Daughters from Marketers' Schemes* (2006).

3. Robin Bernstein uses the term "racial innocence" to challenge the universalization of childhood innocence as based in both marked and unmarked whiteness. Like dominant understandings of beauty and fashion cultures, childhood innocence is most often rooted in "the performed transcendence of social categories of class, gender, and, most importantly . . . race" (6).

4. Dixit's stories have appeared in *Fiction on a Stick: New Stories by Minnesota Writers* and *In Search of Her Mother's Ashes: Stories from South Asian Women in Canada and the United States*. "Pageant" appears in the latter collection. Dixit is currently writing a novel.

5. Thus, though the form and structure of these pageants might very well resemble those of more mainstream ones, it is important to distinguish their ongoing cultural relevance when compared to mainstream pageants such as Miss America, Miss USA, and Miss Universe, which might now be considered retrograde, rearguard, or even kitschy among national and global audiences.

6. See Gopinath, "Queer"; Stewart, *Space*; Halberstam, *Queer Time*; Gray; Johnson; Herring; Desai and Joshi; and Hettne et al.

7. Leslie Bow's book *Partly Colored* (2010) and the anthology *Asian Americans in Dixie: Race and Migration in the South* (2013), edited by Khyati Joshi and Jigna Desai, are the only full-length studies on Asian Americans in the US South.

8. The IFC, which was formed in 1974, sponsored the first Miss India USA pageant in 1980 in New York City. The IFC launched the first Miss India Worldwide competition in 1990 to expand the national reach of the US-based pageant to a global Indian diaspora. The Miss India Worldwide competition attests to the way that the US-based diasporic pageant itself has become a globalized cultural form that parallels the global visibility of Indian beauty pageants such as *Femina* Miss India.

9. Miss India USA began as part of New York City's India Day festival in 1974 and has staged national-level competitions in New Jersey, California, Texas, and Florida but none to date in what is often considered the "deep" US South.

10. While there is, as yet, no existing scholarship that addresses how regional differences shape narratives of diasporic authenticity, the sheer proliferation of South Asian American scholarship that privileges diasporic populations in the tri-state area speaks to this regional bias. See, for example, Gopinath, *Impossible*; Das Gupta; Maira, *Desis*; Rana; and Sudhakar. Though Bakirathi Mani's book *Aspiring to Home* examines what she calls "locality," which refers to "domestic, public, or virtual spaces" (4), such spaces are distinct from regions, which I understand as actual geographic locales.

11. Mani notes that in 1999 Miss India USA did not include representation from several midwestern and southern states, including Kentucky ("Beauty" 745).

12. In Daniel Friedman and Sharon Grimberg's documentary film *Miss India Georgia* (1999), for instance, the pageant contestant Mini Rao's family experiences

downward mobility upon their immigration to the United States and struggles to afford the financial costs associated with Mini's participation in the pageant. Yet the film also reveals that Mini's parents socialize almost exclusively with wealthy Indian American doctors and engineers, in part because this group of coethnics represents for them a professional class to which they once belonged on the subcontinent.

13. The internalization of this model minority project by working-class South Asians whose labor supports the lives of upwardly mobile South Asians demands further exploration within the context of what Aihwa Ong calls "latitudinal citizenship" (*Neoliberalism* 121).

14. It is also worth noting here that Miss Kentucky's performance of the ghazal for two men recalls the mythical figure of the ghazal-singing Indian courtesan, in which the courtesan's performance is marked as a labor of intimacy and nostalgia.

15. See Uberoi; and Mankekar. Dixit also notes the popularity of Bollywood performances in South Asian cultural shows organized on high school and college campuses: "In my school's annual Diwali and Holi programs, there were many dance performances of Bollywood songs. The shows usually began with some sort of classical dance performance, but the main event seemed to be these Bollywood numbers" (Dixit, interview).

16. Jan Susina notes that in 1994 AG developed a primary school curriculum, combining social studies, language arts, and literature, on the basis of the school stories in the AG collection. AG's founder, Pleasant Rowland, herself was a previous language-arts editor and textbook author (131).

17. The swadeshi movement involved Indians boycotting British goods, institutions, and laws.

18. Despite the hugely popular success of the AG brand in the United States, surprisingly little feminist scholarship currently exists on the US-based dolls. None exists on the Girls of Many Lands line, though this is perhaps a symptom of the short-lived nature of the series and therefore its more restricted visibility within girl consumer and literary cultures.

19. Though non-Indians do wear the sari, it became strongly associated with an Indian identity after the 1947 partition of the Indian subcontinent into India and Pakistan.

20. AG launched its first doll, Felicity, a girl living in pre-Revolutionary America, in 1986. AG produced several other "historical" girl dolls, ranging from the late eighteenth century to the late twentieth century, each with an accompanying historical narrative (and other accessories). In 1998, Rowland sold AG, which was then owned by the Pleasant Company, to Mattel.

21. As the Indian media scholar Arvind Rajagopal has succinctly put it, the national advertising ethos reflected this shift from a closed to an open economy with a corresponding shift in advertising rhetoric, from "Be Indian. Buy Indian" to "To Buy is Indian" (73).

22. Certainly, Indie's youth makes her economic citizenship tenuous, since the right to work is contingent on legal age requirements for securing employment. However, I am less concerned with Indie's legal right to work since she is clearly old enough to secure a babysitting job and since she is seeking an unpaid internship, rather than a salaried career, as a fashion reporter.

23. See, for example, Christine So's *Economic Citizens* (2009) and Lisa Park's *Consuming Citizenship* (2005). For these critics, Asian American participation in circuits

of economic exchange belies the possibilities of their abstract citizenship in the face of histories of state exclusion.

24. I here paraphrase Pierre Bourdieu's definition of social capital in *Distinction: A Social Critique in the Judgment of Taste* (1979).

25. South Asian Americans' absence from histories of fashion labor in the United States contrasts sharply with the British Asian fashion designers whose stylistic innovation around the Punjabi or salwar-kameez suit spearheaded its popularity within transnational fashion economies. See, for example, Bhachu.

26. There is an emerging body of sociological scholarship on the aesthetic and affective labor of fashion models. However, little of it addresses racial differences within the US fashion industry. Even less elaborates on racial differences beyond the black-white color line, never mind the increasingly visible presence of nonwhite international fashion models. See, for example, Mears; and Wissinger, "Always."

27. Beri's biography shares much in common with Indie's, suggesting that Daswani's reference to Beri as an Indian fashion designer is perhaps more than arbitrary. Like Indie, Beri has described fashion as an area of academic inquiry that conflicted with the professional labor that she felt pressed to enter as a child growing up in a newly liberalized India. Despite possessing a childhood ambition to be a doctor, Beri claims, "My doctoral ambitions were somewhat thwarted by the fact that I spent more time musing over how the wardrobe of the medical team should look rather than over the more noble and gory aspects of the trade. Mentally, I was always designing the doctor's overcoat with an interesting pocket detail for his stethoscope. My mind would buzz with designs for dressing up the nurses, designing starched headgear and improvising their aprons, adding frills at the hem" (*Ritu Beri*).

4 / Oppositional Economies of Fashion in Experimental Feminist Visual Media

1. I am here referring to Frederic Jameson's definition of postmodern parody, or pastiche, which he describes as a "neutral practice of . . . mimicry, without any of parody's ulterior motives, amputated of the satiric impulse, devoid of laughter" (17).

2. For more on debates about "cultural appropriation" versus "cultural appreciation" regarding the racialized and ethnicized fashion trends, see Pham, "Fashion's."

3. The bindi's resurgence as ethnic style has prompted some recent fashion writers to claim that when it comes to the popularity of Indo-chic, its resurgence "has a lot to do with a new nostalgia for the '90s" (Sidell), and that while "we've felt the subtle breeze of a '90s revival in the air for a few seasons now . . . never has its presence been so ubiquitous as now" (Wilson).

4. For an example of a refutation of the cultural appropriation argument, see Joshi.

5. Anxiety about authenticity extends to Western fashion industrialists and entrepreneurs designing and selling Asian-inspired fashions. Tu describes the way that in the early 1990s fashion designers saw themselves as striving toward an "aesthetic of realism" (114) so that readers who encountered Asian-chic in magazines were "encouraged to think of these designers as something like ethnographers and their creations as something like cultural artifacts" (111). Similarly, Maira describes the way that white henna artists in the 1990s often saw themselves not as fashion experts but as recuperating a lost art that Asian and Arab women are either too modernized to learn and care about or too repressed to enjoy, even as they express "anxiety about cultural borrowing" ("Indo-chic" 226).

6. See, for example, Gopinath, *Impossible*; Bhattacharjee; and Maira, *Desis*.

7. Minh-Ha Pham uses the term "exploitation chic" to describe the transformation of non-Western and nonwhite sartorial practices into global fashion trends ("Fashion's").

8. Other similarities include stolen film and Internet footage and hand-held video recording.

9. Of course, when viewed from the perspective of twenty-first-century new media technologies, such as high-resolution imaging and retinal display, these artworks may also read as "low resolution" or as bearing the mark of technological patina.

10. *Dothead* was originally shown at an awards ceremony at New York University, from which Khurana received her master's in studio art and art criticism in 2001.

11. Khurana has uploaded the three loops of *Dothead* onto her website, so that viewers can watch them all simultaneously ("Dothead"). However, the simultaneity of two-dimensional web-based viewing clearly does not produce the same effect as a live viewing of the installation.

12. Here I follow the lead of fashion studies scholars such as Minh-Ha Pham, who has argued that critiques of racialized fashion trends are most useful when they produce an "inappropriate discourse" of fashion by focusing on "what cannot be integrated into and continue to maintain the existing power structure of the high fashion system" ("Fashion's").

13. Daniel Miller has recently argued for the agency of objects. Critiquing what he describes as the "tyranny of the subject" within new material culture studies, in which objects simply represent subjects, Miller draws from Bruno Latour's philosophy of materiality to argue that "where material forms have consequences for people that are autonomous from human agency, they may be said to possess the agency that causes these effects" ("Materiality" 11). His examples are a plant that refuses to grow despite consistent watering or a computer that crashes in the middle of using it.

14. I am struck by the similarities between Khurana's racial fantasy of countersurveillance of the bindi and the racial fantasy of the bindi as an object of retributive violence in Sarat Chandra's short story "Dot Busters." Published in 1998, just three years before *Dothead* made its first official debut on the diasporic arts scene, "Dot Busters" explores how the targeting of the bindi as an object of racial violence produces a fashion dilemma for the bindi-wearing South Asian woman. In Chandra's story, Radha, a newly arrived South Asian immigrant, struggles with the decision of whether to wear her bindi as she traverses various public spaces in and around Jersey City, New Jersey. The bindi becomes a dilemma of embodiment for Radha after the Dotbusters verbally and physically harass her while she is grocery shopping. The attack on Radha follows on the heels of the Dotbusters' racial attacks on other South Asian women in Radha's immigrant community who also wear the bindi in public. Warned by her husband not to appeal to the police for legal protection because of their tenuous status as noncitizen immigrants, Radha temporarily abandons wearing the bindi in order to avoid future incidents of racial violence but resumes wearing it with T-shirts and jeans by the end of the story, when she is sexually assaulted by a Dotbusters gang member. Emboldened by her desire to protect her small son from witnessing her impending rape, Radha fights back. She uses the sharp end of the bracelet she is wearing to mutilate her attacker's penis, lifts the "kumkum dot from her forehead and smack[s] it" on her attacker's forehead while yelling, "Show your friends what a dot can do!" (34),

and escapes in her car. In "smack[ing]" her bindi onto the forehead of her white, male perpetrator, Radha uses the bindi—once a material object that subjects her to surveillance and violence—as a material object of retributive violence.

15. Khurana's racial fantasy of sartorial countersurveillance continues to play out in a more sustained way on the second channel of the installation. When viewed independently from the two-channel display, this channel cuts back and forth from Khurana's bindi to Madonna's and Stefani's performances of Indo-chic in their music videos. The images of Madonna and Stefani are overlaid with text that reads, "Women who are displaying their Hindu-ness by dressing in saris, wearing a bindi, are defined as targets for racial violence, as opposed to Indian women who dress in Western clothing." To the racially conscious viewer, the text contains a clear nativist logic—that if Indian women who choose to wear the bindi (and the sari) simply abandoned their everyday habits of dress, they could avoid being the targets of violence. Yet because this text appears underneath the images of Madonna and Stefani, and not Khurana, these frames produce a fantasy of Madonna and Stefani as "targets for racial violence" through their donning of the bindi and henna.

16. Thing.net, which began as an online bulletin-board system in 1991 and then took the form of an experimental arts website in 1995, is often hailed as launching online new-media art.

17. These features—photos, videos, chat rooms, gift shops, and real-time webcasts—are fairly standard conventions of amateur online porn. See Patterson, esp. 110–12.

18. The images of South Asian women are taken from Asian porn websites (Murthy, interview). Users are clued into this when, after viewing all nine porn artists, the message "BindiGirl's harem captured from 'the net'" appears.

19. As Shimizu notes, "Asian/American women comprise their own special genre in American pornography" (140).

20. I am not constructing a cause-effect relationship between Murthy's biracial identity and the framework of hybridity. Indeed, hybridity can be—and has been—deployed as a framework through which to understand South Asian cultural identities in South Asia *and* in the diaspora. More recently, bloggers of South Asian descent living in South Asia and the diaspora have argued for the bindi's inherent hybridity and are therefore critical of "cultural appropriation" arguments. For example, the South Asian American political blogger Jaya Sundaresh's reflections on bindi-chic resonate with those of Murthy: "The bindi has lost whatever religious significance it once had to Hindus some time ago, and is now used mostly for decoration. Madonna and Gwen Stefani didn't turn the bindi into a fashion statement when they adopted it in the 90s—we desi women already did so years before that." Yet many of these bloggers maintain that the bindi's stylishness still remains questionable when worn on South Asian bodies.

21. Though the origins of tantra are diverse—originating in Persia and then finding expression in Buddhist and other Indian sacred texts—tantra generally refers to sacred sexuality.

22. Haraway understands blasphemy as rooted in the figure of the cyborg (part [human/animal] organism, part machine). Cyborg feminism is a "rhetorical strategy and a political method" committed to "partiality, irony, intimacy, and perversity" (151).

23. The dots in Baldessari's photographs are actually price stickers, much like the ones found on discounted items in stores. They are thus linked to mass production even before they appear as part of pop art.

24. The proliferation of racialized cyberporn that "traffic[s] in racial and colonialist fictions and fantasies" does much to dispel the cybercultural fantasy of consumption-as-democratization (Pham, "Blog" 3).

25. Kusama herself "stridently denied any connection with feminism," but as the art critic Bree Richards contends, her art clearly "reference[s] feminism's history in art" and has been a clear, if understudied, influence among female artists who "embrace new media technologies and tropes."

26. Kusama's proliferative, repetitive, and multiplied dot aesthetic in fact came to dominate much pop art of the 1960s, most famously in the artwork of Andy Warhol.

27. The art critic Reuben Keehan describes Kusama's use of polka dots as "dissembl[ing]" and "obliterat[ing]" identity altogether.

28. The desacralization of the bindi in the blurring of the bindi with dots is visually resonant with the diasporic Pakistani visual artist Shahzia Sikander's use of the bindi and benday dots in her series of Mughal-inspired miniatures, "Venus's Wonderlands" and "Fleshly Weapons." See A. Patel.

29. It is also possible that Murthy's visual aesthetics of the bindi redirect the question of labor as residing elsewhere, namely, in the laboring body of the South Asian sex worker. That is, the bindi's appearance in *Bindigirl* brings into view a body that is normally invisible in discussions of orientalist consumer economies. In addition to the exploited South Asian female garment worker or the immigrant entrepreneurial businessperson who sells Indo-chic, *Bindigirl* posits the online South Asian female sex worker as a laboring body in these economies.

5 / Histories of the Cloth and Sartorial Sentiment in Shailja Patel's *Migritude*

1. Even after the events of 9/11, Indo-chic thrived. For more on the impact of 9/11 on Asian-chic designs, see Tu 118–20.

2. I discuss some of Negritude's prevailing features in what follows, but a fuller discussion of Negritude is beyond the scope of this chapter.

3. Its premiere at the La Peña underscored this fact. The La Peña was formed by a group of multiracial Latin Americans and North Americans as a response to a US-backed military coup that overthrew Chilean president Salvador Allende's socialist government in 1973. Since its founding, the La Peña has had a history of promoting existing and experimental cultural forms (La Peña Cultural Center).

4. Parijat Desai, a Bay Area–based South Asian American dancer, choreographed the performance.

5. For an analysis of Patel's early performance of excerpts of *Migritude* at Artwallah, see Mani, *Aspiring* 203–5.

6. In this way, Patel has been compared to the writer-activist Arundhati Roy, who has claimed that her politics have never been separate from her fictional writing. In her manifesto *Power Politics*, Roy writes, "I'm wondering why it should be that the person who wrote *The God of Small Things* is called a writer, and the person who wrote the political essays called an activist. *The God of Small Things* is a work of fiction, but it is no less political than any of my essays" (11).

7. Part of this oversight regarding the role of saris in the performance might have to do with the fact that Patel's book-length prose poem *Migritude* has received much more critical attention than the live performance has. In the printed version

of *Migritude*, the sari is the focal point of only three sections—"History of Paisley," "Swore I'd Never Wear Clothes I Couldn't Run or Fight In," and "Born to a Law"—all of which are part of the stage performance as well.

8. I borrow from Robin Bernstein's understanding of material objects as "scriptive things." A script "broadly structures" the way an object can be used but does not determine the possible uses of an object (11).

9. "Could commodities themselves speak, they would say: Our use value may be a thing that interests men. It is no part of us as objects. What, however, does belong to us is our [exchange] value" (Marx 83).

10. This little-known history of paisley is also the subject of the Kashmiri American poet Agha Shahid Ali's poem "The History of Paisley."

11. See writes within the context of Filipino American diasporic visual and performance art.

12. This sari's uniform structure marks it as distinct from garments such as pants, shirts, or most notably, the popular South Asian salwar kameez, which is not uniform in length, fit, and cut.

13. For the details of this history, see Nair; and Metcalf.

14. Patel's citation of the Mau Mau uprising might also be a tacit way of acknowledging historical links between Kenyan state nationalisms and British imperialisms. The historian Vijay Prashad has argued, "We tend to remember [Amin's expulsion of Asians from Uganda in 1972] only as an example of Idi Amin's heinousness, and we forget the hand of the British, who did two things: They created the idea that *desis* are only temporary workers whose culture is so transient that they can only make their lives in their homeland, and second, they made it very difficult for the Asians to enter Britain (whose 'Commonwealth' was shown to be an utter sham by this episode). The social being of the desi is structured by this imperial racism" (*Karma* 101).

15. These debates were most visible in the then-emerging discipline of feminist anthropology, though they also influenced more humanistic disciplines such as literary studies. See, for example, Gayatri Spivak's 1988 essay "Can the Subaltern Speak?" as a seminal example of these debates.

16. While it is generally agreed that Negritude as a literary political movement is linked most explicitly with Francophone writers such as Aimé Césaire, Léopold Sédar Senghor, and Léon Damas, its formation is geographically heterogeneous, historically contested, and politically and aesthetically diverse. It includes among its influences writers of the US Harlem Renaissance, such as Langston Hughes, Richard Wright, and Claude McKay, as well as those from the Spanish-speaking Caribbean, Haiti, and female Francophone Caribbean writers. For a few exemplary studies of Negritude, see Kesteloot; and Sartre. For an important historical intervention into the masculinist genealogy of the movement, see Sharpley-Whiting's *Negritude Women* and "Femme Négritude," as well as Edwards, esp. chap. 3.

17. Ngai's definition of tone departs from the classical literary definition of tone as an attitude that a writer/speaker takes toward his or her audience and instead focuses on tone as that which allows critics to characterize an artwork in affective terms.

18. While Patel does not cite Lorde in particular as an inspiration for her feminist poetics, she does claim a politicized identity as a "woman of color" in the United States, an identity that she traces to her encounters with the seminal women-of-color feminist anthology, *This Bridge Called My Back* (1984), edited by Cherríe Moraga and

Gloria Anzaldúa. As Patel explains, "*This Bridge Called My Back* was a major influence for me, as it was for a whole generation of young feminists of color. It gave me language and conceptual tools for my experience. . . . I do consider myself a woman of color in the U.S., because that is the first line of perception I encounter when I walk down the street" (145).

19. Lorde goes on to suggest that translating anger into action can help to identify "who are our allies with whom we have grave differences, and who are our genuine enemies" (8).

20. I am thinking here specifically of guilt as a form of racial objectification in which Patel might have otherwise trafficked, given the way that histories of race and class consolidated Asians' settler status in East Africa.

21. Indeed, we might read this generational narrative as itself proximate to these collective histories.

22. "The Mother" is the first of four installments of *Migritude*. Patel has also completed the second installment, called "The Father."

23. Keane provides the following example: "Western slacks treat the legs independently of one another. This permits a longer gait than does a Javanese sarong, inviting (but not determining) athleticism and giving them the potential for becoming . . . symbols understood as icons, of, say, 'freedom'" (194–95).

24. Even the popularity of Indo-chic style does not, according to Loomba, fully allow for the sari's insertion into performances of fashionability. She notes that the salwar kameez and not the sari has been more adaptable to both Indian and Western contemporary fashion trends (291–92).

25. For an incisive reading of the multiple ways in which the sari functions as an extension of the Indian woman's body, see D. Miller, introduction.

26. This is not to discount the way that sartorial judgments about sari colors, fabrics, design, and tying abound on the subcontinent, though these judgments tend to center on sari style as rural versus urban, cosmopolitan versus provincial, regional versus national, etc.

27. Though Patel's mother is not represented visually within *Migritude*, her voice in these letters is performed aurally through the voice of the Bay Area–based actor and director Vidhu Singh.

28. In "Shilling Love," Patel describes normative love, in the form of filial affection, as "emotions without consequences." *Migritude* was written after Patel's migration to the United States, where she now resides, and Patel associates this love with American families for whom love can be captured by a mere "I love you" (25), uttered with impunity. For Patel, the financial wealth of the US nation-state enables these families to express love without the risk of economic and political upheaval that might otherwise threaten the transparency of that love.

29. This is very likely due to the fact that the construction of "homeland" within concepts of diaspora rarely take into account multiple migrations and therefore multiple homelands.

30. Patel replicates in the prose poem this moment of sari display in a section called "What Came Out of the Suitcase." Patel details the appearance of each of her eighteen saris, along with her own and others' affective responses to each of them (65–70).

Epilogue

1. This is a phrase that, as Puar observes, became a "central organizing refrain for numerous national Sikh advocacy groups" after 9/11 (*Terrorist* 166).

2. Assessments about the incommensurability of turbans with fashionability and modernity are, of course, rooted in the colonial and postcolonial Indian state's historical and ongoing vilification and disenfranchisement of Sikh populations and the way that such histories inform the racialization of Sikhs in the diaspora.

3. As just three recent examples, see the South Asian Canadian artist Meera Sethi's street-style project *Upping the Aunty*, her collective visual art project *Unstitched: The Sari Project*, and the South Asian American beauty blog *Dark, Lovely, and South Asian* (http://darklovelyandsouthasian.tumblr.com/).

Bibliography

Abu-Lughod, Lila. "Do Muslim Women Really Need Saving? Anthropological Reflections on Cultural Relativism and its Others." *American Anthropologist* 104.3 (2002): 783–90.

Ahmed, Sara. *The Cultural Politics of Emotion*. London: Routledge, 2004.

———. *The Promise of Happiness*. Durham: Duke UP, 2010.

———. *Strange Encounters: Embodied Others in Post-coloniality*. London: Routledge, 2000.

Al-'Azm, Sadik Jalal. "Orientalism and Orientalism in Reverse." *Orientalism: A Reader*. New York: NYU P, 2000. 217–38.

Alessandrini, Anthony. "Reading Bharati Mukherjee, Reading Globalization." *World Bank Literature*. Ed. Amitava Kumar. Minneapolis: U of Minnesota P, 2003. 265–79.

Alexander, M. Jacqui. *Pedagogies of Crossing: Meditations on Feminism, Sexual Politics, and the Sacred*. Durham: Duke UP, 2005.

Alexander, Meena. *Manhattan Music*. New York: Mercury House, 1997.

———. *Words Matter: Conversations with Asian American Writers*. Ed. King-Kok Cheung. Honolulu: U of Hawaii P, 2001.

Ali, Agha Shahid. "A History of Paisley." *The Country without a Post Office*. New Delhi: Ravi Dayal, 1998.

Althusser, Louis. *Lenin and Philosophy and Other Essays*. Trans. Ben Brewster. New York: Monthly Review Press, 1971.

Anand, Anita. *The Beauty Game*. New Delhi: Penguin Books India, 2002.

Aneja, Anu. "*Jasmine*: The Sweet Scent of Exile." *Pacific Coast Philology* 28.1 (1993): 72–80.

Appadurai, Arjun. *Modernity at Large: Cultural Dimensions of Globalization*. Minneapolis: U of Minnesota P, 1996.

Aran, Ishra. "Take That Dot Off Your Forehead and Quit Trying to Make Bindis Happen." *Jezebel* 4 April 2014. Web. 12 Dec. 2014.

"Arundhati Roy." *People* 11 May 1998: 161.

Banet-Weiser, Sarah, and Roopali Mukherjee. "Introduction: Commodity Activism in Neoliberal Times." *Commodity Activism: Cultural Resistance in Neoliberal Times.* Ed. Mukherjee and Banet-Weiser. New York: NYU P, 2012. 1–17.

Barthes, Roland. *The Fashion System.* Trans. Matthew Ward and Richard Howard. Berkeley: U of California P, 1990.

Bascara, Victor. *Model Minority Imperialism.* Minneapolis: U of Minnesota P, 2006.

Baynton, Douglas. C. "Disability and the Justification of Inequality in American History." *The Disability Studies Reader.* 4th ed. New York: Routledge, 2013. 17–33.

Berlant, Lauren. "Cruel Optimism." *The Affect Theory Reader.* Ed. Melissa Gregg and Gregory J. Seigworth. Durham: Duke UP, 2007. 93–117.

———. *The Female Complaint: The Unfinished Business of Sentimentality in American Culture.* Durham: Duke UP, 2008.

Bernstein, Robin. *Racial Innocence: Performing American Childhood from Slavery to Civil Rights.* New York: NYU P, 2011.

Bhachu, Parminder. *Dangerous Designs: Asian Women Fashion the Diaspora Economies.* London: Routledge, 2003.

Bhattacharjee, Ananya. "The Habit of Ex-Nomination: Nation, Woman, and the Indian Immigrant Bourgeoisie." *Public Culture* 5.1 (1992): 19–44.

Bordo, Susan. *Unbearable Weight: Feminism, Western Culture, and the Body.* Berkeley: U of California P, 1993.

Bourdieu, Pierre. *Distinction: A Social Critique of the Judgment of Taste.* 1979. Trans. Richard Nice. Cambridge: Harvard UP, 1984.

———. *Sociology in Question.* Trans. Richard Nice. London: Sage, 1993.

Bow, Leslie. *Partly Colored: Asian Americans and Racial Anomaly in the Segregated South.* New York: NYU P, 2010.

Boym, Svetlana. "On Diasporic Intimacy: Ilya Kabakov's Installations and Immigrant Homes." *Intimacy.* Ed. Lauren Berlant. Chicago: U of Chicago P. 226–52.

Brand, Peg Zeglin, ed. *Beauty Matters.* Bloomington: Indiana UP, 2000.

Brennan, Teresa. *The Transmission of Affect.* Ithaca: Cornell UP, 2004.

Brontë, Charlotte. *Jane Eyre.* London: Smith Elder, 1847.

Brooklynwala. "Turbans on the Runway: What Does It Mean for Sikhs?" *Langar Hall* (blog) 10 July 2012. Web. 13 Sept. 2013.

Brown, Wendy. *Edgework: Critical Essays on Knowledge and Politics.* Princeton: Princeton UP, 2005.

Butler, Pamela, and Jigna Desai, "Manolos, Marriage, and Mantras: Chick-Lit Criticism and Transnational Feminism." *Meridians: Feminism, Race, Transnationalism* 8.2 (2008): 1–31.

Carter-Sanborn, Kristin. "We Murder Who We Were: *Jasmine* and the Violence of Identity." *American Literature* 66.3 (1994): 573–93.

Césaire, Aimé. *Notes of a Return to My Native Land.* Trans. and ed. Clayton Eshleman and Annette Smith. Middleton, CT: Wesleyan UP, 2001.

Chakrabarty, Dipesh. *Provincializing Europe: Postcolonial Thought and Historical Difference.* Princeton: Princeton UP, 2000.

Chandra, G. S. Sharat. "Dot Busters." *Sari of the Gods.* Minneapolis: Coffee House, 1998. 23–34.

Chatterjee, Partha. *A Nation and Its Fragments: Colonial and Postcolonial Histories.* Princeton: Princeton UP, 1993.

Cheah, Peng. "Introduction Part II: The Cosmopolitical Today." *Cosmopolitics: Thinking and Feeling beyond the Nation.* Ed. Cheah and Bruce Robbins. Minneapolis: U of Minnesota P, 1998. 20–44.

Chen, Nancy. "'Speaking Nearby.' A Conversation with Trinh T. Minh-Ha." *Visual Anthropology Review* 8.1 (Spring 1992): 82–91.

Chen, Tina. *Double Agents: Acts of Impersonation in Asian American Literature and Culture.* Stanford: Stanford UP, 2005.

Cheng, Anne. "Wounded Beauty: An Exploratory Essay on Race, Beauty, and the Aesthetic Question." *Tulsa Studies in Women's Literature* 19.2 (2000): 191–217.

"Chitra Divakaruni: The Road to *Shadowland.*" *Language Arts* 87.3 (2010): 215–18.

Chow, Rey. *The Protestant Ethnic and the Spirit of Capitalism.* New York: Columbia UP, 2002.

Chu, Patricia. "Women's Plots: Edith Maude Eaton and Bharati Mukherjee." *Assimilating Asians: Gendered Strategies of Authorship in Asian America.* Durham: Duke UP, 2000. 90–138.

Chuh, Kandice. *Imagine Otherwise: On Asian Americanist Critique.* Durham: Duke UP, 2003.

Clough, Patricia, and Janet Halley, eds. *The Affective Turn: Theorizing the Social.* Durham: Duke UP, 2007.

Cvetkovich, Ann. *An Archive of Feelings: Trauma, Sexuality, and Lesbian Public Cultures.* Durham: Duke UP, 2003.

Das Gupta, Monisha. *Unruly Immigrants: Rights, Activism, and Transnational South Asian Politics in the United States.* Durham: Duke UP, 2006.

Daswani, Kavita. *Indie Girl.* New York: Simon Pulse, 2007.

Dave, Shilpa. " 'Community Beauty: Transnational Performances and Cultural Citizenship in 'Miss India Georgia.'" *LIT* 12 (2001): 335–58.

Dave, Shilpa, Pawan Dhingra, et al. "De-Privileging Positions: Indian Americans, South Asian Americans, and the Politics of Asian American Studies." *Journal of Asian American Studies* 3.1 (2000): 67–100.

Deleuze, Gilles, and Félix Guattari. *A Thousand Plateaus: Capitalism and Schizophrenia.* Minneapolis: U of Minnesota P, 1987.

Desai, Jigna. "Bollywood, USA." *Transnational South Asians: The Making of a Neo-Diaspora*. Ed. Susan Koshy and R. Radhakrishnan. Oxford: Oxford UP, 2008. 345–67.

Desai, Jigna, and Khyati Y. Joshi. Introduction. Joshi and Desai 1–30.

Devil's Food Cake. "Friday Fancy...Jhumpa Lahiri." *The Most Cake* 28 Oct. 2011. Web. 12 Dec. 2012. http://themostcake.co.uk/culture/friday-fancy-jhumpa-lahiri/.

Dewey, Susan. *Making Miss India Miss World: Constructing Gender, Power, and the Nation in Postliberalization India*. Syracuse: Syracuse UP, 2008.

Dimock, Wai Chee. "Transnational Beauty: Aesthetics and Treason, Kant and Pound." *Through Other Continents: American Literature Across Deep Time*. Princeton: Princeton UP, 2007. 107–22.

Divakaruni, Chitra Banerjee. *Arranged Marriage*. New York: Anchor, 1995.

———. *The Mistress of Spices*. New York: Anchor, 1997.

———. *Neela: Victory Song*. Middleton, WI: Pleasant, 2002.

Dixit, Pallavi Sharma. "Pageant." *Her Mother's Ashes 3: Stories by South Asian Women in Canada and the United States*. Ed. Nurjehan Aziz. Toronto: TSAR, 2009. 3–10.

———. Personal interview. 2 Oct. 2012.

Doane, Mary Ann. "Film and the Masquerade: Theorizing the Female Spectator." *Screen* 23.3–4 (1982): 74–87.

Dolby, Nadine, and Fazal Rizvi. "Introduction: Youth, Mobility, and Identity." *Youth Moves: Identities and Education in Global Perspective*. Ed. Dolby and Rizvi. New York: Routledge, 2008. 1–14.

"Dothead." Swati Khurana's website. n.d. Web. 10 Mar. 2011. http://swati-khurana.com/portfolio/video/dothead.

Dothead. Dir. Swati Khurana. 2001. DVD.

Du Bois, W. E. B. *The Souls of Black Folk*. Chicago: A. C. McClurg, 1903.

Dulaara. Dir. Vimal Kumar. Shivam Chitrya, 1994. DVD.

Edmonds, Alexander. *Pretty Modern: Beauty, Sex, and Plastic Surgery in Brazil*. Durham: Duke UP, 2010.

Edwards, Brent Hayes. *The Practice of Diaspora: Literature, Translation, and the Rise of Black Internationalism*. Cambridge: Harvard UP, 2003.

Eng, David. *The Feeling of Kinship: Queer Liberalism and the Racialization of Intimacy*. Durham: Duke UP, 2010.

———. *Racial Castration: Managing Masculinity in Asian America*. Durham: Duke UP, 2001.

English, James F. *The Economy of Prestige: Prizes, Awards, and the Circulation of Cultural Value*. Cambridge: Harvard UP, 2008.

Entwistle, Joanne, and Elizabeth Wissinger, eds. *Fashioning Models: Image, Text, Industry*. London: Berg, 2012.

Etcoff, Nancy. *Survival of the Prettiest*. New York: Anchor, 2000.

Fanon, Frantz. *Black Skin, White Masks*. Rev. ed. New York: Grove, 2008.

Fashion. Dir. Madhur Bhandarkar. Pacific Eastern Imports, 2007. DVD.

Flynn, Sean. "Women We Love: Jhumpa Lahiri." *Esquire* 1 Oct. 2000: 172–73.

Foucault, Michel. *The History of Sexuality, an Introduction: Volume I.* New York: Random House, 1978.

——. *Technologies of the Self: A Seminar with Michel Foucault.* Ed. Luther H. Martin, Huck Gutman, and Patrick H. Hutton. Amherst: U of Massachusetts P, 1988.

Freeman, Elizabeth. *Time Binds: Queer Temporalities, Queer Histories.* Durham: Duke UP, 2010.

Fung, Richard. "Working through Cultural Appropriation." *Fuse* 16.5–6 (1993): 16–24.

Ghosh, Bishnupriya. *Global Icons: Apertures to the Popular.* Durham: Duke UP, 2011.

Ghosh, Shohini. "Queer Pleasures for Queer People: Film, Television, and Queer Sexuality in India." *Queering India: Same-Sex Love and Eroticism in Indian Culture and Society.* Ed. Ruth Vanita. New York: Routledge, 2002. 127–48.

Gilbert, Sandra M., and Susan Gubar. *The Madwoman in the Attic: The Woman Writer and the Nineteenth-Century Literary Imagination.* New Haven: Yale UP, 1979.

Gill, Harjant. "Unthreatening the Sikh Turban." *Anthropology News* 30 Aug. 2012. 1–3.

Gilroy, Paul. *Postcolonial Melancholia.* New York: Columbia UP, 2005.

Godsell, Oliver. "John Baldessari: Connecting the Dots." *Artwrite* 49 18 Sept. 2012. Web. 3 Mar. 2013. https://artwrite49.wordpress.com/john-baldessari-connecting-dots/.

Good Hair. Dir. Jeff Stilson. United Artists, 2009. DVD.

Gopinath, Gayatri. *Impossible Desires: Queer Diasporas and South Asian Public Cultures.* Durham: Duke UP, 2005.

——. "Queer Regions: Locating Lesbians in *Sancharram*." *A Companion to Lesbian, Gay, Bisexual, and Transgender Studies.* Ed. George E. Haggerty and Molly McGarry. Oxford, UK: Blackwell, 2007. 341–54.

Gray, Mary. *Out in the Country: Youth, Media, and Queer Visibility in Rural America.* New York: NYU P, 2009.

Grewal, Inderpal. *Transnational America: Feminisms, Diasporas, Neoliberalisms.* Durham: Duke UP, 2005.

Grzegorczyck, Blanka. "Rewriting Colonial Histories in Historical Fictions for the Young: From Below and Above." *Bookbird* 3 (2012): 34–46.

Gundara, Jagdish. Rev. of *Migritude*, by Shailja Patel. *Intercultural Education* 22.3 (2011): 225–26.

Gunga Din. Dir. George Stevens. RKO Radio Pictures, 1939. Film.

Hafiz, Yasmine. "Nina Davuluri's 2014 Win Prompts Twitter Backlash against Indians, Muslims." *Huffington Post* 16 Sept. 2013.

Hair India. Dir. Raffaele Brunetti and Marco Leopardi. B&B Film, 2008. DVD.

Halberstam, Judith. *In a Queer Time and Place*: New York: NYU P, 2005.

——. *The Queer Art of Failure*. Durham: Duke UP, 2011.

Hall, Stuart. "Cultural Identity and Diaspora." *Identity and Difference*. Ed. Kathryn Woodward. London: Sage, 1997. 51–58.

——. "Race, Articulation, and Societies Structured in Dominance." 1980. *Black British Cultural Studies: A Reader*. Ed. Houston A. Baker, Manthia Diawara, and Ruth H. Lindeborg. Chicago: U of Chicago P, 1996.

Hall, Stuart, and Paul DuGay, eds. *Questions of Cultural Identity*. London: Sage, 1996.

Hancock, Geoff. "An Interview with Bharati Mukherjee." *Canadian Fiction Magazine* 59 (1987): 37.

Hanley, Robert. "3 Indicted in Beating of Indian Doctor." *New York Times* 12. Sept. 1992. Web. 11 Mar. 2013. http://www.nytimes.com/1992/09/12/nyregion/3-indicted-in-beating-of-indian-doctor.html.

Haraway, Donna. "Cyborg Manifesto: Science, Technology, and Socialist Feminism in the Late Twentieth Century." *Simians, Cyborgs, and Women: The Reinvention of Nature*. New York: Routledge, 1991. 149–81.

Harmanci, Reyhan. "History Unfolds/'Migritude' Performer Shailja Patel Uses Saris and Letters to Explore Politics, Personal Identity." *SFGate* 30 Nov. 2006. Web. 5 Jan. 2007. http://www.sfgate.com/thingstodo/article/History-unfolds-Migritude-Performer-Shailja-2483793.php.

Hartman, Saidiya. *Scenes of Subjection: Slavery, Terror, and Self-Making in Nineteenth Century America*. Oxford: Oxford UP, 1997.

Hattori, Tomo. "Model Minority Discourse and Asian American Jouis-Sense." *differences: A Journal of Feminist Cultural Studies* 11.2 (1999): 228–47.

Helgesson, Stefan. Rev. of *Migritude*, by Shailja Patel. *Journal of Postcolonial Writing* July 2012: 331–32.

Herring, Scott. *Another Country: Queer Anti-urbanism*. New York: NYU P, 2010.

Hettne, Bjorn, Andras Innotai, and Osvaldo Sunkel, eds. *Globalism and the New Regionalism*. London: Macmillan, 1999.

Hickman, Jennifer. "Consuming: Multimedia, Gender, and Identity." *NYFA Quarterly* Nov. 1999. Web. 10 Oct. 2012.

Hutcheon, Linda. *A Theory of Parody: The Teachings of Twentieth-Century Art Forms*. Urbana: U of Illinois P, 2000.

Indiana Jones and the Temple of Doom. Dir. Steven Spielberg. Paramount Pictures, 1984. Film.

Inness, Sherrie. *Delinquents and Debutantes: Twentieth Century American Girls' Culture*. New York: NYU P, 1998.

Jakhar, Deepti. "Haute Turbanators: Ace French Designer Jean Paul Gaultier's Sikh-Inspired Line Reflects His Love for India." *DailyMail.com India* 29 June 2012. Web. 1 Dec. 2014.

Jameson, Frederic. *Postmodernism, or, the Cultural Logic of Late Capitalism*. Durham: Duke UP, 1991.

Jevens, Susan. Personal interview. 13 Dec. 2010.

Jiwani, Yasmin, Candis Steenbergen, and Claudia Mitchell, eds. *Girlhood: Redefining the Limits*. Montreal: Black Rose Books, 2006.

John, Mary E., and Janaki Nair. *A Question of Silence: The Sexual Economies of Modern India*. Delhi: Zed Books, 2000.

"John Baldessari." *Art 21*. n.d. Web. 13 June 2014. http://www.pbs.org/art21/artists/john-baldessari.

Johnson, Colin. *Just Queer Folks: Gender and Sexuality in Rural America*. Philadelphia: Temple UP, 2013.

Joshi, Anjali. "Why the Bindi Is NOT an Example of Cultural Appropriation." *Huffington Post* 15 Apr. 2014.

Joshi, Khyati Y., and Jigna Desai, eds. *Asian Americans in Dixie: Race and Migration in the South*. Urbana: U of Illinois P, 2013.

Kachka, Boris. "What Is Jhumpa Lahiri's Hook?" *New York* 31 Mar. 2008. Web. 3 Sept. 2012. http://nymag.com/arts/books/profiles/45571/.

Kalra, Virinder S. "Locating the Sikh Pagh." *Sikh Formations: Religion, Culture, Theory* 1.1 (2005): 75–92.

Kant, Immanuel. *Observations on the Feeling of the Beautiful and Sublime*. 1764. Trans. John T. Goldthwait. Berkeley: U of California P, 1991.

Kawamura, Yuniya. *Fashion-ology: An Introduction to Fashion Studies*. New York: Berg, 2005.

Keane, Webb. "Signs Are Not the Garb of Meaning: On the Social Analysis of Material Things." *Materiality*. Ed. Daniel Miller. Durham: Duke UP, 2005. 182–205.

Keehan, Reuben. "Specific Obsessions: Reading Kusama through Minimalism." *Yayoi Kusama: Look Now, See Forever*. N.p. N.d. Web. 4 Apr. 2013. http://interactive.qag.qld.gov.au/looknowseeforever/essays/specific-obsessions/.

Kesteloot, Lilyan. *Black Writers in French: A Literary History of Negritude*. Trans. Ellen Conroy Kennedy. Philadelphia: Temple UP, 1974.

Khal Naaikaa. Dir. Saawan Kumar Tok. DEI, 1993. DVD.

Khal Nayak. Dir. Subhash Ghai. Mukta Arts, 1993. DVD.

Khilnani, Sunil. *The Idea of India*. New York: Farrar, Straus, and Giroux, 1999.

Khuddar. Dir. Iqbal Durrani. DEI, 1998. DVD.

Khurana, Swati. Personal interview. 19 July 2012.

Kibria, Nazli. "Not Asian, Black or White? Reflections on South Asian American Racial Identity." *Amerasia Journal* 22.2 (1996): 77–86.

King-O'Riain, Rebecca Chiyoko. *Pure Beauty: Judging Race in Japanese-American Beauty Pageants*. Minneapolis: U of Minnesota P, 2006.

Klein, Melanie. *Cold War Orientalism: Asia in the Middlebrow Imagination, 1945–1961*. Berkeley: U of California Press, 2003.

Koshy, Susan. "The Geography of Female Subjectivity." *Contemporary American Women Writers: Gender, Class, Ethnicity*. Ed. Lois Parkinson Zamora. London: Longman, 1998. 138–53.

———. "Minority Cosmopolitanism." *PMLA* 126.3 (2011): 592–609.

———. "Morphing Race into Ethnicity: Asian Americans and Critical Transformations of Whiteness." *boundary 2* 28.1 (2001): 153–94.

———. *Sexual Naturalization: Asian Americans and Miscegenation.* Stanford: Stanford UP, 2005.

———. "Why the Humanities Matter for Race Studies Today." *PMLA* 123.5 (2008): 1542–49.

Küchler, Susanne, and Daniel Miller, eds. *Clothing as Material Culture.* Oxford, UK: Berg, 2005.

Lahiri, Jhumpa. "Interpreter of Maladies." *Interpreter* 43–69.

———. *Interpreter of Maladies: Stories of Bengal, Boston and Beyond.* 1999. New Delhi: HarperCollins, 2003.

———. *The Namesake.* Boston: Houghton Mifflin, 2003.

———. "Sexy." *Interpreter* 83–110.

———. "This Blessed House." *Interpreter* 136–57.

———. "The Treatment of Bibi Haldar." *Interpreter* 158–72.

———. *Unaccustomed Earth.* New York: Knopf, 2008.

Lal, Vinay. *The Other Indians: A Political and Cultural History of South Asians in America.* Ed. Don T. Nakanishi and Russell C. Leong. Los Angeles: UCLA Asian American Studies Center, 2008.

Lamb, Sharon, and Lyn Mikel Brown. *Packaging Girlhood: Rescuing Our Daughters from Marketers' Schemes.* New York: St. Martin's, 2006.

La Peña Cultural Center. "La Historia." 2012. Web. 2 May 2013. http://lapena.org/la-pena-history/.

Lara, Adair. "Lahiri Finds Writing Life No Easier after Pulitzer." *SFGate* 7 Oct. 2003. Web. 31 July 2012. http://www.sfgate.com/entertainment/article/Lahiri-finds-writing-life-no-easier-after-Pulitzer-2583747.php.

Larsen, Nella. *Passing.* New York: Knopf, 1929.

Leeds, Maxine. *Ain't I a Beauty Queen? Black Women, Beauty, and the Politics of Race.* New York: Oxford UP, 2002.

Levander, Caroline F. *Cradle of Liberty: Race, the Child, and National Belonging from Thomas Jefferson to W. E. B. Du Bois.* Durham: Duke UP, 2007.

Li, David Leiwei. *Imagining the Nation: Asian American Literature and Cultural Consent.* Stanford: Stanford UP, 1998.

Lipsitz, George. *The Possessive Investment in Whiteness: How White People Benefit from Identity Politics.* Philadelphia: Temple UP, 1998.

Loomba, Ania. "The Long and Saggy Sari." *Women: a Cultural Review* 8.3 (1997): 278–92.

Lorde, Audre. "The Uses of Anger." *Women's Studies Quarterly* 9.3 (1981): 7–10.

Low, Gail Ching-Liang. "In a Free State: Post-Colonialism and Postmodernism in Bharati Mukherjee's Fiction." *Women: A Cultural Review* 4.1 (1993): 8–17.

Lowe, Lisa. *Immigrant Acts: On Asian American Cultural Politics.* Durham: Duke UP, 1996.

Lukose, Ritty. "The Children of Liberalization: Youth Agency and Globalization in India." *Youth Moves: Identities and Education in Global Perspective.* Ed. Nadine Dolby and Fazal Rizvi. New York: Routledge, 2008. 133–49.

Lyons, Janet. *Manifestoes: Provocations of the Modern.* Ithaca: Cornell UP, 1999.

Machida, Margo. *Unsettled Visions: Contemporary Asian American Artists and the Social Imaginary.* Durham: Duke UP, 2009.

"Madhuri's Million Dollar Smile Immortalized." *The Anokhi Blog* 13 Mar. 2012. Web. 12 Dec. 2012. http://www.anokhimagazine.com/anokhi-blog/madhuris-million-dollar-smile-imortalized.

Madonna. "Frozen." *Ray of Light.* Maverick Records, 1998. Music video.

Maira, Sunaina. *Desis in the House: Indian American Youth Culture in New York City.* Philadelphia: Temple UP, 2002.

———. "'Good' and 'Bad' Muslim Citizens: Feminists, Terrorists, and U.S. Orientalisms." *Feminist Studies* 35.3 (2009): 631–56.

———. "Indo-chic: Late Capitalist Orientalism and Imperial Culture." *Alien Encounters: Popular Culture in Asian America.* Ed. Mimi Nguyen and Thuy Linh Nguyen Tu. Durham: Duke UP, 2007. 221–45.

———. *Missing: Youth, Citizenship, and Empire after 9/11.* Durham: Duke UP, 2009.

Mani, Bakirathi. *Aspiring to Home: Becoming South Asian in America.* Stanford: Stanford UP, 2012.

———. "Beauty Queens: Gender, Ethnicity, and Transnational Modernities at the Miss India USA Pageant." *positions: asia critique* 14.3 (2006): 717–47.

———. "The Imagination of South Asian America: Cultural Politics in the Making of Diaspora." Ph.D. diss., Stanford University, 2002.

Mankekar, Purnima. "Brides Who Travel: Gender, Transnationalism, and Nationalism in Hindi Film." *positions: asia critique* 7.3 (1999): 731–62.

Mannur, Anita. *Culinary Fictions: Food in South Asian Diasporic Culture.* Philadelphia: Temple UP, 2010.

Mannur, Anita, and Pia Sahni. "'What Can Brown Do for You?' Indo-chic and the Fashionability of South Asian Inspired Styles." *Journal of South Asian Popular Culture* 9.2 (2011): 177–90.

Manuel, Peter. "The Popularization and the Transformation of the Light Classical Urdu *Ghazal* Song." *Gender, Genre, and Power in South Asian Expressive Traditions.* Ed. Arjun Appadurai, Frank J. Korom, and Margaret A. Mills. Philadelphia: U of Pennsylvania P, 1991. 347–61.

Mao, Douglas. "The Labor Theory of Beauty: Aesthetic Subjects, Blind Justice." *Aesthetic Subjects.* Ed. Pamela Matthews and David McWhirter. Minneapolis: U of Minnesota P, 2003. 190–229.

Marx, Karl. *Capital: Critique of Political Economy: Volume I.* 1867. Trans. Samuel Moore and Edward Aveling. Moscow: Progress, 1887.

Massumi, Brian. *Parables for the Virtual: Movement, Affect, Sensation.* Durham: Duke UP, 2002.

Mazzarella, William. *Shoveling Smoke: Advertising and Globalization in Contemporary India*. Durham: Duke UP, 2003.

McLaren, Peter. "White Terror and Oppositional Agency: Towards a Critical Multiculturalism." *Multicultural Education, Critical Pedagogy, and the Politics of Difference*. Ed. Christine E. Sleeter and Peter McLaren. Albany: State U of New York P, 1995. 33–70.

Mears, Ashley. *Pricing Beauty: The Making of a Fashion Model*. Berkeley: U of California Press, 2011.

Mehta, Monika. "What Is Behind Film Censorship? The *Khalnayak* Debates." *Jouvert: A Journal of Postcolonial Studies* 5.3 (2001): 1–12.

Metcalf, Thomas. *Imperial Connections: India in the Indian Ocean Arena*. Berkeley: U of California Press, 2007.

"Migritude." Shailja Patel's website. N.d. Web. July 2009. shailja.com/about/migritude.html.

Migritude. By Shailja Patel. Dir. Kim Cook. La Peña Arts Center, Oakland, CA, 6 Nov. 2006. Performance and DVD.

Miller, Daniel. Introduction. *Clothing as Material Culture*. Ed. Susanne Kuchler and Daniel Miller. Oxford, UK: Berg, 2003. 1–21.

———. "Materiality: An Introduction." *Materiality*. Ed. Miller. Durham: Duke UP, 2005. 1–50.

Miller, Toby. *Cultural Citizenship: Cosmopolitanism, Consumerism, and Television in a Neoliberal Age*. Philadelphia: Temple UP, 2006.

Mishra, Vijay. *Bollywood Cinema: Temples of Desire*. New York: Routledge, 2002.

Miss India Georgia. Dir. Daniel Friedman and Sharon Grimberg. Urban Life Productions, 1997. DVD.

Moallem, Minoo. *Between Warrior Brother and Veiled Sister: Islamic Fundamentalism and the Politics of Patriarchy in Iran*. Berkeley: U of California P, 2005.

Monegato, Emanuele. "On *Migritude*, Part I; When Saris Speak—The Mother: A Conversation with Shailja Patel." *Other Modernities* 15 July 2008.

Moraga, Cherríe, and Gloria Anzaldúa, eds. *This Bridge Called My Back: Writings by Radical Women of Color*. 2nd ed. New York: Kitchen Table, 1984.

Moran, Joe. *Star Authors: Literary Celebrity in America*. London: Pluto, 2000.

Mukherjee, Bharati. "American Dreamer." *Mother Jones* 22.1 (1997): 1–6.

———. "Beyond Multiculturalism: Surviving the Nineties." *Journal of Modern Literature* 20.1 (1996): 29–34.

———. "Jasmine." *The Middlemen and Other Stories*. New York: Grove, 1988. 125–38.

———. *Jasmine*. New York: Grove, 1989.

———. *Miss New India*. New York: Houghton Mifflin, 2011.

Mukhi, Sunita Sunder. "'Underneath My Blouse Beats My Indian Heart': Sexuality, Nationalism, and Indian Womanhood in the United States." *A Patchwork Shawl: Chronicles of South Asian Women in America*. Ed. Shamita Das Dasgupta. New Brunswick: Rutgers UP, 1998. 186–205.

Muñoz, José Esteban. "Feeling Brown: Ethnicity and Affect in Ricardo Bracho's *The Sweetest Hangover* (and Other STDS)." *Theatre Journal* 52.1 (2000): 67–79.

Murthy, Prema. *Bindigirl.* Thing.net 1999. Web. 15 Feb. 2013. http://www.thing. net/~bindigrl/.

———. Personal interview. 29 June 2012.

Naipaul, V. S. *A House for Mr. Biswas.* 1961. London: Vintage, 2001.

Nair, Savita. "Shops and Stations: Rethinking Power and Privilege in British/ Indian East Africa." *India in Africa, Africa in India.* Bloomington: Indiana UP, 2008. 77–94.

Nakamura, Lisa. *Digitizing Race: Visual Cultures of the Internet.* Minneapolis: U of Minnesota P, 2007.

The Namesake. Dir. Mira Nair. Fox Searchlight Pictures, 2006. DVD.

Nehamas, Alexander. *Only the Promise of Happiness: The Place of Beauty in a World of Art.* Princeton: Princeton UP, 2010.

Ngai, Sianne. *Ugly Feelings.* Cambridge: Harvard UP, 2005.

Nguyen, Mimi. "The Biopower of Beauty: Humanitarian Imperialisms and Global Feminisms in an Age of Terror." *Signs: Women, Culture, and Society* 36.2 (2011): 359–83.

Nguyen, Viet Thanh. *Race and Resistance: Literature and Politics in Asian America.* Oxford: Oxford UP, 2002.

Niessen, Sandra, Ann Marie Leshkowich, and Carla Jones. *Re-Orienting Fashion: The Globalization of Asian Dress.* Oxford, UK: Berg, 2003.

Ninh, erin Khuê. "Gold Digger: Reading the Marital and National Romance in Bharati Mukherjee's *Jasmine.*" *MELUS: Multi-Ethnic Literature of the U.S.* 38.3 (Fall 2013): 146–59.

No Doubt. "I'm Just a Girl." *Tragic Kingdom.* Interscope Records, 1995. Music video.

Norris, Lucy. *Recycling Indian Clothing: Global Contexts of Reuse and Value.* Bloomington: Indiana UP, 2010.

Omi, Michael, and Howard Winant. *Racial Formation in the United States: From the 1960s to the 1990s.* New York: Routledge, 1994.

Ong, Aihwa. *Flexible Citizenship: The Cultural Logics of Transnationality.* Durham: Duke UP, 1999.

———. *Neoliberalism as Exception: Mutations in Citizenship and Sovereignty.* Durham: Duke UP, 2006.

Ong, Aihwa, and Stephen Collier. Introduction. *Global Assemblages: Technology, Politics, and Ethics as Anthropological Problems.* Ed. Ong and Collier. Malden, MA: Blackwell, 2005. 3–21.

Osterweil, Ara. "Andy Warhol's *Blow Job*: Toward the Recognition of a Pornographic Avant-garde." *Porn Studies.* Ed. Linda Williams. Durham: Duke UP, 2004. 432–60.

Osuri, Goldie. "Ash-Coloured Whiteness: The Transfigurations of Aishwarya Rai." *Journal of South Asian Popular Culture* 6.2 (2008): 109–23.

Oza, Rupal. *The Making of Neoliberal India: Nationalism, Gender, and the Paradoxes of Globalization*. New York: Routledge, 2006.

Parameswaran, Radhika. "E-Racing Color: Gender and Transnational Visual Economies of Beauty in India." *Circuits of Visibility: Gender and Transnational Media Cultures*. New York: NYU P, 2011. 68–86.

Park, Lisa. *Consuming Citizenship: Children of Asian Immigrant Entrepreneurs*. Stanford: Stanford UP, 2005.

Parreñas, Rhacel Salazar. *Servants of Globalization: Women, Migration, and Domestic Work*. Stanford: Stanford UP, 2001.

Parreñas, Rhacel, and Eileen Borris, eds. *Intimate Labors: Cultures, Technologies, and the Politics of Care*. Stanford: Stanford UP, 2010.

Patel, Alpesh. "Queer Desi Visual Culture across the Brown Atlantic." PhD diss., U of Manchester, 2011.

Patel, Shailja. *Migritude*. New York: Kaya, 2010. Web. 8 Oct. 2006. http://www.shailja.com.

———. Personal interview. 30 Sept. 2008.

Patterson, Zabet. "Going On-line: Consuming Pornography in the Digital Era." *Porn Studies*. Ed. Linda Williams. Durham: Duke UP, 2004. 104–23.

Peiss, Kathy. *Hope in a Jar: The Making of America's Beauty Culture*. Philadelphia: U of Pennsylvania P, 1998.

Pham, Minh-Ha T. "Blog Ambition: Fashion, Feelings, and the Political Economy of the Digital Raced Body." *Camera Obscura 76* 26.1 (2011): 1–38.

———. "Fashion's Cultural Appropriation Debate: Pointless." *Atlantic* 15 May 2014. Web. 14 Nov. 2014. http://www.theatlantic.com/entertainment/archive/2014/05/cultural-appropriation-in-fashion-stop-talking-about-it/370826/.

Pinto, Rochelle. "Singh Street Style." *Vogue India*. 17 June 2013. Web. 15 Jan. 2015.

Prashad, Vijay. "Speaking of Saris." *Migritude*. By Shailja Patel. New York: Kaya, 2010. i–v.

———. *The Karma of Brown Folk*. Minneapolis: U of Minnesota P, 2000.

"Pratibha Parmar." Carroll/Fletcher Onscreen. 3 July 2014. Web. http://carroll-fletcheronscreen.com/2014/07/03/pratibha-parma/.

Premnath, Gautam. "The Weak Sovereignty of the Postcolonial Nation-State." *World Bank Literature*. Ed. Amitava Kumar. Minneapolis: U of Minnesota P, 2003. 253–64.

Puar, Jasbir. "'I Would Rather Be a Cyborg than a Goddess': Intersectionality, Assemblage, and Affective Politics." European Institute for Progressive Cultural Policies, 5 Feb. 2011. http://www.eipcp.net/transversal/0811/puar/en.

———. *Terrorist Assemblages: Homonationalism in Queer Times*. Durham: Duke UP, 2007.

Puchner, Martin. *Poetry of the Revolution: Marx, Manifestoes, and the Avant-Gardes*. Princeton: Princeton UP, 2005.

Qureshi, Regula Burckhardt. "In Search of Begum Akhtar: Patriarchy, Poetry, and Twentieth-Century Indian Music." *world of music* 43.1 (2001): 93–137.

Radhakrishnan, Smitha. *Appropriately Indian: Gender and Culture in a New Transnational Class.* Durham: Duke UP, 2011.

Rai, Amit. *Untimely Bollywood: Globalization and India's New Media Assemblage.* Durham: Duke UP, 2010.

Rajagopal, Arvind. *Politics after Television: Hindu Nationalism and the Reshaping of the Public in India.* Cambridge: Cambridge UP, 2001.

Rajan, Gita, and Shailja Sharma. "Theorizing Recognition: South Asian Authors in a Global Milieu." *New Cosmopolitanisms: South Asians in the U.S.* Ed. Rajan and Sharma. Stanford: Stanford UP, 2006. 150–70.

Rajghatta, Chidanand. "Indian Touch Breathes Life into Moribund Miss America Pageant." *Times of India* 16 Sept. 2013.

——. "Racist Slurs Mar Triumph of First Miss America of Indian Origin." *Times of India* 17 Sept. 2013.

Ramamurthy, Priti. "All-Consuming Nationalism: The Indian Modern Girl in the 1920s and 1930s." *The Modern Girl around the World: Consumption, Modernity, and Globalization.* Ed. Modern Girl Around the World Research Group. Durham: Duke UP, 2008. 147–73.

Rana, Junaid. *Terrifying Muslims: Race and Labor in the South Asian Diaspora.* Durham: Duke UP, 2011.

Rangappa, Asha. "Miss America and the Indian Beauty Myth." *Huffington Post* 17 Sept. 2013.

Reckitt, Helena. "From Bindi Girls to Space Invaders: Prema Murthy." *Art Asia Pacific* 39 (Winter 2004): 34–35.

Reddy, Vanita. "Beauty and the Limits of National Belonging in Bharati Mukherjee's *Jasmine.*" *Contemporary Literature* 54.2 (2013): 337–68.

——. "Come for the Saris, Stay for the Politics." Interview with Shailja Patel. *Migritude.* New York: Kaya, 2010. 141–47.

——. "Jhumpa Lahiri's Feminist Cosmopolitics and the Transnational Beauty Assemblage." *Meridians.* 11.2 (2013): 29–59.

——. "The Nationalization of the Global Indian Woman: Geographies of Beauty in *Femina.*" *Journal of South Asian Popular Culture* 4.1 (2006): 61–85.

Richards, Bree. "Yayoi Kusama: Performing the Body." *Yayoi Kusama: Look Now, See Forever.* N.p. N.d. Web. 4 Apr. 2013. http://interactive.qag.qld.gov.au/looknowseeforever/essays/performing-the-body/.

Ritu Beri. Home page. RB Productions. n.d. Web. 25 Sept. 2012. http://rituberi.com/flash/home.html.

Rizvi, Uzma Z. "Seducing Structures and Stiches: Reappropriating Love, Desire, and the Image." *Love Letters and Other Necessary Fictions.* Mumbai: Chatterjee and Lal, 2010.

Roach, Joseph. *It.* Ann Arbor: U of Michigan P, 2007.

Robbins, Bruce. *Feeling Global: Internationalism in Distress.* New York: NYU P, 1999.

——. "Introduction Part I: Actually Existing Cosmopolitanism." *Cosmopoli-*

tics: Thinking and Feeling beyond the Nation. Ed. Peng Cheah and Robbins. Minneapolis: U of Minnesota P, 1998. 1–19.

Rodriguez, Richard. *Brown: The Last Discovery of America.* New York: Penguin, 2002.

Roots of Love: On Sikh Hair and Turban. Dir. Harjant Gill. Tilotama Productions, 2010. DVD.

Roy, Anindyo. "The Aesthetics of an (Un)Willing Immigrant: Bharati Mukherjee's *Days and Nights in Calcutta* and *Jasmine.*" *Bharati Mukherjee: Critical Perspectives.* Ed. Immanuel Nelson. New York: Garland, 1993. 127–42.

Roy, Arundhati. *The God of Small Things.* New York: Random House, 1997.

———. *Power Politics.* London: South End, 2001.

Roy, Sandip. "Indians Back Off: Nina Davuluri Is an American Story." *Huffington Post* 17 Sept. 2013.

Said, Edward. *Orientalism.* New York: Vintage, 1978.

Sanchez-Eppler, Karen. *Dependent States: The Child's Part in Nineteenth Century American Culture.* Chicago: U of Chicago P, 2005.

Sari Red. Dir. Pratibha Parmar. Women Make Movies, 1988. DVD.

Sartre, Jean Paul. "Black Orpheus." *Massachusetts Review* 6.1 (1961): 13–52.

Scarry, Elaine. *On Beauty and Being Just.* Princeton: Princeton UP, 1999.

Schlund-Vials, Cathy. *Modeling Citizenship: Jewish and Asian American Writing.* Philadelphia: Temple UP, 2011.

Scruton, Roger. *Beauty: A Very Short Introduction.* Oxford: Oxford UP, 2011.

See, Sarita. *The Decolonized Eye: Filipino American Art and Performance.* Minneapolis: U of Minnesota P, 2009.

———. "How to Make Thick Thin: The Vertical Seamlessness of Swati Khurana's Collages." *Out of the Archive: Process and Progress.* Ed. See and Angel Velasco Shaw. New York: Asian American Arts Center, 2009.

Seiter, Ellen. *Sold Separately: Children and Parents in Consumer Culture.* New Brunswick: Rutgers UP, 1993.

Shah, Priya. "Mr. Khan Goes to Washington: The Bollywood Media Assemblage, Affect, and the State." Paper presented at the Cultural Studies Association conference, San Diego, CA, 29 Mar. 2012.

"Shailja Patel." *Spark* companion website, KQED Arts, Mar. 2007. Web. Feb. 2015. http://www.kqed.org/arts/programs/spark/profile.jsp?essid=14612.

Sharpley-Whiting, T. Denean. "Femme Négritude: Jane Nardal, La Dépêche Africaine, and the Francophone New Negro." *Souls: A Critical Journal of Black Politics, Culture, and Society* (Fall 2000): 8–17.

———. *Negritude Women.* Minneapolis: U of Minnesota P, 2002.

Shimizu, Celine Parreñas. *The Hypersexuality of Race: Performing Asian/American Women on Screen and Scene.* Durham: Duke UP, 2007.

Shohat, Ella, ed. *Talking Visions: Multicultural Feminism in a Transnational Age.* Cambridge: MIT P, 1998.

Shohat, Ella, and Robert Stam. *Race in Translation: Culture Wars around the Postcolonial Atlantic.* New York: NYU Press, 2012.

Shukla, Sandhya. *India Abroad: Diasporic Cultures of Postwar America and England.* Princeton: Princeton UP, 2003.

Sidell, Misty White. "Indian-Inspired Bindis a Hot Trend in Winter Bling." *The Daily Beast* 4 Jan. 2013. Web. 15 Apr. 2013. http://www.thedailybeast.com/articles/2013/01/04/indian-inspired-bindis-a-hot-trend-in-winter-bling.html.

Silverman, Kaja. *Male Subjectivities at the Margins.* New York: Routledge, 1992.

Singh-Sohal, Jay. *Turbanology: Guide to Sikh Identity.* Birmingham, UK: Dot Hyphen, 2012.

Siu, Lok. "The Queen of the Chinese Colony: Contesting Nationalism, Engendering Diaspora." *Asian Diasporas: New Formations, New Conceptions.* Ed. Rhacel Parreñas and Lok Siu. Stanford: Stanford UP, 2007. 105–40.

Smith, Neil. "Scale Bending and the Fate of the National." *Scale and Geographic Inquiry.* Ed. Eric Sheppard and Robert B. McMaster. Malden, MA: Blackwell, 2004. 192–212.

So, Christine. *Economic Citizens: A Narrative of Asian American Visibility.* Philadelphia: Temple UP, 2008.

Spivak, Gayatri. "Can the Subaltern Speak?" *Marxism and the Interpretation of Culture.* Ed. Cary Nelson and Lawrence Grossberg. London: Macmillan, 1988. 271–316.

Srikanth, Rajini. *The World Next Door: South Asian American Literature and the Idea of America.* Philadelphia: Temple UP, 2004.

Staiger, Janet, Ann Cvetkovich, and Ann Reynolds. "Introduction: Political Emotions and Public Feelings." *Political Emotions.* Ed. Staiger, Cvetkovich, and Reynolds. New York: Routledge, 2010. 1–17.

Steinberg, Shirley B., ed. *Kinderculture: The Corporate Construction of Childhood.* 3rd ed. Boulder, CO: Westview, 2011.

Stewart, Kathleen. *Ordinary Affects.* Durham: Duke UP, 2007.

———. *A Space on the Side of the Road: Cultural Politics in an "Other" America.* Princeton: Princeton UP, 1996.

Stoler, Ann. "Tense and Tender Ties: The Politics of Comparison in North American History and Postcolonial Studies." *Haunted by Empire: Geographies of Intimacy in North American History.* Durham: Duke UP, 2006. 23–67.

Sudhakar, Anantha. "Conditional Futures." Ph.D. diss. Rutgers University, 2011.

Sundaresh, Jaya. "Beyond Bindis: Why Cultural Appropriation Matters." *Aerogram* 10 May 2013.

Sunder Rajan, Rajeswari. *Real and Imagined Women: Gender, Culture and Postcolonialism.* London: Routledge, 1993.

Superle, Michelle. *Contemporary English-Language Indian Children's Litera-*

ture: Representations of Nation, Culture, and the New Indian Girl. New York: Routledge, 2011.

Susina, Jan. "American Girls Collection: Barbies with a Sense of History." *Children's Literature Association Quarterly* 24.3 (1999): 130–35.

Swerdlow, J. "Global Culture." *National Geographic* 196.2 (1999): 2–11.

Tarlo, Emma. *Clothing Matters: Dress and Identity in India.* Chicago: U of Chicago P, 1996.

Taylor, Diana. *The Archive and the Repertoire: Performing Cultural Memory in the Americas.* Durham: Duke UP, 2003.

Texeira, Erin. "Indian Immigrants Enter a New Phase: Community Is More Vocal, Politically Active." *Washington Post* 12 Nov. 2006. Web. 11 Mar. 2013. http://www.washingtonpost.com/archive/politics/2006/11/12/indian-immigrants-enter-a-new-phase-span-classbankheadcommunity-is-more-vocal-politically-activespan/o598fe71-3e53-429a-8e5b-00c1943393a4/.

Thrift, Nigel. *Knowing Capitalism.* London: Sage, 2005.

———. "Understanding the Material Practices of Glamour." *The Affect Theory Reader.* Ed. Melissa Gregg and Gregory J. Seigworth. Durham: Duke UP, 2010. 289–308.

Traffic Signal. Dir. Madhur Bhandarkar. Percept Picture, 2008. DVD.

Tu, Thuy Linh Nguyen. *The Beautiful Generation: Asian Americans and the Fashion Industry.* Durham: Duke UP, 2010.

Tulshyan, Ruchika. "Why We Need an Indian Miss America." *Forbes* 16 Sept. 2013.

"Turbanology." Companion website for *Turbanology: Sikhs Unwrapped* exhibition. n.d. Web. http://dothyphen.co.uk/turbanology/.

"Turbanology: Material Witness." Companion website for *Turbanology: Sikhs Unwrapped* exhibition. n.d. Web. ttp://dothyphen.co.uk/turbanology/exhibition/material-witness/.

Uberoi, Patricia. "The Diaspora Comes Home: Disciplining Desire in *DDLJ.*" *Contributions to Indian Sociology* 32.2 (1998): 305–36.

"Unaccustomed Earth, by Jhumpa Lahiri." *Books to the Ceiling* 10 May 2008. Web. 12 Dec. 2012. https://robertarood.wordpress.com/2008/05/10/unaccustomed-earth/.

Vadhera, Shalini. *Passport to Beauty: Secrets and Tips from Around the World for Becoming a Global Goddess.* New York: St. Martin's, 2006.

Vertovec, Stephen, and Robin Cohen. "Introduction: Conceiving Cosmopolitanism." *Conceiving Cosmopolitanism: Theory, Context, and Practice.* Ed. Vertovec and Cohen. Oxford: Oxford UP, 2002.

Visweswaran, Kamala. "Diaspora by Design: Flexible Citizenship and South Asians in U.S. Racial Formations." *Diaspora: A Journal of Transnational Studies* 6.1 (1997): 5–29.

Warhol-Down, Robyn. "Jasmine Reconsidered: Narrative Discourse and Multicultural Subjectivity." *Contemporary Women's Writing* 2.1 (2008): 1–16.

Waters, Mary. "Optional Ethnicities: For Whites Only?" *Women's Lives: Multicultural Perspectives.* Ed. Gwyn Kirk and Margo Okazawa-Rey. New York: McGraw-Hill, 2007. 113–19.

Weingus, Leigh. "9 Disney Princesses Transformed into Indian Brides." *Huffington Post* 15 Jan. 2015.

Wilk, Richard. "Connections and Contradictions: From the Crooked Tree Cashew Queen to Miss World Belize." *Beauty Queens on the Global Stage: Gender, Contests, and Power.* Ed. Colleen Ballerino Cohen, Richard Wilk, and Beverly Stoeltje. New York: Routledge, 1996. 217–32.

Williams, Linda. "Porn Studies: Proliferating Pornographies On/Scene: An Introduction." *Porn Studies.* Ed. Williams. Durham: Duke UP, 2004. 1–23.

Williams, Raymond. *Marxism and Literature.* Oxford: Oxford UP, 1977.

Wilson, Gaby. "Katy Perry Channels Late-'90s Gwen Stefani with Bindi." *MTV Style* 6 Apr. 2012. Web. 15 Apr. 2013. http://style.mtv.com/2012/04/06/katy-perry-gwen-stefani-bindi/.

Wissinger, Elizabeth. "Always on Display: Affective Production in the Modeling Industry." *The Affective Turn: Theorizing the Social.* Ed. Patricia Ticineto Clough and Jean Halley. Durham: Duke UP, 2007. 231–60.

———. *The Modeling Life.* New York: NYU P, forthcoming.

Woolf, Naomi. *The Beauty Myth: How Images of Beauty Are Used against Women.* New York: Harper Perennial, 1991.

Wu, Judy Tzu-Chun. "'Loveliest Daughter of Our Ancient Cathay': Representations of Gender and Ethnic Identity in the Miss Chinatown U.S.A. Beauty Pageant." *Journal of Social History* 31.1 (1997): 5–31.

"You're the Inspiration." *Vogue India* Aug. 2009. Web. 12 Dec. 2012.

Index

Note: "n" after a page number indicates a note; "f" indicates a figure.

About the Author

Vanita Reddy is an Assistant Professor of English at Texas A&M University.

Ko-lin Chin, *Smuggled Chinese: Clandestine Immigration to the United States*

Evelyn Hu-DeHart, ed., *Across the Pacific: Asian Americans and Globalization*

Soo-Young Chin, *Doing What Had to Be Done: The Life Narrative of Dora Yum Kim*

Robert G. Lee, *Orientals: Asian Americans in Popular Culture*

David L. Eng and Alice Y. Hom, eds., *Q & A: Queer in Asian America*

K. Scott Wong and Sucheng Chan, eds., *Claiming America: Constructing Chinese American Identities during the Exclusion Era*

Lavina Dhingra Shankar and Rajini Srikanth, eds., *A Part, Yet Apart: South Asians in Asian America*

Jere Takahashi, *Nisei/Sansei: Shifting Japanese American Identities and Politics*

Velina Hasu Houston, ed., *But Still, Like Air, I'll Rise: New Asian American Plays*

Josephine Lee, *Performing Asian America: Race and Ethnicity on the Contemporary Stage*

Deepika Bahri and Mary Vasudeva, eds., *Between the Lines: South Asians and Postcoloniality*

E. San Juan Jr., *The Philippine Temptation: Dialectics of Philippines–U.S. Literary Relations*

Carlos Bulosan and E. San Juan Jr., eds., *The Cry and the Dedication*

Carlos Bulosan and E. San Juan Jr., eds., *On Becoming Filipino: Selected Writings of Carlos Bulosan*

Vicente L. Rafael, ed., *Discrepant Histories: Translocal Essays on Filipino Cultures*

Yen Le Espiritu, *Filipino American Lives*

Paul Ong, Edna Bonacich, and Lucie Cheng, eds., *The New Asian Immigration in Los Angeles and Global Restructuring*

Chris Friday, *Organizing Asian American Labor: The Pacific Coast Canned-Salmon Industry, 1870–1942*

Sucheng Chan, ed., *Hmong Means Free: Life in Laos and America*

Timothy P. Fong, *The First Suburban Chinatown: The Remaking of Monterey Park, California*

William Wei, *The Asian American Movement*

Yen Le Espiritu, *Asian American Panethnicity*

Velina Hasu Houston, ed., *The Politics of Life*

Renqiu Yu, *To Save China, To Save Ourselves: The Chinese Hand Laundry Alliance of New York*

Shirley Geok-lin Lim and Amy Ling, eds., *Reading the Literatures of Asian America*

Karen Isaksen Leonard, *Making Ethnic Choices: California's Punjabi Mexican Americans*

Gary Y. Okihiro, *Cane Fires: The Anti-Japanese Movement in Hawaii, 1865–1945*

Sucheng Chan, *Entry Denied: Exclusion and the Chinese Community in America, 1882–1943*